TEACHINGS OF PRESIDENTS OF THE CHURCH

JOSEPH FIELDING SMITH

Published by
The Church of Jesus Christ of Latter-day Saints
Salt Lake City, Utah

Books in the *Teachings of Presidents of the Church* Series

Teachings of Presidents of the Church: Joseph Smith (item number 36481)
Teachings of Presidents of the Church: Brigham Young (35554)
Teachings of Presidents of the Church: John Taylor (35969)
Teachings of Presidents of the Church: Wilford Woodruff (36315)
Teachings of Presidents of the Church: Lorenzo Snow (36787)
Teachings of Presidents of the Church: Joseph F. Smith (35744)
Teachings of Presidents of the Church: Heber J. Grant (35970)
Teachings of Presidents of the Church: George Albert Smith (36786)
Teachings of Presidents of the Church: David O. McKay (36492)
Teachings of Presidents of the Church: Joseph Fielding Smith (36907)
Teachings of Presidents of the Church: Harold B. Lee (35892)
Teachings of Presidents of the Church: Spencer W. Kimball (36500)

To obtain copies of these books, go to your local distribution center or visit store.lds.org. The books are also available electronically at LDS.org.

Your comments and suggestions about this book would be appreciated. Please submit them to Curriculum Development, 50 East North Temple Street, Salt Lake City, UT 84150-0024 USA.

Email: cur-development@ldschurch.org

Please give your name, address, ward, and stake. Be sure to include the title of the book. Then offer your comments and suggestions about the book's strengths and areas of potential improvement.

Contents

Joseph Fielding Smith

Introduction

The First Presidency and the Quorum of the Twelve Apostles have established the *Teachings of Presidents of the Church* series to help you draw closer to your Heavenly Father and deepen your understanding of the restored gospel of Jesus Christ. As the Church adds volumes to this series, you will build a collection of gospel reference books for your home. The volumes in this series are designed to be used for personal study and for Sunday instruction. They can also help you prepare other lessons or talks and answer questions about Church doctrine.

This book features the teachings of President Joseph Fielding Smith, who served as President of The Church of Jesus Christ of Latter-day Saints from January 23, 1970, to July 2, 1972.

Personal Study

As you study the teachings of President Joseph Fielding Smith, prayerfully seek the inspiration of the Holy Ghost. The questions at the end of each chapter will help you understand President Smith's teachings and apply them in your life. As you study these teachings, you may want to think about ways to share them with family members and friends. This will strengthen your understanding of what you read.

Teaching from This Book

This book has been designed for use at home and at church. In high priests groups, elders quorums, and Relief Societies, two Sunday lessons each month will normally be taught from chapters in the book. Because the book contains more chapters than can be covered in 12 months, ward and stake leaders may determine which chapters will best meet the needs of the members they serve.

The following guidelines may help you teach from the book:

Prepare to Teach

Seek the guidance of the Holy Ghost as you prepare to teach. Prayerfully study the assigned chapter to become confident in your understanding of President Smith's teachings. You will teach with greater sincerity and power when his words have influenced you personally (see D&C 11:21).

If you are teaching a Melchizedek Priesthood or Relief Society lesson, you should not set this book aside or prepare a lesson from other materials. Prayerfully select from the chapter those teachings that you feel will be most helpful to those you teach. Some chapters contain more material than you will be able to discuss during class time.

Encourage participants to study the chapter before the lesson and to bring their books with them. When they do so, they will be better prepared to participate in discussions and edify one another.

In your preparation to teach, give special attention to the "Suggestions for Study and Teaching" at the end of each chapter. Under this heading, you will find questions, related scriptures, and teaching helps. The questions and related scriptures correlate specifically with the chapter in which they are found. The teaching helps can guide you in all your efforts to help others find joy in learning and living the gospel.

Introduce the Chapter

As you introduce the chapter, and throughout the lesson, work to establish an atmosphere in which the Spirit can touch the hearts and minds of those you teach. To start the lesson, help those you teach focus on the teachings of the chapter. Consider the following ideas:

- Read and discuss the section titled "From the Life of Joseph Fielding Smith" at the beginning of the chapter.
- Discuss a picture or scripture from the chapter.
- Sing a related hymn together.
- Briefly share a personal experience about the topic.

Lead a Discussion about President Smith's Teachings

As you teach from this book, invite others to share their thoughts, ask questions, and teach one another. When they actively participate, they will be more prepared to learn and to receive personal revelation. Allow good discussions to continue rather than trying to cover all the teachings. To encourage discussion, use the questions at the end of each chapter. You may also develop your own questions especially for those you are teaching.

The following options may give you additional ideas:

- Ask participants to share what they have learned from their personal study of the chapter. It may be helpful to contact a few participants during the week and ask them to come prepared to share what they have learned.

- Assign participants to read selected questions at the end of the chapter (either individually or in small groups). Ask them to look for teachings in the chapter that relate to the questions. Then invite them to share their thoughts and insights with the rest of the group.

- Read together a selection of President Smith's statements from the chapter. Ask participants to share examples from the scriptures and from their own experience that illustrate what President Smith taught.

- Ask participants to choose one section and read it silently. Invite them to gather in groups of two or three people who chose the same section and discuss what they have learned.

Encourage Sharing and Application

President Smith's teachings will be most meaningful for participants who share them with others and apply them in their lives. Consider the following ideas:

- Ask participants how they can apply President Smith's teachings in their responsibilities at home and in the church. For example, you might help them ponder and discuss how they can apply his teachings as husbands, wives, parents, sons, daughters, home teachers, or visiting teachers.

- Encourage participants to share some of President Smith's teachings with family members and friends.

- Invite participants to apply what they have learned and share their experiences at the beginning of the next class.

Conclude the Discussion

Briefly summarize the lesson or ask one or two participants to do so. Testify of the teachings you have discussed. You may also want to invite others to share their testimonies.

Information about the Sources Quoted in This Book

The teachings in this book are direct quotations from President Joseph Fielding Smith's sermons, articles, books, letters, and journals. Quotations from published sources have retained the punctuation, spelling, capitalization, and paragraphing of the original sources unless editorial or typographic changes have been necessary to improve readability. For this reason, you may notice minor inconsistencies in the text. For example, the word *gospel* is lowercased in some quotations and capitalized in others.

Also, President Smith often used terms such as *men, man,* or *mankind* to refer to all people, both male and female. He frequently used the pronouns *he, his,* and *him* to refer to both genders. This was common in the language of his era. Despite the differences between these language conventions and current usage, President Smith's teachings apply to both women and men.

Historical Summary

The following chronology provides a brief historical framework for the teachings of President Joseph Fielding Smith in this book.

July 19, 1876	Born in Salt Lake City, Utah, to Julina Lambson Smith and Joseph F. Smith.
July 19, 1884	Baptized and confirmed by his father. Receives his first personal copy of the Book of Mormon from his father.
April 6, 1893	Attends the dedication of the Salt Lake Temple.
1896	Receives the Melchizedek Priesthood and the temple endowment.
April 26, 1898	Marries Louie Emily Shurtliff in the Salt Lake Temple.
May 1899 to July 1901	Serves as a full-time missionary assigned to England.
1901 to 1910	Serves in many Church callings, including as president in a priesthood quorum, a member of the Young Men's Mutual Improvement Association general board, a high councilor, and a member of a general Church committee assigned to prepare materials in defense of the Church.
October 1901	Begins employment in the Church Historian's office.

1902	Publishes a family history booklet titled *Asael Smith of Topsfield, Massachusetts, with Some Account of the Smith Family.* This is his first of many publications, including 25 books and numerous articles for Church magazines and periodicals.
April 8, 1906	Sustained in general conference as Assistant Church Historian, a position he holds until March 1921.
March 30, 1908	Louie Shurtliff Smith dies after suffering from a severe illness related to her third pregnancy.
November 2, 1908	Marries Ethel Georgina Reynolds in the Salt Lake Temple.
April 7, 1910	Ordained an Apostle by his father.
October 1918	Records a revelation on the redemption of the dead as dictated by his father, who is the President of the Church at the time. This revelation is now found in Doctrine and Covenants 138.
January 6, 1919	Appointed as a counselor in the presidency of the Salt Lake Temple, a position he holds until 1935.
March 17, 1921	Named as Church Historian, a position he holds until 1970.
1934	Named as president of the Genealogical Society of Utah, a position he holds until 1961.
August 26, 1937	Ethel Reynolds Smith dies after suffering with an illness for four years.
April 12, 1938	Marries Jessie Ella Evans in the Salt Lake Temple.

May to November 1939	Fills a special assignment in Europe with Jessie, visiting England, Scotland, Holland, Belgium, France, Switzerland, Italy, Sweden, Norway, Denmark, Czechoslovakia, Austria, and Germany. Directs the evacuation of all American missionaries from Europe after the outbreak of World War II.
June 8, 1945	Called to serve as president of the Salt Lake Temple, a position he holds until 1949.
October 6, 1950	Set apart as Acting President of the Quorum of the Twelve Apostles.
April 9, 1951	Sustained as President of the Quorum of the Twelve Apostles.
July to August 1955	Fills a special assignment in Asia, with Jessie accompanying him. Dedicates Guam, Korea, Okinawa, and the Philippines for the preaching of the gospel.
September 1958	Attends the dedication of the London England Temple.
October 1960 to January 1961	Accompanied by Jessie, visits Church leaders and missionaries in Central and South America.
May 1963	Officiates at the laying of the cornerstone of the Oakland California Temple.
September 1963	Dedicates the Pioneer Monument in Kansas City, Missouri, and the Liberty Jail Historic Site in Liberty, Missouri.
October 29, 1965	Called to serve as a Counselor in the First Presidency under the direction of President David O. McKay.

January 18, 1970	Becomes the senior Apostle and presiding leader of the Church at the death of President David O. McKay.
January 23, 1970	Set apart as President of The Church of Jesus Christ of Latter-day Saints.
April 6, 1970	Sustained as President of the Church in general conference.
August 3, 1971	Jessie Evans Smith dies.
August 27–29, 1971	Presides at the Church's first area conference, which is held in Manchester, England.
January 18, 1972	Offers the dedicatory prayer for the Ogden Utah Temple.
February 9, 1972	Presides at the dedication of the Provo Utah Temple. Having written the dedicatory prayer, assigns President Harold B. Lee to offer the prayer.
July 2, 1972	Dies in Salt Lake City, Utah, 17 days before his 96th birthday.

The Life and Ministry of Joseph Fielding Smith

President Joseph Fielding Smith "used three great words that I can never forget," recalled President Gordon B. Hinckley. Those words were "true and faithful." President Hinckley said, "In his public addresses, in his private conversation, in his prayers to the Lord, he pleaded that we might be true and faithful."[1] President Thomas S. Monson shared a similar memory: "Even in his advanced years, [he] always prayed, 'May we be true and faithful to the end.'"[2]

"True and faithful." For President Joseph Fielding Smith, this was more than an often-repeated phrase. It was a heartfelt expression of his hope for all people. It was also a description of his life, from his childhood through his service as President of The Church of Jesus Christ of Latter-day Saints.

"A Child of Promise"

Joseph Fielding Smith "was born as a child of promise," said Elder Bruce R. McConkie of the Quorum of the Twelve Apostles. Elder McConkie, a son-in-law to President Smith, explained that Julina Lambson Smith "had three daughters but no sons, and so she went before the Lord and, like Hannah of old, 'vowed a vow.' [1 Samuel 1:11.] Her promise: that if the Lord would give her a son, 'she would do all in her power to help him be a credit to the Lord and to his father.' The Lord hearkened to her prayers, and she kept her promise to him."[3] On July 19, 1876, Julina and her husband, Joseph F. Smith, welcomed a newborn son into their family. They named him Joseph Fielding Smith Jr., after his father.

At birth, Joseph Fielding Smith joined a family rich in faith, service, and leadership. His grandfather Hyrum Smith was the Prophet Joseph Smith's brother and a valiant witness of the Restoration of

1

*Joseph Fielding Smith's parents, President Joseph F.
Smith and Julina Lambson Smith*

the gospel. The Lord appointed Hyrum to "be a prophet, and a seer, and a revelator unto [His] church," saying that Hyrum's name would "be had in honorable remembrance from generation to generation, forever and ever" (D&C 124:94, 96). With his brother Joseph, Hyrum sealed his testimony with his blood, martyred by a mob on June 27, 1844 (see D&C 135).

Joseph Fielding Smith's father, Joseph F. Smith, shouldered heavy responsibilities from the time he was a child. The firstborn child of Hyrum and Mary Fielding Smith, he was five years old when his father was martyred and nine years old when he helped his widowed mother drive her wagon from Nauvoo, Illinois, to the Salt Lake Valley. He later served as a missionary and as a member of the Quorum of the Twelve Apostles. He was a Counselor in the First Presidency when his son Joseph was born. From October 17, 1901, to November 19, 1918, he served as President of the Church.

Joseph Fielding Smith's mother, Julina Lambson Smith, was part of one of the early pioneer families in the Salt Lake Valley. From the age of nine, she was raised in the home of her uncle George A. Smith, who was a member of the Quorum of the Twelve Apostles at the time, and her aunt Bathsheba W. Smith. (Elder Smith later served as First Counselor in the First Presidency under President Brigham Young, and Sister Smith later served as Relief Society general president.) As an adult, Julina was a devoted wife and mother and a dedicated member of Relief Society. She was known for her compassion and skill as a midwife, bringing "nearly 1,000 babies into the world" and caring for their mothers.[4] From October 1910 to April 1921, she served as second counselor in the Relief Society general presidency.

Work and Play as a Young Man

Joseph learned how to work at an early age. His family owned a farm in Taylorsville, Utah, about 10 miles (16 kilometers) from their home, where he and his brothers helped with irrigating, harvesting hay, and taking care of livestock. At home, the family cared for a large vegetable garden, several fruit trees, three long rows of grapes, a flock of chickens, three cows, and a few horses. President

Joseph F. Smith practiced plural marriage, so the family had many mouths to feed and many hands to help with the work. Because Joseph Fielding Smith was one of the oldest sons in the large family, he was given some responsibilities that normally would have been given to an adult. In addition to these responsibilities, he always kept up with his studies for school.

Joseph's first work outside the home and the family farm was with his mother. He often drove a horse and carriage to help her fulfill her duties as a midwife. In his late teens, he found employment at Zion's Cooperative Mercantile Institution (ZCMI), where he put in long and physically demanding days. He later recalled: "I worked like a work horse all day long and was tired out when night came, carrying sacks of flour and sacks of sugar and hams and bacons on my back. I weighed 150 pounds [68 kilograms], but I thought nothing of picking up a 200-pound sack [91 kilograms] and putting it on my shoulders."[5]

To balance his heavy work responsibilities, Joseph found some time to play. He and his siblings liked to play nighttime games around the house, hiding among the grapevines—"especially when the grapes were ripe."[6] He also loved to play baseball. Each ward had an organized baseball team, and he enjoyed these friendly rivalries.

Gospel Study and Spiritual Growth

Although baseball was important to young Joseph Fielding Smith, he sometimes left games early, pulled away by an interest that was even more important to him. At such times, he could be found secluded "in the hayloft or in the shade of a tree to get back to his reading" of the Book of Mormon.[7] "From my earliest recollection," he later said, "from the time I first could read, I have received more pleasure and greater satisfaction out of the study of the scriptures, and reading of the Lord Jesus Christ, and of the Prophet Joseph Smith, and the work that has been accomplished for the salvation of men, than from anything else in all the world."[8] He began to establish a pattern of personal gospel study when he received his first copy of the Book of Mormon at age eight. He eagerly read the

Young Joseph Fielding Smith sometimes left baseball games early
so he could read the Book of Mormon in his family's hayloft.

standard works and Church publications. He carried a pocket-sized edition of the New Testament so he could read during lunch breaks and as he walked to and from his job at ZCMI. Steadily and persistently, he added to the strength of his testimony of the restored gospel.

But Joseph's spiritual growth was not confined to silent personal study. He faithfully participated in Church meetings and classes, and he received priesthood ordinances and blessings. He was especially drawn to the temple. The Salt Lake Temple had been under construction for 23 years when he was born. "Through his youth Joseph had watched with keen interest the daily progress in construction on this magnificent edifice. He had seen the last of the huge granite stones brought in by railroad cars from the rock quarry. . . . [He] had seen the majestic spires finally take shape. . . . [He said,] 'I used to wonder whether I would ever live long enough to see the temple completed.'"[9]

On April 6, 1893, Joseph attended the first dedicatory session of the Salt Lake Temple. President Wilford Woodruff, the fourth President of the Church, presided at the session and offered the dedicatory prayer. Seated on the stand to the left of President Woodruff was his Second Counselor, President Joseph F. Smith.

When Joseph Fielding Smith was 19 years old, he received a patriarchal blessing. This blessing, pronounced by his uncle John Smith, who was then serving as Church Patriarch, added to Joseph's spiritual strength. Joseph was told:

"It is thy privilege to live to a good old age and the will of the Lord that you should become a mighty man in Israel. . . .

"It shall be thy duty to sit in counsel with thy brethren and to preside among the people. It shall be thy duty also to travel much at home and abroad, by land and water, laboring in the ministry. And I say unto thee, hold up thy head, lift up thy voice without fear or favor, as the Spirit of the Lord shall direct, and the blessings of the Lord shall rest upon thee. His Spirit shall direct thy mind and give thee word and sentiment, that thou shalt confound the wisdom of the wicked and set at naught the counsels of the unjust." [10]

Later that year, after his 20th birthday, he received new opportunities for service and spiritual growth. He was ordained to the office of elder in the Melchizedek Priesthood, and he received the temple endowment. Toward the end of his life, when he was serving as President of the Church, he declared: "How grateful I am that I hold the holy priesthood. I have sought all my days to magnify my calling in that priesthood and hope to endure to the end in this life and to enjoy the fellowship of the faithful saints in the life to come." [11]

Courtship and Marriage

As young Joseph Fielding Smith helped support his family, studied the gospel, and prepared for priesthood blessings, his efforts did not go unnoticed by a young woman named Louie Shurtliff. Louie, whose parents lived in Ogden, Utah, came to live with the Smith family so she could attend the University of Utah, which at the time was located across the street from the Smiths' home.

At first, Joseph and Louie's relationship was nothing more than a formal friendship, but it gradually deepened into a courtship. Because the couple had little money, their courtship was confined mostly to reading together in the family parlor, talking with one another, taking walks together, and attending Church socials. Joseph also enjoyed listening to Louie play the piano. Occasionally they went to a performance at a local theater. By the end of Louie's second year of studies at the university, their courtship had blossomed into love—so much that Joseph rode his bicycle the 100-mile (160-kilometer) round trip, over rutted dirt roads, to see her in Ogden once or twice when school was not in session.[12]

Eventually, Louie and Joseph discussed marriage. However, a question remained in their minds: would Joseph be called to serve a mission? In those days, young men and women desiring to serve missions did not approach their bishops to be recommended for such calls. The processing of mission calls was done entirely through the office of the President of the Church. A young man never knew when he might find a mission call in the mailbox.

Louie graduated from the university in the spring of 1897 and moved back to Ogden with her parents. One year later, with apparently no mission call forthcoming, the couple decided to move forward with marriage plans. As Joseph later said, "I persuaded her to change her place of residence, and on the 26th day of April, 1898, we went to the Salt Lake Temple and were married for time and all eternity by my father, President Joseph F. Smith."[13] As Joseph and Louie began their life together, they lived in a small apartment in the Smith family's home.

Heeding the Missionary Call

In the early days of the Church, married men were often called to serve full-time missions, so Joseph and Louie were not surprised when, on March 17, 1899, a mission call signed by President Lorenzo Snow arrived in the mail. But Joseph might have been somewhat surprised at his assigned field of labor. Before receiving the call, he had had a conversation with President Franklin D. Richards, President of the Quorum of the Twelve Apostles, about the

Elder Joseph Fielding Smith as a full-time missionary

possibility of receiving a mission call. Joseph later recalled: "[He] asked me where I'd like to go. I told him I had no choice particularly, only to go where I was sent. But he said, 'You must have some place where you would prefer to go to.' I said, 'Well, I'd prefer to go to Germany.' So they sent me to England!"[14]

Louie decided to live with her parents while Joseph was away. This, she felt, would help her endure the loneliness of being separated from her husband. And she would work in her father's store, earning money to help fund Joseph's mission.[15]

On May 12, 1899, one day before departing for the mission field, Elder Smith and other missionaries received instructions from President Joseph F. Smith and Elders George Teasdale and Heber J. Grant of the Quorum of the Twelve Apostles. This was the extent of their training before they departed as full-time missionaries. At this meeting, each missionary received an official missionary certificate. Elder Smith's read:

"This certifies that the bearer Elder Joseph F. Smith Jr. is in full faith and fellowship with The Church of Jesus Christ of Latter-day Saints and by the General Authorities of said Church has been duly appointed a Mission to Great Britain to Preach the Gospel and administer in all the Ordinances thereof pertaining to his office.

"And we invite all men to give heed to his Teachings and Counsels as a man of God, sent to open to them the door of Life and Salvation—and to assist him in his travels, in whatsoever things he may need.

"And we pray God, The Eternal Father, to bless Elder Smith and all who receive him and minister to his comfort, with the blessings of Heaven and Earth, for time and all eternity, in the name of Jesus Christ, Amen.

"Signed at Salt Lake City, Utah, May 12th, 1899, in behalf of said Church. Lorenzo Snow, George Q. Cannon, Jos. F. Smith, First Presidency."[16]

The next day, the family gathered at home to bid farewell to Joseph and to an older brother who had also been called to serve in England. However, one family member was absent from the gathering. Joseph's younger sister Emily was hiding, ashamed about something she had done a few years earlier. When Joseph and Louie had been courting, Joseph sometimes sent Emily and other little children to bed early so he could spend time alone with his sweetheart. Frustrated with this perceived injustice, Emily had often prayed that the Lord would send her brother away on a mission. Now that he really was leaving, she felt guilty about the part she might have played in his departure.[17]

Joseph and Louie knew that the call to serve in England had come from the Lord. Joseph was eager to do his duty, and Louie was pleased that her husband would serve a mission, but they both struggled with the idea of being separated. When the time came for Elder Smith to leave for the train depot, "Louie tried to be brave, tried not to let Joseph see her cry. But it was hard to conceal red eyes. And Joseph was already so homesick just at the thought of leaving that he did not feel much like talking with anyone. . . . There was a lump in Joseph's throat as he paused at the front door of the old home on First North Street and kissed each of his loved ones goodbye: Mama, Papa, brothers and sisters, aunties, and last of all, Louie. 'Goodbye Louie, my precious. God bless you and keep you safe for me.'"[18]

Planting Gospel Seeds in England

From the time his train—uncomfortable and filled with tobacco smoke—sped away from home, Elder Smith dedicated himself to his mission. His journal entries and the letters he sent and received revealed the difficulties he faced as a missionary and the faith and devotion with which he faced them.

At the end of his first day of missionary work in England, he wrote in his journal: "This has been a very important day in my short life. I came from my home less than a month ago for the purpose of preaching the gospel of our Lord. . . . I have been out tracting today and delivered 25 tracts [pamphlets]. It is the first of this kind of work that I ever tried to do and it did not come to me very easy. . . . I bore my testimony to the world for the first time today, but will be able to do so better. With the help of the Lord I shall do his will as I was called to do."[19]

When his father sent him a few dollars for necessities, he replied: "I shall be very careful of the means you send me. I do not spend anything unless I have a good reason for it." He also told his father of his determination to learn and teach the gospel: "I am here to preach the gospel and I hope I will be able to do that well. . . . It is my desire to improve my mind and talents while I am here, that I may always be useful for something in life. . . . I want to be right on all things and nothing gives me more pleasure than to learn something about the gospel. My desire is to become acquainted with it and gain wisdom."[20]

President Joseph F. Smith wrote the following words of commendation in a letter to Elder Joseph Fielding Smith: "I like your spirit, I have faith in your integrity, and I have pleasure and satisfaction in you. I want you to cultivate wisdom and deliberate judgment and patience as well as the Holy Spirit and the love of God."[21] Louie's father, Lewis Shurtliff, also expressed confidence in Elder Smith: "I have always felt that you would fill a glorious mission and gain an experience that will fit you for the exalted station that you are destined to fill in the future."[22]

In letters to Louie, Joseph always expressed his love for her. He often enclosed pressed flowers inside his "warm and affectionate letters."[23] He also wrote of the challenges he faced: "There are many in this nation who know the gospel is true that we teach, but they have not the moral courage to come out of the world and embrace it."[24]

Louie sent letters at least once a week. "Remember," she once wrote, "I am here to love and pray for you and that I never forget you for one single moment. . . . Bless you, my own precious husband, is my prayer always."[25] Louie was clear about her devotion to her husband, and she was equally clear about her devotion to the Lord and His work. She consistently reminded Joseph not to allow homesickness to weaken his resolve to serve.

Elder Smith needed such encouragement, for he rarely found anyone who would receive the message of the restored gospel. Years later, he "told his son Joseph that conditions were so bad and the people so disinterested that he reached a frame of mind where he thought that he could not continue. One night he lay awake thinking of the need to work for passage home."[26] But inspired by encouragement from loved ones and strengthened by their prayers and his own desire to serve, he overcame such thoughts. He knew that the Lord had called him, and he knew that he needed to work diligently for the good of the people he served and for the good of his family. He wrote: "I would rather stay here forever than come home without an honorable record and release. . . . I pray that I may have the spirit of the gospel and a love for my fellow man that I may be able to stay here until I am released honorably. If it were not for the many prayers that are offered up for me at home as well as my own I could not succeed."[27]

Elder Joseph Fielding Smith was honorably released from his mission on June 20, 1901. In his two years of diligent service, "he did not make one convert, did not have opportunity to perform one

Louie Shurtliff Smith

baptism, although he did confirm one convert."[28] However, he and his companions had planted gospel seeds, helping many people find greater peace and understanding, and he had grown personally as a student and teacher of the gospel and as a priesthood leader.

A New Home and New Responsibilities

Joseph arrived in Salt Lake City on July 9, 1901. After spending a few days with Louie's family in Ogden, Joseph and Louie returned to their home with the Smiths and resumed their life together. Their marriage was characterized by faith, diligence, and service, as they worked to establish a home and family and to serve in the Church.

Soon after Joseph returned home, he began looking for a job so he could support his family. With help from a family member, he secured a temporary job at the Salt Lake County clerk's office. About five weeks later, he accepted a position in the Church Historian's office. As he learned more about the history of the Church, he also became more aware of people who sought to discredit the Church and its leaders. He worked tirelessly to provide information in defense of the faith. This was the beginning of service that would bless the Church for years to come.

In the spring of 1902, Louie was pregnant. She and Joseph were grateful for their little apartment, but they looked forward to building their own home. Joseph's secure employment allowed them to start making plans. They hired a building firm and made arrangements for Joseph to do much of the work himself, thus cutting expenses. Their first child, a daughter named Josephine, was born in September 1902, and they moved into their new home about 10 months later. In 1906, after Louie suffered through a difficult pregnancy, they welcomed another daughter into their home and named her Julina.

Joseph was always willing to participate in the Lord's work of salvation, and he received many opportunities to do so. In 1902 he was called to serve as one of the presidents of the twenty-fourth quorum of the seventy, including duties as the quorum instructor. (At that time, the Church had more than 100 quorums of the seventy. The members of those quorums were not General Authorities.) Joseph was also called to serve on the general board of the Young Men's Mutual Improvement Association and as a member of the high council of the Salt Lake Stake. He was ordained a high priest by his brother Hyrum, a member of the Quorum of the Twelve Apostles. In the April 1906 general conference, he was sustained as an Assistant Church Historian, and the following January he was appointed to a special committee whose purpose was "to prepare data for a defense of the church against assaults made upon it by its enemies."[29]

When Joseph's father was serving as President of the Church, Joseph often helped him with correspondence and other administrative duties, and he occasionally accompanied his father on Church assignments. Once Joseph even traveled in President Smith's place. He recorded: "I went to Brigham City [Utah] at the request of my father to dedicate the Second Ward meeting house in Brigham City. They were very desirous of having *him* offer the dedicatory prayer, but as he was suffering from a severe cold he sent me in his stead." When the stake president and a bishop met Joseph at the train station, they were not happy to see him.[30] The stake president reportedly said: "I could bawl. We were expecting the President of the Church and we get a boy instead." According to one account of the story, Joseph quipped in reply, "I could bawl too." [31]

Although much of Joseph's Church duties took him away from home, he and Louie also found time to serve together and enjoy each other's company. In his journal entry for November 1, 1907, he wrote, "With Louie, I spent the greater part of the day in the Salt Lake Temple, one of the happiest days of our lives and the most profitable to us." [32]

Trials and Blessings

Joseph set many of his Church responsibilities aside in March 1908, feeling a need to stay home with Louie as much as possible. She was suffering from a severe, unremitting illness related to the early stages of her third pregnancy. Despite prayers, priesthood blessings, solicitous care from her husband, and careful attention from doctors, she continued to worsen. She died on March 30.

In his grief, Joseph wrote: "During this month which has been one of constant anxiety and worry for me, I have passed through trials and experiences of the deepest and most painful kind. And through it all I have depended on the Lord for strength and comfort. After suffering most excruciating pain for three or four weeks and after an illness covering a period of nearly two months my beloved wife was released from her suffering . . . and departed from me and our precious babies, for a better world, where we patiently and in sorrow await a meeting which shall be most glorious." Joseph said that his wife "died firm in the faith and true to every principle of the gospel." [33]

Joseph was soon overwhelmed with the task of raising two little girls in a motherless home. His parents invited the young family to live with them. Even with this help, the widower realized that his little children needed the care of a loving mother.

As he did with all important decisions, Joseph made this issue a matter of fervent prayer. Ethel Georgina Reynolds, a clerk in the Church Historian's office, became the answer to his prayers. Joseph invited her to join him and his daughters on an outing in the

Ethel Reynolds Smith

park on July 6, 1908. The outing was successful, as all four of them enjoyed each other's company. Ten days later, Joseph and Ethel enjoyed a date together without the children, and soon thereafter they were engaged to be married.

Ethel and Joseph were sealed in the Salt Lake Temple on November 2, 1908. Years later in a letter to Ethel, Joseph wrote, "You do not know how often I have thanked the Lord that I made no mistake when I needed a companion. You were sent to me."[34] In addition to being a loving companion to Joseph, Ethel quickly became a second mother to Josephine and Julina.

Service as a Member of the Quorum of the Twelve Apostles

Just before general conference in April 1910, President John R. Winder, First Counselor in the First Presidency, died. Elder John Henry Smith, who had been serving in the Quorum of the Twelve, was called to serve in the First Presidency, leaving a vacancy in the Quorum of the Twelve. The First Presidency and the Quorum of the Twelve met in the Salt Lake Temple to discuss men who would be qualified to fill that vacancy. After counseling together for about an hour, they were unable to "reach any unanimity of feeling on the matter. Finally President Joseph F. Smith retired to a room by himself and knelt in prayer for guidance. When he returned he somewhat hesitatingly asked the 13 other brethren whether they would be willing to consider his son Joseph Fielding Smith Jr. for the position. He was reluctant to suggest it, he said, because his son Hyrum was already a member of the council and his son David was a Counselor in the Presiding Bishopric. Church members, he feared, would be disgruntled to have another of his sons appointed as a general authority. Nevertheless he felt inspired to offer Joseph's name for consideration. The other men seemed immediately receptive to the suggestion and sustained President Smith in it.

"Apparently President Smith confided the choice of Joseph to his [Joseph's] mother prior to the conference announcement. Joseph's sister Edith S. Patrick says, 'I remember mother telling us that in 1910 father came home from his temple council meeting and seemed very worried. When asked what was troubling him, he said that Joseph had been chosen as one of the Twelve. He said the brethren had unanimously selected him and he said now he, as the president, would be severely criticized, having his son made an apostle. Mother told him not to worry one minute as to what people might say. She knew the Lord had chosen him and said she knew he would be a credit to his calling.'

". . . It was the custom at that time *not* to notify the chosen person in advance but rather to let him hear of his appointment when his name was read in conference for a sustaining vote. Thus it was that when Joseph Fielding left for conference on April 6, 1910, he had no knowledge of having been selected." As he entered the Tabernacle, an usher said to him, "Well Joseph, who is the new apostle to be?" He responded: "I don't know. But it won't be you and it won't be me!"

Just before the name of the newest member of the Quorum of the Twelve was read, Joseph felt a prompting from the Spirit that the name might be his own. Still, he later said that when his name was announced, "I was so startled and dumbfounded I could hardly speak."

*The Quorum of the Twelve Apostles in 1921. Elder Joseph
Fielding Smith is standing on the far left.*

Later that day, he went home to share the news with Ethel, who
had not been able to attend the meeting. He began by saying: "I
guess we'll have to sell the cow. I haven't time to take care of it any
more!"[35]

During his 60 years as a member of the Quorum of the Twelve
Apostles, Joseph Fielding Smith saw many changes in the world.
For example, when he was called to the apostleship, many people
still used the horse and carriage as their primary means of transportation. At the end of his service in the quorum, he often traveled to
assignments by jet plane.

Elder Smith held many positions of trust and responsibility while
serving as a member of the Quorum of the Twelve. For the first
eight years of his ministry as an Apostle, he served unofficially as
a secretary for his father. He served in this capacity until his father
passed away in November 1918. In this role, Joseph Fielding Smith
acted as scribe when his father dictated the vision of the redemption of the dead, now found in Doctrine and Covenants 138.

Elder Smith served as Assistant Church Historian, as Church Historian for almost 50 years, as a counselor in the Salt Lake Temple
presidency, as president of the Salt Lake Temple, as president of

the Utah Genealogical and Historical Society, as the first editor and business manager of the *Utah Genealogical and Historical Magazine,* and as the chairman of the Executive Committee of the Church Board of Education. He also served as the chairman of the Church Publications Committee, an assignment that required him to read thousands of pages of manuscripts before they were prepared as lesson manuals and other Church publications.

He was set apart as Acting President of the Quorum of the Twelve on October 6, 1950, and he served in that capacity until April 1951, when he was set apart as President of the Quorum of the Twelve. He served in that capacity from April 1951 to January 1970, when he became President of the Church. From 1965 to 1970, he also served as a Counselor in the First Presidency while continuing in his responsibilities as President of the Quorum of the Twelve.

A Ministry of Stern Warnings and Gentle Forgiveness

In his first address at general conference, Elder Joseph Fielding Smith spoke directly to anyone who would "raise his voice against the actions of the authorities who preside over the Church." He issued this stern declaration: "I wish to raise a warning voice to all such who hold membership in the Church, and say unto them, that they had better repent and turn unto the Lord, lest His judgments come upon them, lest they lose the faith and be turned from the truth." [36]

Throughout his ministry, he continued to raise a voice of warning. He once said: "I have considered that it has been my mission, having been so impressed, I think, by the Spirit of the Lord in my travels in the stakes of Zion, to say unto the people that *now* is the day of repentance. . . . I feel that it is my mission to cry repentance and to call upon the people to serve the Lord." [37]

This no-nonsense, straightforward approach to teaching was tempered by gentleness and kindness. Elder Boyd K. Packer once witnessed this in a meeting when Joseph Fielding Smith was chairman of the Church's Missionary Committee. "A report was presented concerning an accident involving two missionary elders in a Church-owned automobile. An elderly vegetable vendor had run a stop sign with his truck. The missionary car was struck broadside and totally wrecked. The driver of the truck was cited by the police. He had no insurance. Fortunately, neither missionary was seriously injured.

"President Smith sat silent as the members of the committee considered the matter. After some discussion they instructed the managing director of the Missionary Department to retain an attorney and press the matter in court.

"Only then was President Smith asked if he agreed with that course of action. Quietly he said: 'Yes, we could do that. And if we press with all vigor, we might even succeed in taking the truck away from the poor man; then how would he make a living?'

" 'We looked at each other, a little ashamed,' Elder Packer said. 'Then we allowed that the Church could buy another missionary car, go about its work, and leave the matter alone.' "[38]

"A Kind, Loving Husband and Father"

When Elder Smith was called to the apostleship, he had three children: Josephine and Julina and Ethel's firstborn child, Emily. Seven months later, the family welcomed another daughter, Ethel and Joseph named her Naomi. Because of complications at birth, Naomi had to struggle for her life, and the family feared that she might not live long. But, as her father later said, she "was saved through the power [of] prayer and administration after it appeared that breath could not enter her body."[39] Ethel later gave birth to seven other children: Lois, Amelia, Joseph, Lewis, Reynolds, Douglas, and Milton.

President Smith's assignments as an Apostle often took him away from home for long periods of time. But when he was home, he focused his attention on his family. His wife Ethel described him as "a kind, loving husband and father whose greatest ambition in life is to make his family happy, entirely forgetful of self in his efforts to do this."[40]

The children in the Smith family were amused by the impression some people had of their father—as a severe, stern man. "One time . . . after he had preached a rather vigorous sermon on the importance of properly governing one's children, an annoyed woman approached two of his little daughters and expressed sympathy for them [and said,] 'I'll bet your daddy beats you!'" In response to this accusation, the girls just giggled. They knew their father much better than she did—he would never hurt them. When he came home from his long trips, "it was happy times, from the moment they eagerly met him at the train depot until they sadly bade him farewell again several days hence." They played games, made pies and ice cream, went on picnics, rode the train, and visited nearby canyons and lakes. They enjoyed hearing stories about his Church assignments all over the world.[41] They also worked together, staying busy with chores around the house.[42]

President Smith's sons played sports, and he attended their games whenever he could.[43] He also enjoyed playing sports with them, particularly handball. He had fun with them, but he was competitive. His sons Reynolds and Lewis remembered times when the two of them teamed up against their father. He let them choose which hand he could use during the game. Even with one hand behind his back, he always "soundly trounced them both."[44]

Sadness and Hope

Elder Smith's assignments away from home were difficult for Ethel and the children, and the weeks of separation were also painful for him. On April 18, 1924, he was traveling by train to preside at a stake conference. Ethel was seven months pregnant at the time, doing her best to care for the children at home. In a letter to her, he said, "I am thinking of you and wish I could be with you constantly for the next few weeks, to help take care of you."[45] As he thought of home, he closed the letter with a poem he had written. Some of the words to that poem now appear in many Church hymnbooks under the title "Does the Journey Seem Long?"

> Does the journey seem long,
> The path rugged and steep?
> Are there briars and thorns on the way?
> Do sharp stones cut your feet
> As you struggle to rise
> To the heights thru the heat of the day?

Is your heart faint and sad,
Your soul weary within,
As you toil 'neath your burden of care?
Does the load heavy seem
You are forced now to lift?
Is there no one your burden to share?

Let your heart be not faint
Now the journey's begun;
There is One who still beckons to you.
So look upward in joy
And take hold of his hand;
He will lead you to heights that are new—

A land holy and pure,
Where all trouble doth end,
And your life shall be free from all sin,
Where no tears shall be shed,
For no sorrows remain.
Take his hand and with him enter in.[46]

Beginning in 1933, the happiness in the Smith home was some-times interrupted by a heavy "burden of care," as Elder Smith had expressed in his poem nine years earlier. Ethel began to suffer from "a terrible illness which she could not understand. At times she was plunged into the depths of depression and at other times her mind raced beyond control forcing her exhausted body to do more and more. The tender love and support of her family, prayers, and blessings, even hospitalizations did not seem to help."[47] After four years of suffering, she died on August 26, 1937. Writing of her death, her bereaved husband recorded, "A better woman could not be found, or truer wife and mother."[48] In the depths of his sorrow, he felt the comforting knowledge that he and Ethel Reynolds Smith were bound together for the eternities by a sacred sealing covenant.

A New Friendship Leads to Marriage

When Ethel died, five children still lived in the Smith home. Two of them would soon move away—Amelia was engaged to be married, and Lewis was preparing to serve a full-time mission.

This would leave 16-year-old Reynolds, 13-year-old Douglas, and 10-year-old Milton. Concerned about these motherless sons, Joseph Fielding Smith pondered the idea of marrying again.

With this idea in mind, Elder Smith soon focused his attention on Jessie Ella Evans, a famous soloist with the Mormon Tabernacle Choir. Jessie had sung a solo at Ethel's funeral services, and Elder Smith had sent her a note to express his appreciation. That note had led to conversations by telephone. Elder Smith and Jessie had not known one another before this exchange, but they quickly became good friends.

Elder Smith spent days thinking and praying about the possibility of asking Jessie to marry him. Finally he wrote her a letter in which he hinted that he would like to have a more personal friendship with her. Four days later, he worked up the courage to deliver the letter in person. He took it to the city and county offices, where she worked as the county recorder. Later he recorded the following in his journal: "Went to *County Recorder's* office. . . . *Had interview with recorder, very important,* and left her the letter I wrote."[49] Following a week in which he traveled by train to stake conference meetings, Elder Smith returned home and once again visited with Jessie.

In his typical straightforward style, Elder Smith wrote in his journal, "Met Miss Jessie Evans and had [an] *important* interview with her." With mutual feelings of admiration, they made arrangements for him to meet Jessie's mother and for Jessie to meet his children. Less than a month later, on November 21, 1937, she accepted an engagement ring. The two were sealed in the Salt Lake Temple on April 12, 1938, by President Heber J. Grant, the seventh President of the Church.[50]

Elder Francis M. Gibbons, who served as a secretary to the First Presidency when President Smith was President of the Church, described the relationship between Joseph Fielding Smith and Jessie Evans Smith: "Despite a difference of twenty-six years in their ages and differences in temperament, background, and training, Joseph Fielding and Jessie Evans Smith were remarkably compatible. She was an irrepressible extrovert, full of fun and good humor, who enjoyed the limelight of public attention. Joseph, on the other hand,

Joseph Fielding Smith and Jessie Evans Smith at the piano

was a quiet, retiring introvert, dignified and detached, who always seemed somewhat uncomfortable in a public setting and who never sought to call attention to himself. The thing that bridged the wide gulf between these two disparate personalities was the genuine love and respect they had for each other."[51] This love and respect extended to Jessie's mother, Jeanette Buchanan Evans, with whom Jessie had been living until the marriage. Sister Evans joined her daughter to live in the Smith home and helped care for the children.

Ministering to a World in Turmoil

The new Sister Smith, addressed as Aunt Jessie by Elder Smith's children and grandchildren, frequently joined her husband as he traveled to stake conferences. Local leaders often invited her to sing in meetings, and occasionally she persuaded her husband to sing a duet with her. In 1939, President Heber J. Grant assigned Elder and Sister Smith to tour all of the Church's missions in Europe.

Although World War II had not yet erupted when the Smiths arrived in Europe, tensions between the nations were increasing.

On August 24, while the Smiths were in Germany, the First Presidency instructed Elder Smith to see that all missionaries in Germany were transferred to neutral countries. He coordinated this work from Copenhagen, Denmark. During this transferral of missionaries, Wallace Toronto, the mission president in Czechoslovakia, found it necessary to send his wife, Martha, and their children to Copenhagen for safety. He remained behind to ensure the safe evacuation of four missionaries who had been detained. Days passed without any word from them. Martha later recalled:

"The day finally came when all trains, ferries, and boats made their last runs from Germany and we prayed that Wally [President Toronto] and his four young charges would be on that last ferry as it headed for its home port. Seeing that I was very worried and getting more upset by the minute, President Smith came over to me, put his protecting arm around my shoulders and said, 'Sister Toronto, this war will not start until Brother Toronto and his missionaries arrive in this land of Denmark.' As the day advanced into early evening, a telephone call came. . . . It was Wally! The five of them had come out of Czechoslovakia with the British Legation on a special train that had been sent in for them, boarded the last ferry from Germany, and they were now on the coast [of Denmark] waiting for transportation to Copenhagen. The relief and happiness felt in the mission home and among the 350 missionaries was like a dark cloud lifting to reveal sunshine."[52]

Elder Smith was grateful to the people of Denmark, who allowed so many evacuated missionaries into their country. At the outbreak of the war, he prophesied that because of their generosity, the Danish people would not suffer for lack of food during the war. Years later, "the people of Denmark had survived the war perhaps better than those of any other European nation. The Danish Saints had even sent welfare packages to distressed Latter-day Saints in Holland and Norway. Membership had steadily increased, and tithing receipts in the Danish Mission had more than doubled. . . . The Danish Saints considered their circumstances a direct fulfillment of [the] prophecy that Elder Joseph Fielding Smith had made."[53]

As the war began, Elder Smith organized the evacuation of the 697 American missionaries serving in Europe. Because some of the missionaries had served as district and branch leaders, Elder Smith transferred those leadership responsibilities to local members. After fulfilling these duties, Elder Smith sailed for the United States with Jessie. They took a train from New York and arrived home seven months after they had left.

Although Elder Smith was happy that the American missionaries were able to return safely to their homes, he expressed concern for the innocent people now caught in the tragedy of war in their homelands. He wrote: "My heart was sick every time we held a meeting and shook hands with the people at its close. They all greeted us warmly, and their [friendship] meant more to me than they perhaps realized. Some of them shed tears and said they were looking for grave trouble, and we would never meet again in this life. I feel sorry for them now, and pray each day that the Lord will protect them through this dreadful time."[54]

Elder Smith's son Lewis, who was in England when World War II began, was part of the last group of missionaries to return home.[55] About two and a half years later, Lewis crossed the Atlantic Ocean again, this time to serve in the military. "This condition brought sadness to us all," wrote Elder Smith. "It is a shame that the clean and the righteous are forced into a conflict of world proportions, because of the wickedness of men."[56]

On January 2, 1945, Elder Smith received a telegram informing him that his son had been killed in the service of his country. He wrote: "This word came to us as a most severe shock as we had high hopes that soon he would be back in the United States. We had felt that he would be protected as he has escaped several times before from danger. It was hard for us to realize that such a thing could happen. . . . As severe as the blow is, we have the peace and happiness of knowing that he was clean and free from the vices so prevalent in the world and found in the army. He was true to his faith and is worthy of a glorious resurrection, when we shall be reunited again."[57]

A Trusted Teacher and Leader

As a member of the Quorum of the Twelve, Joseph Fielding Smith often stood before Latter-day Saints to testify of Jesus Christ, teach the restored gospel, and call the people to repentance. He delivered more than 125 sermons in general conference, participated in thousands of stake conferences, and spoke at events such as genealogy conferences and radio broadcasts. He also taught by the written word. For many years he wrote a feature in the Church's *Improvement Era* magazine, answering questions submitted by readers. He also wrote other articles for Church magazines and the Church section of the *Deseret News*. During his service as an Apostle, from 1910 to 1972, his writings were published in 25 books, including *Essentials in Church History, Doctrines of Salvation, Church History and Modern Revelation,* and *Answers to Gospel Questions.*

Through listening to his sermons and reading his writings, Church members came to trust President Smith as a gospel scholar. Even more, they learned to trust and follow the Lord. As President N. Eldon Tanner said, Joseph Fielding Smith "influenced the lives of hundreds of thousands of people as he lived and taught by word and pen every principle of the gospel. He left no doubt in the minds of anyone that he knew that God is a living God and that we are his spirit children; that Jesus Christ is the Only Begotten Son of God in the flesh; that he gave his life for us that we might enjoy immortality; and that by accepting and living the gospel we may enjoy eternal life."[58]

Elder Bruce R. McConkie observed:

"The life and labors of President Joseph Fielding Smith were characterized by three things:

"1. His love of the Lord and the absolute, unswerving fidelity with which he sought to signify that love by keeping his commandments and doing ever those things which would please the Lord.

"2. His loyalty to the Prophet Joseph Smith and the everlasting truths restored through him; to his grandfather, the Patriarch Hyrum Smith, . . . [who] met a martyr's death; and to his father, President Joseph F. Smith, whose name is enshrined forever in the celestial city as one who endured valiantly in the cause of him whose blood was shed that we might live.

"3. His own gospel scholarship and spiritual insight; his own unwearying diligence as a preacher of righteousness; and his own course of feeding the hungry, clothing the naked, visiting the widow and the fatherless, and manifesting pure religion by precept as well as by example."[59]

President Smith's brethren in the Quorum of the Twelve saw him as a wise, compassionate leader. In recognition of his 80th birthday, the other members of the Quorum of the Twelve published a tribute to him. As part of that tribute, they said:

"We who labor in the Council of the Twelve under his leadership have occasion to glimpse the true nobility in his character. Daily we see continuing evidences of his understanding and thoughtful consideration of his fellow workers in making our assignments and in co-ordinating our efforts to the end that the work of the Lord might move forward. We only wish that the entire Church could feel the tenderness of his soul and his great concern over the welfare of the unfortunate and those in distress. He loves all the saints and never ceases to pray for the sinner.

"With remarkable discernment, he seems to have but two measures in arriving at final decisions. What are the wishes of the First Presidency? Which is best for the kingdom of God?"[60]

President of the Church

On a Sabbath morning, January 18, 1970, President David O. McKay's mortal life came to an end. The responsibility of Church leadership now rested on the Quorum of the Twelve Apostles, with 93-year-old Joseph Fielding Smith as their President.

On January 23, 1970, the Quorum of the Twelve met and officially sustained President Smith in his calling as President of The Church of Jesus Christ of Latter-day Saints. President Smith selected Harold B. Lee as First Counselor and N. Eldon Tanner as Second Counselor. Then all three men were set apart to fulfill their new responsibilities.

President Joseph Fielding Smith and his Counselors in the First Presidency:
President Harold B. Lee (center) and President N. Eldon Tanner (right)

Elder Ezra Taft Benson, who was present at that meeting, re-called: "We had a wonderful spirit of unity in our meeting and great evidence of affection as the brethren threw their arms around each other as the new leadership was selected and set apart."[61]

Elder Boyd K. Packer shared his personal witness of President Smith's calling:

"I left the office one Friday afternoon thinking of the weekend conference assignment. I waited for the elevator to come down from the fifth floor.

"As the elevator doors quietly opened, there stood President Joseph Fielding Smith. There was a moment of surprise in seeing him, since his office is on a lower floor.

"As I saw him framed in the doorway, there fell upon me a pow-erful witness—there stands the prophet of God. That sweet voice of Spirit that is akin to light, that has something to do with pure intelligence, affirmed to me that this was the prophet of God."[62]

Under President Smith's leadership, the Church continued to grow. For example, 81 stakes were created, including the first stakes in Asia and Africa, and Church membership passed 3 million. Two temples were dedicated—in Ogden, Utah, and Provo, Utah.

Even as the Church grew worldwide, President Smith emphasized the importance of individual homes and families. He reminded Latter-day Saints that "the Church organization really exists to assist the family and its members in reaching exaltation."[63] He taught: "The family is the most important organization in time or in eternity. . . . It is the will of the Lord to strengthen and preserve the family unit."[64] In an effort to strengthen families and individuals, the Church placed greater emphasis on family home evening, a program that had been encouraged since 1909, when President Smith's father was President of the Church. Under the leadership of President Joseph Fielding Smith, Mondays were officially designated for family home evening. On those nights, no Church meetings were to be held, and local Church facilities were closed.

Despite his advanced age, President Smith approached his calling with childlike humility and youthful energy. In the two years and five months he served as the Church's prophet, seer, and revelator, Latter-day Saints across the world were inspired by his messages.

He declared that "we are the spirit children of God our Heavenly Father"[65] and that "we must believe in Christ and pattern our lives after him."[66] He testified that Joseph Smith "beheld and stood in the actual presence of God the Father and his Son Jesus Christ"[67] and became "the revealer of the knowledge of Christ and of salvation to the world for this day and generation."[68]

He encouraged the Saints to "forsake many of the ways of the world"[69] but to love all people in the world—"to see the good in people even though we are trying to help them overcome one or two bad habits."[70] He reminded them that one way to show this "spirit of love and brotherhood" is to share the gospel—to "invite all men everywhere to give heed to the words of eternal life revealed in this day."[71]

He reached out to the youth of the Church, meeting with large congregations of young Latter-day Saints and encouraging them to "stand firm in the faith despite all opposition."[72]

He spoke often to priesthood holders, reminding them that they had been "called to represent the Lord and hold his authority" and exhorting them to "remember who [they] are and act accordingly."[73]

He encouraged all Latter-day Saints to receive temple blessings, be true to temple covenants, and return to the temple to receive sacred ordinances for their ancestors. Before dedicating the Ogden Utah Temple, he said, "May I remind you that when we dedicate a house to the Lord, what we really do is dedicate ourselves to the Lord's service, with a covenant that we shall use the house in the way he intends that it shall be used."[74]

"Keep the commandments," he urged. "Walk in the light. Endure to the end. Be true to every covenant and obligation, and the Lord will bless you beyond your fondest dreams."[75]

Quoting President Brigham Young, President Harold B. Lee described President Smith's influence and leadership: "President Young said this: 'If we live our holy religion and let the Spirit reign, it will not become dull or stupid, but as the body approaches dissolution, the Spirit takes a firmer hold on that enduring substance behind the veil, drawing from the depths of that eternal fountain of life sparkling gems of intelligence, which surround the frail and shrinking tabernacle with a halo of immortal wisdom.'

"This we have witnessed time and again, as we were engaged in discussing very serious matters—decisions that should only be made by the President of the Church. It was then that we saw this sparkling wisdom come to light as he [President Smith] recounted undoubtedly beyond his own present understanding things that he called up from the depths of his soul."[76]

"Called by the Lord . . . to Other and Greater Labors"

On August 3, 1971, Jessie Evans Smith passed away, leaving President Joseph Fielding Smith as a widower for the third time. As a result, President Smith went to live with his daughter Amelia

McConkie and her husband, Bruce. His other children regularly took turns visiting him and taking him for rides. He continued to go to his office each weekday, attend meetings, and travel on Church business.

On June 30, 1972, President Smith left his office on the first floor of the Church Administration Building toward the end of the day. With his secretary, D. Arthur Haycock, he went to the Church Historian's office, where he had labored prior to becoming President of the Church. He desired to greet all those who served there. After shaking their hands, he went to the basement of the building to shake the hands of the telephone operators and others who worked in that area to show his appreciation. This was his last day at the office.

On Sunday, July 2, 1972, just 17 days before his 96th birthday, he attended sacrament meeting in his home ward. Later that afternoon he visited his firstborn child, Josephine, with his son Reynolds. That evening, as he sat in his favorite chair in the McConkie home, he passed away peacefully. As his son-in-law later said, President Smith had been "called by the Lord whom he loved so much and served so well to other and greater labors in his eternal vineyard."[77]

President Harold B. Lee, who was now the senior Apostle on the earth, visited the McConkie home when he heard of President Smith's passing. He "walked quietly to the couch, and, kneeling, took one of the Prophet's hands in his. He remained in that position for some time, not speaking, in prayer or meditation. He then arose to express his condolences to the family, his admiration for their father, and his admonition to them that they honor President Smith by living worthily."[78]

Tributes to "a Devoted Man of God"

At President Smith's funeral services, President N. Eldon Tanner referred to him as "a devoted man of God, one who has served so nobly both God and his fellowmen and who has led by example his family and all over whom he has been called to preside; one of whom it can truthfully be said he was a man without guile and without pride. It could never be said of him," observed President

Tanner, "that he 'loved the praise of men more than the praise of God' [John 12:43]."[79]

President Harold B. Lee said: "Brother Tanner and I have loved this man these last two and a half years. It hasn't been pretended. He begat love, because he loved us, and we have stood by him, as he stood by and trusted us."[80]

A newspaper that had been critical of President Smith, even questioning his call to the Twelve over 60 years earlier, now published the following tribute: "Joseph Fielding Smith, a man stern in devotion to his creed, yet tender in regard for essential needs of people everywhere, gave wise counsel to his associates, loving care to his family and exalted leadership to his church responsibilities. He will be missed, but remembered with special esteem."[81]

Perhaps the most meaningful tribute was the declaration of a family member, President Smith's son-in-law Bruce R. McConkie, who described him as "a son of God; an apostle of the Lord Jesus Christ; a prophet of the Most High; and above all, a father in Israel!" Elder McConkie prophesied, "For years to come his voice will speak from the dust as generations yet unborn learn the doctrines of the gospel from his writings."[82]

As you study this book, the teachings of President Joseph Fielding Smith will help fulfill that declaration. His voice will "speak from the dust" to you as you "learn the doctrines of the gospel."

Notes

1. Gordon B. Hinckley, "Believe His Prophets," *Ensign,* May 1992, 52.

2. Thomas S. Monson, in "News of the Church," *Ensign,* May 1996, 110.

3. Bruce R. McConkie, "Joseph Fielding Smith: Apostle, Prophet, Father in Israel," *Ensign,* Aug. 1972, 29.

4. Julina Lambson Smith, in Joseph Fielding Smith Jr. and John J. Stewart, *The Life of Joseph Fielding Smith* (1972), 52.

5. Joseph Fielding Smith, in *The Life of Joseph Fielding Smith,* 65.

6. Joseph Fielding Smith Jr. and John J. Stewart, *The Life of Joseph Fielding Smith,* 51.

7. Joseph Fielding Smith Jr. and John J. Stewart, *The Life of Joseph Fielding Smith,* 57.

8. In Conference Report, Apr. 1930, 91.

9. Joseph Fielding Smith Jr. and John J. Stewart, *The Life of Joseph Fielding Smith,* 62.

10. Joseph Fielding Smith Jr. and John J. Stewart, *The Life of Joseph Fielding Smith,* 71–72.

11. Joseph Fielding Smith, in Conference Report, Oct. 1970, 92.

12. See Joseph Fielding Smith Jr. and John J. Stewart, *The Life of Joseph Fielding Smith,* 73–74; Francis M. Gibbons, *Joseph Fielding Smith: Gospel Scholar, Prophet of God* (1992), 52–53.

13. Joseph Fielding Smith, in *The Life of Joseph Fielding Smith,* 75.

14. Joseph Fielding Smith, in *The Life of Joseph Fielding Smith,* 79.

15. See *The Life of Joseph Fielding Smith,* 80.

16. In *The Life of Joseph Fielding Smith,* 81.

17. See *The Life of Joseph Fielding Smith,* 82.

18. Joseph Fielding Smith Jr. and John J. Stewart, *The Life of Joseph Fielding Smith,* 83.

19. Joseph Fielding Smith, in *The Life of Joseph Fielding Smith,* 90.

20. Joseph Fielding Smith, in *The Life of Joseph Fielding Smith,* 117; see also page 116.

21. Joseph F. Smith, in *The Life of Joseph Fielding Smith,* 116.

22. Lewis Shurtliff, in *The Life of Joseph Fielding Smith,* 112–13.

23. Joseph Fielding Smith Jr. and John J. Stewart, *The Life of Joseph Fielding Smith,* 113.

24. Joseph Fielding Smith, in *The Life of Joseph Fielding Smith,* 96.

25. Louie Smith, in *The Life of Joseph Fielding Smith,* 113–14.

26. Joseph Fielding Smith Jr. and John J. Stewart, *The Life of Joseph Fielding Smith,* 92.

27. Joseph Fielding Smith, in *The Life of Joseph Fielding Smith,* 115.

28. See *The Life of Joseph Fielding Smith,* 91.

29. In Francis M. Gibbons, *Joseph Fielding Smith: Gospel Scholar, Prophet of God,* 124.

30. See Joseph Fielding Smith, in *The Life of Joseph Fielding Smith,* 152–53.

31. See *Joseph Fielding Smith: Gospel Scholar, Prophet of God,* 113.

32. Joseph Fielding Smith, in *The Life of Joseph Fielding Smith,* 160.

33. Joseph Fielding Smith, in *The Life of Joseph Fielding Smith,* 162.

34. Joseph Fielding Smith, in *The Life of Joseph Fielding Smith,* 169.

35. Joseph Fielding Smith Jr. and John J. Stewart, *The Life of Joseph Fielding Smith,* 174–76.

36. In Conference Report, Oct. 1910, 39.

37. In Conference Report, Oct. 1919, 88–89.

38. Lucile C. Tate, *Boyd K. Packer: A Watchman on the Tower* (1995), 176.

39. Joseph Fielding Smith, in *Joseph Fielding Smith: Gospel Scholar, Prophet of God,* 162.

40. Ethel Smith, in Bryant S. Hinckley, "Joseph Fielding Smith," *Improvement Era,* June 1932, 459.

41. See *The Life of Joseph Fielding Smith,* 14.

42. See *The Life of Joseph Fielding Smith,* 234.

43. See *The Life of Joseph Fielding Smith,* 15.

44. See *The Life of Joseph Fielding Smith,* 237.

45. Joseph Fielding Smith, in *The Life of Joseph Fielding Smith,* 188–89.

46. *Hymns,* no. 127.

47. Joseph Fielding Smith Jr. and John J. Stewart, *The Life of Joseph Fielding Smith,* 242–43.

48. Joseph Fielding Smith, in *The Life of Joseph Fielding Smith,* 249.

49. Joseph Fielding Smith, in *Joseph Fielding Smith: Gospel Scholar, Prophet of God,* 275.

50. See *The Life of Joseph Fielding Smith,* 251–58.

51. Francis M. Gibbons, *Joseph Fielding Smith: Gospel Scholar, Prophet of God,* 278–79.

52. Martha Toronto Anderson, *A Cherry Tree Behind the Iron Curtain* (1977), 32.

53. Sheri L. Dew, *Ezra Taft Benson: A Biography* (1987), 204.

54. Joseph Fielding Smith, in *The Life of Joseph Fielding Smith,* 282–83.

55. See *Joseph Fielding Smith: Gospel Scholar, Prophet of God,* 315.

56. Joseph Fielding Smith, in *Joseph Fielding Smith: Gospel Scholar, Prophet of God,* 332.

57. Joseph Fielding Smith, in *The Life of Joseph Fielding Smith,* 287–88.

58. N. Eldon Tanner, "A Man without Guile," *Ensign,* Aug. 1972, 33.

59. Bruce R. McConkie, "Joseph Fielding Smith: Apostle, Prophet, Father in Israel," *Ensign,* Aug. 1972, 28.

60. Quorum of the Twelve Apostles, "President Joseph Fielding Smith," *Improvement Era,* July 1956, 495.

61. Ezra Taft Benson, in Sheri L. Dew, *Ezra Taft Benson,* 411.

62. Boyd K. Packer, "The Spirit Beareth Record," *Ensign,* June 1971, 87.

63. Joseph Fielding Smith, in "Message from the First Presidency," *Ensign,* Jan. 1971, inside front cover and page 1.

64. Joseph Fielding Smith, "Counsel to the Saints and to the World," *Ensign,* July 1972, 27.

65. Joseph Fielding Smith, *Sealing Power and Salvation,* Brigham Young University Speeches of the Year (Jan. 12, 1971), 2.

66. Joseph Fielding Smith, "The Plan of Salvation," *Ensign,* Nov. 1971, 5.

67. Joseph Fielding Smith, "To Know for Ourselves," *Improvement Era,* Mar. 1970, 3.

68. Joseph Fielding Smith, "The First Prophet of the Last Dispensation," *Ensign,* Aug. 1971, 7.

69. Joseph Fielding Smith, "Our Responsibilities as Priesthood Holders," *Ensign,* June 1971, 49.

70. Joseph Fielding Smith, "My Dear Young Fellow Workers," *New Era,* Jan. 1971, 4.

71. Joseph Fielding Smith, "I Know That My Redeemer Liveth," *Ensign,* Dec. 1971, 27.

72. Joseph Fielding Smith, "President Joseph Fielding Smith Speaks on the New MIA Theme," *New Era,* Sept. 1971, 40.

73. Joseph Fielding Smith, in Conference Report, Oct. 1970, 92.

74. Joseph Fielding Smith, in "Ogden Temple Dedicatory Prayer," *Ensign,* Mar. 1972, 6.

75. Joseph Fielding Smith, "Counsel to the Saints and to the World," 27.

76. Harold B. Lee, "The President— Prophet, Seer, and Revelator," *Ensign,* Aug. 1972, 35.

77. Bruce R. McConkie, "Joseph Fielding Smith: Apostle, Prophet, Father in Israel," 24.

78. Francis M. Gibbons, *Joseph Fielding Smith: Gospel Scholar, Prophet of God,* 495.

79. N. Eldon Tanner, "A Man without Guile," *Ensign,* Aug. 1972, 32.

80. Harold B. Lee, "The President— Prophet, Seer, and Revelator," 39.

81. *Salt Lake Tribune,* July 4, 1972, 12.

82. Bruce R. McConkie, "Joseph Fielding Smith: Apostle, Prophet, Father in Israel," 24, 27.

Our Father in Heaven

*"It is my desire to remind you of the nature
and kind of being that God is, so that you may
worship him in spirit and in truth and thereby
gain all of the blessings of his gospel."*

From the Life of Joseph Fielding Smith

President Joseph Fielding Smith marveled at the technological advances of his day. "Great progress has been made in mechanics, chemistry, physics, surgery, and other things," he said. "Men have built great telescopes that have brought the hidden galaxies to view. They have, by the aid of the microscope, discovered vast worlds of microorganisms. . . . They have discovered means to control disease. . . . They have invented machines more sensitive than the human touch, more far-seeing than the human eye. They have controlled elements and made machinery that can move mountains, and many other things have they done too numerous to mention. Yes, this is a wonderful age." However, he was concerned about another trend he saw in the world. He lamented: "All of these discoveries and inventions have not drawn men nearer to God! Nor created in their hearts humility and the spirit of repentance, but to the contrary, to their condemnation. . . . Faith has not increased in the world, nor has righteousness, nor obedience to God."[1]

In contrast to the world's growing indifference toward God, President Smith demonstrated a closeness to his Father in Heaven. One of his grandsons recalled: "My mother was an excellent cook, and my grandfather ate frequently at our house. Quite often he would be invited by my father to ask a blessing on the food. His prayers were always very personal—as if talking to a friend."[2]

Through Joseph Smith's First Vision, "the true knowledge of God" was restored.

Teachings of Joseph Fielding Smith

─────────────── ⟨⟨⟨⟩ **1** ⟨⟨⟩⟩ ───────────────

**Beginning with Joseph Smith's First Vision, the true
knowledge of God has been restored in our day.**

I am very grateful for the first vision, in which the Father and the
Son appeared to the youthful prophet and again restored to man
the true knowledge of God.[3]

It should be remembered that the entire Christian world in 1820
had lost the true doctrine concerning God. The simple truth which
was understood so clearly by the apostles and saints of old had
been lost in the mysteries of an apostate world. All the ancient
prophets, and the apostles of Jesus Christ had a clear understanding that the Father and the Son were separate personages, as our
scriptures so clearly teach. Through apostasy this knowledge was
lost. . . . God had become a mystery, and both Father and Son were
considered to be one unknowable effusion of spirit, without body,
parts, or passions. The coming of the Father and the Son placed on
the earth a divine witness who was able by knowledge to restore
to the world the true nature of God.[4]

The [first] vision of Joseph Smith made it clear that the Father and
the Son are separate personages, having bodies as tangible as the
body of man. It was further revealed to him that the Holy Ghost is
a personage of Spirit, distinct and separate from the personalities
of the Father and the Son [see D&C 130:22]. This all-important truth
staggered the world; yet, when we consider the clear expressions
of holy writ, it is a most astounding and wonderful fact that man
could have gone so far astray. The Savior said, "My Father is greater
than I;" [John 14:28] and he invited his disciples, after his resurrection, to handle him and see that it was he, for, said he, "A spirit
hath not flesh and bones, as ye see me have." [Luke 24:39.] The
apostles clearly understood the distinct entities of the Father, Son,
and Holy Ghost, to which they constantly refer in their epistles; and
Paul informed the Corinthians of the fact that when all things are
subjected to the Father, "then shall the Son also himself be subject
unto him that put all things under him, that God may be all in all."
[1 Corinthians 15:28.]

Joseph Smith beheld the Father and the Son; therefore he could testify with personal knowledge that the scriptures were true wherein we read: "So God created man in his own image, in the image of God created he him; male and female created he them." [Genesis 1:27.] This was to be understood literally, and not in some mystical or figurative sense.[5]

2

To exercise faith in God and worship Him, we must have an understanding of His characteristics.

One of our revelations tells us that if we are to be glorified in Christ, as he is in the Father, we must understand and know both how to worship and what we worship. (See D&C 93:19–20.)

It is my desire to remind you of the nature and kind of being that God is, so that you may worship him in spirit and in truth and thereby gain all of the blessings of his gospel.

We know that God is known only by revelation, that he stands revealed or remains forever unknown. We must go to the scriptures—not to the scientists or philosophers—if we are to learn the truth about Deity. Indeed, John's great prophecy about the restoration of the gospel by an angel who should fly in the midst of heaven says that it was to occur so that men could come to a knowledge of the true God and be taught: "Fear God, and give glory to him . . . and worship him that made heaven, and earth, and the sea, and the fountains of waters." (Rev. 14:7.) In other words, beginning with the restoration of the gospel in this dispensation, men once again would be called upon to worship and serve their Creator rather than the false concepts of Deity that prevail in the world.

In every age the Lord's prophets have been called upon to combat false worship and proclaim the truth about God. In ancient Israel there were those who worshiped images and pagan gods, and Isaiah asked: "To whom then will ye liken God? or what likeness will ye compare unto him?

"Hast thou not known? hast thou not heard, that the everlasting God, the Lord, the Creator of the ends of the earth, fainteth not, neither is weary? there is no searching of his understanding." (Isa. 40:18, 28.)

Much of the world today does not have this knowledge of God, and even in [the Church] there are those who have not perfected their understanding of that glorious being who is our Eternal Father. To those without this knowledge we might well say: "Why dost thou limit the glory of God? Or why should ye suppose that he is less than he is? Hast thou not known? Hast thou not heard, that the everlasting God, the Lord, the Creator of the ends of the earth, is infinite and eternal; that he has all power, all might, and all dominion; that he knows all things, and that all things are present before his face?"

In section 20 of the Doctrine and Covenants, which directed the Prophet Joseph Smith to organize the Church again in this dispensation, we have a revealed summary of some of the basic doctrines of salvation. As to Deity the revelation says: " there is a God in heaven, who is infinite and eternal, from everlasting to everlasting the same unchangeable God, the framer of heaven and earth, and all things which are in them." (D&C 20:17.) . . .

God is our Father; he is the being in whose image man is created. He has a body of flesh and bones as tangible as man's (D&C 130:22), and he is the literal and personal father of the spirits of all men. He is omnipotent and omniscient; he has all power and all wisdom; and his perfections consist in the possession of all knowledge, all faith or power, all justice, all judgment, all mercy, all truth, and the fullness of all godly attributes. . . . If we are to have that perfect faith by which we can lay hold upon eternal life, we must believe in God as the possessor of the fullness of all these characteristics and attributes. I say also that he is an infinite and eternal being, and as an unchangeable being, he possesses these perfected powers and attributes from everlasting to everlasting, which means from eternity to eternity.[6]

We know that our Heavenly Father is a glorified, exalted personage who has all power, all might, and all dominion, and that he knows all things. We testify that he, through his Only Begotten Son, is the Creator of this earth and of worlds without number.[7]

──────────── ⌒⌒〉3〈⌒⌒ ────────────

God is a personal being and the Father of our spirits.

We are the spirit children of God our Heavenly Father. . . . We are members of his family. . . . We dwelt with him for long ages in our premortal life. . . . He ordained a plan of progression and salvation which would enable us, if faithful and true in all things, to advance and progress until we become like him.[8]

We are taught in the Scriptures that God is literally, and not in a figurative sense, our very eternal Father. The words of our Redeemer spoken to Mary near the tomb from which he had risen and gained the victory over death, are most sublime and filled with glorious meaning: "Touch me not; for I am not yet ascended to my Father: but go to my brethren, and say unto them, I ascend unto my Father, and your Father; and to my God, and your God." [John 20:17.] In these words the truth of the Fatherhood of God is emphatically pronounced by his only begotten Son, who declares that he is our Brother and that we have the same eternal Father.[9]

I am grateful that the knowledge of God and his laws has been restored in our day and that we who are members of the Church know he is a personal being and not, as some sectarians have said, "a congeries [a disorderly collection] of laws floating like a fog in the universe." I am grateful that we know he is our Father in heaven, the Father of our spirits, and that he ordained the laws whereby we can advance and progress until we become like him. And I am grateful that we know he is an infinite and eternal being who knows all things and has all power and whose progression consists not in gaining more knowledge or power, not in further perfecting his godly attributes, but in the increase and multiplying of his kingdoms.[10]

──────────── ⌒⌒〉4〈⌒⌒ ────────────

Heavenly Father loves us and is interested in each of us.

There comes to my mind an expression in the Pearl of Great Price, in the vision of Moses, which was given at a time when Moses was caught up into an exceeding high mountain and saw God face to face and talked with him. The Lord showed unto Moses

*Moses, here pictured overlooking the promised land, received
a vision in which he learned of God's work and glory.*

the "workmanship of his hands," and Moses beheld the world, and
all the children of men to the latest generations. [See Moses 1:1–8,
27–29.]

And the Lord said to Moses:

"For behold there are many worlds that have passed away by
the word of my power. And there are many that now stand, and
innumerable are they unto man, but all things are numbered unto
me, for they are mine and I know them.

"And it came to pass that Moses spake unto the Lord, saying: Be merciful unto thy servant, O God, and tell me concerning this earth and the inhabitants thereof, and also the heavens, and then thy servant will be content.

"And the Lord God spake unto Moses, saying: The heavens, they are many, and they cannot be numbered unto man; but they are numbered unto me, for they are mine." [Moses 1:35–37.]

. . . The thought comes to mind that notwithstanding the countless number of worlds and the great magnitude of many of them, they are a means to an end, and not the end itself. The Father is creating worlds for the purpose of peopling them—placing upon them his sons and his daughters. We are informed in section 76 of the Doctrine and Covenants, that by and through the Son of God, the "worlds are and were created, and the inhabitants thereof are begotten sons and daughters unto God." [D&C 76:24.]

We learn from these scriptures from which I have read and from other revelations from the Lord, that man is the most important of all our Father's creations. In the same vision given to Moses, the Father said: "And as one earth shall pass away, and the heavens thereof, even so shall another come; and there is no end to my works, neither to my words. For behold, this is my work and my glory—to bring to pass the immortality and eternal life of man." [Moses 1:38–39.]

From this, and other scripture, I say, we learn that the great work of the Father is to bring to pass the salvation of his children giving unto each that reward which each merits according to his works. I feel most assuredly that our Father in heaven is far more interested in a soul—one of his children—than it is possible for an earthly father to be in one of his children. His love for us is greater than can be the love of an earthly parent for his offspring.[11]

———————— 5 ————————

Heavenly Father weeps over His disobedient children.

We are informed that when the Lord spoke to Enoch and showed to him the nations of the earth and explained to him the nature of the punishment that should befall them for their transgressions of his commandments, that the Lord wept and showed his sorrow in tears for their disobedience. Because of this, Enoch marvelled and thought it strange that the Lord could weep.

Here is the passage:

"And it came to pass that the God of heaven looked upon the residue of the people, and he wept; and Enoch bore record of it, saying: How is it that the heavens weep, and shed forth their tears as the rain upon the mountains?

"And Enoch said unto the Lord: How is it that thou canst weep, seeing thou art holy and from all eternity to all eternity?

"And were it possible that man could number the particles of the earth, yea millions of earths like this, it would not be a beginning to the number of thy creations; and thy curtains are stretched out still; and yet thou art there, and thy bosom is there and also thou art merciful and kind forever." [See Moses 7:28–30.]

And the Lord answered: ". . . Behold these thy brethren; they are the workmanship of mine own hands, and I gave unto them their knowledge, in the day I created them; and in the Garden of Eden, gave I unto man his agency;

"And unto thy brethren have I said, and also given commandment, that they should choose me, their Father; but behold they are without affection, and they hate their own blood." [Moses 7:32–33.]

These are reasons why the Lord wept and why the heavens wept.

I was asked by a brother one time if a man could be perfectly happy in the celestial kingdom if one of his children was not permitted to enter there. I told him that I supposed that any man who was so unfortunate as to have one of his children barred from the celestial kingdom would, of course, have feelings of sorrow because of that condition; and that is just the position our Father in heaven is in. Not all of his children are worthy of celestial glory, and many are forced to suffer his wrath because of their transgressions, and this causes the Father and the whole heavens to have sorrow and to weep. The Lord works in accordance with natural law. Man must be redeemed according to law and his reward must be based on the law of justice. Because of this the Lord will not give unto men that which they do not merit, but shall reward all men according to their works.

. . . I am satisfied that our Father in heaven would, if it were possible, save all men and give unto them celestial glory, even the fulness of exaltation. But, he has given unto man his agency and man is under the necessity of obeying the truth according to that which is revealed in order to obtain the exaltation of the righteous.[12]

_____ 6 _____

Heavenly Father has provided the way of redemption so we can be brought back to His presence.

When Adam was in the Garden of Eden he was in the presence of God, our Father. . . . After he was driven out of the Garden of Eden the scene changed. Adam was banished because of his transgression from the presence of the Father. The scriptures say he became spiritually dead—that is, he was shut out from the presence of God.[13]

I know that Jesus Christ is the Son of God and that he received from his Father the power to ransom men from the spiritual and temporal death brought into the world by the fall of Adam.[14]

There was only one way of redemption, one way in which reparation could be made and the body restored again to the spirit; that was by an infinite atonement, and it had to be made by an infinite being, someone not subject to death and yet someone who had the power to die and who also had power over death. And so, our Father in heaven sent us his Son, Jesus Christ, into the world with life in himself. And because he [Jesus Christ] had a mother who had blood in her veins, he had the power to die. He could yield up his body to death and then take it again. Let me read his own words: "Therefore doth my Father love me, because I lay down my life, that I might take it again.

"No man taketh it from me, but I lay it down of myself. I have power to lay it down, and I have power to take it again. This commandment have I received of my Father." (John 10:17–18.)[15]

It was never the intention of our Father in heaven to leave men to grope and feel their way in darkness and that without any light to guide them, and expect them under such conditions to find their way back into his kingdom and into his holy presence. That is not the way of the Lord. All down the ages from the beginning our Father in heaven has shown his kindness for his children and has been willing to give them direction. From the earliest times the heavens have been opened, the Lord has sent messengers from his presence to divinely appointed servants, men holding the authority of the priesthood who have been commissioned to teach the principles of the Gospel, to warn the people and teach them righteousness; and these men have received this knowledge, this inspiration and guidance from these messengers from the presence of God. This is true of our own dispensation. There is no need for men to shut their eyes and feel that there is no light only as they may depend upon their reason, for the Lord has always been willing to lead and direct and show the way. He has sent, as I say, messengers from his presence. He has sent revelation. He has commanded that his word be written, that it be published, so that all the people might know it.[16]

I say to you, and to the whole Church, and, for that matter, to the whole world, that a gracious and loving Father has in these last days spoken again from heaven to his servants the prophets.

His voice has been one inviting all men to come to his Beloved Son, to learn of him, to partake of his goodness, to take his yoke upon them, and to work out their salvation by obedience to the laws of his gospel. His voice has been one of glory and honor, of peace in this life, and of eternal life in the world to come.[17]

Suggestions for Study and Teaching

Questions

- What do you think leads a person to be able to pray to God "as if talking to a friend"? ("From the Life of Joseph Fielding Smith"). Consider ways you can strengthen your relationship with your Heavenly Father.

- President Smith expressed his gratitude for Joseph Smith's First Vision, which restored "the true knowledge of God" (section 1).

What are some truths you know about God the Father and Jesus Christ because of the First Vision?

• Of the characteristics of God that President Smith mentions in section 2, which are most meaningful to you? Why? As you exercise faith in your Heavenly Father, how does it help you to know of His characteristics?

• President Smith testified: "We are the spirit children of God our Heavenly Father. . . . We are members of his family" (section 3). How has this truth influenced you?

• In sections 4 and 5, what expressions help you feel your Heavenly Father's love for you? Why is it important to understand that God loves us and is interested in us individually? How can we help family members and friends feel His love?

• Think about what Heavenly Father has done to help you return to His presence (see section 6). What are your feelings as you think about Heavenly Father sending His Beloved Son? In what ways has Heavenly Father sent "light to guide [you]"?

Related Scriptures

John 3:16; 17:3; 1 Nephi 11:17; Alma 30:44

Teaching Help

"Quite a bit of teaching that is done in the Church is done so rigidly, it's lecture. We don't respond to lectures too well in classrooms. We do in sacrament meeting and at conferences, but teaching can be two-way so that you can ask questions. You can sponsor questions easily in a class" (Boyd K. Packer, "Principles of Teaching and Learning," *Ensign,* June 2007, 87).

Notes

1. In Conference Report, Apr. 1943, 15–16.

2. Unpublished manuscript by Hoyt W. Brewster Jr.

3. In Conference Report, Apr. 1930, 90.

4. *Answers to Gospel Questions,* comp. Joseph Fielding Smith Jr., 5 vols. (1957–66), 3:117.

5. "Origin of the First Vision," *Improvement Era,* Apr. 1920, 496–97; see also *Doctrines of Salvation,* ed. Bruce R. McConkie, 3 vols. (1954–56), 1:2–3.

6. "The Most Important Knowledge," *Ensign,* May 1971, 2–3.

7. "Out of the Darkness," *Ensign,* June 1971, 2.

8. *Sealing Power and Salvation,* Brigham Young University Speeches of the Year (Jan. 12, 1971), 2.

9. "Purpose and Value of Mortal Probation," *Deseret News,* Church section, June 12, 1949, 21; see also *Doctrines of Salvation,* 1:1.

10. "The Most Important Knowledge," 3.

11. In Conference Report, Apr. 1923, 135–36. Note that Moses's vision recorded in Moses 1 is an example of the Savior speaking the words of the Father by divine investiture of authority (see "The Father and the Son: A Doctrinal Exposition by the First Presidency and the Twelve," *Improvement Era,* Aug. 1916, 939; reprinted in *Ensign,* Apr. 2002, 17). The scriptural text and the commentary by Joseph Fielding Smith in this chapter show that the words in Moses 1 represent the mind and will of God the Father.

12. In Conference Report, Apr. 1923, 136–37, 139. See also note 11 in this chapter, which applies also to Enoch's vision recorded in Moses 7.

13. In Conference Report, Oct. 1953, 58.

14. "A Witness and a Blessing," *Ensign,* June 1971, 109.

15. In Conference Report, Apr. 1967, 122.

16. In Conference Report, Oct. 1931, 15.

17. "A Witness and a Blessing," 109.

"All things are concentrated in and around the Lord Jesus Christ, the Redeemer of the world."

Our Savior, Jesus Christ

"Let it be uppermost in your minds, now and at all times, that Jesus is the Christ, the Son of the living God who came into the world to lay down his life that we might live. That is the truth, and is fundamental. Upon that our faith is built."

From the Life of Joseph Fielding Smith

As an Apostle, President Joseph Fielding Smith was true to his calling to be one of the "special witnesses of the name of Christ in all the world" (D&C 107:23). He said: "I try to love Him, our Redeemer, above everything else. It is my duty to. I travel up and down in this country as one of His special witnesses. I couldn't be a special witness of Jesus Christ if I didn't have the absolute and positive knowledge that He is the Son of God and Redeemer of the world."[1]

As a father, President Smith was just as dedicated to his responsibility to testify of the Savior. On July 18, 1948, he sent a letter to his sons Douglas and Milton, who were serving as full-time missionaries. He wrote:

"I sit and reflect at times, and in my reading of the scriptures, I think of the mission of our Lord, what he did for *me,* and when these feelings come upon me I say to myself, I cannot be untrue to him. He loved me with a perfect love, as he has done for all men, especially those who serve him, and I *must* love him with all the love I can, even if it is imperfect, which it should not be. It is wonderful. I did not live in the days of our Savior; he has not come to me in person. I have not beheld him. His Father and he have not felt it necessary to grant me such a great blessing as this. But it is not necessary. I have felt his presence. I know that the Holy Spirit has enlightened my mind and *revealed him unto me,* so that I do love my Redeemer, I hope, and feel it is true, better than everything else in this life. I would not have it otherwise. I want to be true to him. I know he died for me, for you and all mankind that we might live again through the resurrection. I know that he died that I might be forgiven my follies, my sins, and be cleansed from them. How wonderful is this love. How can I, knowing this, do anything else but love him, my Redeemer. I want my boys in the mission fields to feel this same way. I want my children and my grandchildren to feel that way, and never stray from the path of truth and righteousness." [2]

One of President Smith's sons recounted:

"As children, so frequently we would hear him say, 'If only the people in the world would understand the trials, the tribulations, the sins our Lord took upon himself for our benefit.' Whenever he would refer to this, tears would come into his eyes.

"[Once] as I sat alone with my father in his study, I observed that he had been in deep meditation. I hesitated to break the silence, but finally he spoke. 'Oh, my son, I wish you could have been with me last Thursday as I met with my Brethren in the temple. Oh, if you could have heard them testify of their love for their Lord and Savior, Jesus Christ!' And then he lowered his head, and tears streamed from his face and dropped to his shirt. Then, after many seconds, without as much as raising his head, but moving his head back and forth, he said, 'Oh, how I love my Lord and Savior Jesus Christ!'" [3]

Teachings of Joseph Fielding Smith

1

Jesus Christ is the Only Begotten Son of God and the Savior of the world.

May I say, as plainly and as forcefully as I can, that we believe in Christ. We accept him without reservation as the Son of God and the Savior of the world. [4]

We know that salvation is in Christ; that he was the Firstborn Son of the Eternal Father; that he was chosen and foreordained in the councils of heaven to work out the infinite and eternal atonement;

that he was born into the world as the Son of God; and that he has brought life and immortality to light through the gospel.

We believe with perfect surety that Christ came to ransom men from the temporal and spiritual death brought into the world by the fall of Adam and that he took upon himself the sins of all men on condition of repentance. . . .

We believe it is by grace that we are saved after all that we can do [see 2 Nephi 25:23], and that building upon the foundation of the atonement of Christ, all men must work out their salvation with fear and trembling before the Lord [see Philippians 2:12; Mormon 9:27].[5]

The difference between our Savior and the rest of us is that we have had fathers who were mortal and therefore subject to death. Our Savior did not have a mortal Father and therefore death was subject to him. He had power to lay down his life and to take it again [see John 10:17-18], but we do not have power to lay down our lives and to take them again. It is through the atonement of Jesus Christ that we receive eternal life, through the resurrection of the dead and obedience to the principles of the gospel.[6]

He is indeed the only begotten Son of God, and through His grace, and the grace of His Father, hath redeemed us from sin on condition of our repentance. We know that He has risen from the dead, that He has ascended on high, taking captivity captive [see Psalm 68:18], and has become the author of salvation unto all who will believe, who will repent of their sins and accept Him as the Redeemer of the world [see Hebrews 5:9]. Latter-day Saints are not left in doubt regarding these things.[7]

While men may formulate plans, adopt theories, introduce strange works, and gather and teach many peculiar doctrines, one teaching is fundamental, and from it we cannot depart: *all things are concentrated in and around the Lord Jesus Christ, the Redeemer of the world.* We accept him as the Only Begotten of the Father in the flesh, the only one who has dwelt in the flesh who had a Father who was immortal. Because of his birthright and the conditions surrounding his coming to the earth, he became the Redeemer of men; and through the shedding of his blood we are privileged to return into the presence of our Father, on conditions of our repentance and acceptance of the great plan of redemption of which he is the author.[8]

We testify that the gospel of Jesus Christ is the plan of salvation; and that through our Lord's atoning sacrifice all men shall be raised in immortality, to be judged by him according to the deeds done in the flesh; and that those who believe and obey the fullness of gospel law shall be raised also unto eternal life in our Father's kingdom.[9]

2

We become the sons and daughters of Jesus Christ through His Atonement and through our covenants of obedience to Him.

Our Father in heaven is the Father of Jesus Christ, both in the spirit and in the flesh. Our Savior is the Firstborn in the spirit, the Only Begotten in the flesh.[10]

He [Jesus Christ] is our Elder Brother and was honored by the Father with the fulness of authority and power as a member of the grand Presidency, of Father, Son, and Holy Ghost.[11]

Our scriptures teach that Jesus Christ is both the Father and the Son. The simple truth is that he is the Son of God by birth, both in the spirit and in the flesh. He is the Father because of the work that he has performed.[12]

The Savior becomes our Father, in the sense in which this term is used in the scriptures, because he offers us life, eternal life, through the atonement which he made for us. In the wonderful instruction given by King Benjamin we find this: "And now, because of the covenant which ye have made ye shall be called *the children of Christ, his sons, and his daughters;* for behold, this day *he hath spiritually begotten you;* for ye say that your hearts are changed through faith on his name; therefore, *ye are born of him and have become his sons and his daughters.*" [Mosiah 5:7; see also verses 8–11.]

So, we become the children, sons and daughters of Jesus Christ, through our covenants of obedience to him. Because of his divine authority and sacrifice on the cross, we become spiritually begotten sons and daughters, and he is our Father.[13]

*"We become the children, sons and daughters of Jesus
Christ, through our covenants of obedience to him."*

Like the Nephites in King Benjamin's day, we Latter-day Saints
have likewise taken upon ourselves the name of Christ [see Mosiah
5:1–9; 6:1–2]. Each week at the sacrament service, as we are commanded to do, we take upon us his name always to remember him
and that is what the Nephites covenanted to do.[14]

3

The Savior has revealed Himself in this dispensation, and each of us can have an abiding testimony of Him.

We accept Jesus as the Redeemer of the world. We know . . . that
He revealed Himself in this dispensation. We are not dependent

upon the testimonies of . . . ancient worthies, who lived in His day and conversed with Him in His ministry, and to whom He appeared after His resurrection. We have witnesses who have lived in our own day, who have seen Him, who knew that He lives and have testified to us and to the world of this fact. We know their testimonies are true. Joseph Smith was not left alone to bear witness in this dispensation of the mission of Jesus Christ, for the Lord raised up other witnesses who, with the Prophet Joseph Smith, saw the Redeemer, received instruction from Him and beheld Him in the heavens sitting on the right hand side of the Father surrounded by holy angels. They have given us their testimony which shall stand against the world to condemn all those who heed it not.

But neither are we dependent as members of the Church upon the testimonies of Joseph Smith, Oliver Cowdery, Sidney Rigdon or any others now dead, who in this dispensation received wonderful revelations and visions from the Lord by which they knew that Jesus lives and is the Redeemer of the world. We have an individual testimony given through the Spirit of the Lord to all who have lived in accordance with the Gospel. If we have been in harmony with the truth after having been baptized for the remission of our sins, and confirmed by the laying on of hands for the gift of the Holy Spirit, the Lord has revealed unto us individually that these things are true. We are not dependent upon the testimony of anyone else for this knowledge for we know through the Spirit that Jesus is the Christ, the Redeemer of the world.[15]

If there is any one thing that brings joy and peace and satisfaction to the heart of man, beyond anything else that I know of, it is the abiding testimony which I have, and which you have, that Jesus Christ is the Son of God. That is a truth that cannot be changed. Men may attack it; they may ridicule it; they may declare that he is not the Redeemer of the world, that his mission was not true, or that its purpose, through the shedding of his blood, was not to grant unto all men the remission of sins on condition of their repentance. They may refuse to believe in the resurrection from the dead, or even that Christ himself came forth, as the Scriptures declare, after he had been put to death by his enemies; nevertheless the truth remains. He did die for the sins of the world, he did bring to pass redemption from death, he did grant unto men the opportunity of repentance, and remission of sins through their belief and acceptance of the principles of the gospel, and of his mission. These truths are fundamental, they shall endure; they cannot be destroyed no matter what men may say or think.[16]

Let it be uppermost in your minds, now and at all times, that Jesus is the Christ, the Son of the living God who came into the world to lay down his life that we might live. That is the truth, and is fundamental. Upon that our faith is built.[17]

4

We all should pattern our lives after the life of Jesus Christ.

The greatest example ever set for men was that of the Son of God himself. His life was perfect. He did all things well and was able to say to all men, "Follow thou me," [2 Nephi 31:10] and we all should pattern our lives after his.

I shall give you an illustration from his life. He taught the people how to pray and then said: "Verily, verily, I say unto you, ye must watch and pray always, lest ye be tempted by the devil, and ye be led away captive by him. And as I have prayed among you even so shall ye pray in my church, among my people who do repent and are baptized in my name. Behold I am the light; I have set an example for you. . . . Therefore, hold up your light that it may shine unto the world. Behold I am the light which ye shall hold up—that which ye have seen me do. . . ." [3 Nephi 18:15–16, 24.]

Perhaps his most perfect counsel in this respect was given to the Nephite disciples. "What manner of men ought ye to be?" he asked, and then gave this answer: "Verily I say unto you, even as I am." [3 Nephi 27:27.][18]

We must believe in Christ and pattern our lives after him. We must be baptized as he was baptized. We must worship the Father as he did. We must do the will of the Father as he did. We must seek to do good and work righteousness as he did. He is our Exemplar, the great Prototype of salvation.[19]

When you have a problem and need to make a choice, make it by asking yourself, "What would Jesus do?" Then do as he would.

You can feel the joy of his presence and have his inspiration to guide you each day of your lives if you will seek it and live worthy of it. Jesus' love and the comforting strength of his Holy Spirit can be just as real to you as they were to the children he drew close to him when he lived on the earth.[20]

May I say that those who follow his example will become like him and be glorified with him in his Father's kingdom; to gain honor, power, and authority. To certain Nephite disciples who had followed him with full purpose of heart he said: ". . . ye shall be even as I am, and I am even as the Father; and the Father and I are one." [3 Nephi 28:10.] . . .

I pray that we may all walk in his footsteps and keep his commandments so that we may be like him. This is my desire. I hope it is yours.[21]

Suggestions for Study and Teaching

Questions

- How do you think President Smith's children were influenced by his testimony and his expressions of love for the Savior? (See "From the Life of Joseph Fielding Smith.") Consider what you can do to increase your love for the Savior and share your testimony of Him.

- President Smith declared that "all things are concentrated in and around the Lord Jesus Christ" (section 1). In what ways can this truth influence our personal lives? In what ways can it influence our homes?

- In what ways do the teachings in section 2 help you understand your relationship to the Savior? What does it mean to you to take the name of Christ upon yourself?

- President Smith warned that some people will attack and ridicule truths about Jesus Christ and His Atonement (see section 3). How can we fortify our testimonies so we can withstand such challenges? How can parents help children fortify their testimonies?

• Ponder President Smith's counsel to ask "What would Jesus do?" (section 4). What are some specific ways we can pattern our lives after the life of Jesus Christ? When we follow His example, how might we influence the lives of others?

Related Scriptures

John 14:6; 1 Nephi 10:6; Mosiah 3:5–7; Helaman 5:12; 3 Nephi 11:3–7; D&C 34:1–3; 76:22–24; Joseph Smith—History 1:17

Teaching Help

"[Avoid] the temptation to cover too much material. . . . We are teaching people, not subject matter per se; and . . . every lesson outline that I have ever seen will inevitably have more in it than we can possibly cover in the allotted time" (Jeffrey R. Holland, "Teaching and Learning in the Church," *Ensign,* June 2007, 91).

Notes

1. "Message of President Joseph Fielding Smith" (address delivered May 22, 1955, Joseph Fielding Smith Collection, Church History Library), 2.

2. In Joseph Fielding Smith Jr. and John J. Stewart, *The Life of Joseph Fielding Smith* (1972), 387–88; italics in original.

3. In Leon R. Hartshorn, "President Joseph Fielding Smith: Student of the Gospel," *New Era,* Jan. 1972, 63.

4. "The First Prophet of the Last Dispensation," *Ensign,* Aug. 1971, 6.

5. "Out of the Darkness," *Ensign,* June 1971, 2, 4.

6. Personal correspondence, quoted in *Doctrines of Salvation,* ed. Bruce R. McConkie, 3 vols. (1954–56), 1:28–29.

7. In Conference Report, Apr. 1912, 67.

8. "The One Fundamental Teaching," *Improvement Era,* May 1970, 3; italics in original.

9. "Out of the Darkness," 2, 4.

10. Personal correspondence, quoted in *Doctrines of Salvation,* 1:18.

11. "The Spirit of Reverence and Worship," *Improvement Era,* Sept. 1941, 573; see also *Doctrines of Salvation,* 1:15.

12. Personal correspondence, quoted in *Doctrines of Salvation,* 1:28.

13. Personal correspondence, quoted in *Doctrines of Salvation,* 1:29.

14. *Man: His Origin and Destiny* (1954), 117.

15. In Conference Report, Oct. 1914, 98.

16. In Conference Report, Oct. 1924, 100–101.

17. In Conference Report, Oct. 1921, 186; see also *Doctrines of Salvation,* 2:302.

18. "Follow His Example," *New Era,* Aug. 1972, 4.

19. "The Plan of Salvation," *Ensign,* Nov. 1971, 5.

20. "Christmas Message to Children of the Church in Every Land," *Friend,* Dec. 1971, 3.

21. "Follow His Example," 4.

*"We lived and dwelt with [our Father in Heaven] before
the foundations of this earth were laid."*

The Plan of Salvation

*"Our Father in heaven established a plan of salvation
for his spirit children . . . to enable them to advance
and progress until they obtain eternal life."*

From the Life of Joseph Fielding Smith

On April 29, 1901, Joseph Fielding Smith's 18-year-old sister Alice died after an extended illness. Joseph was just finishing a full-time mission in England. His response to the news of Alice's passing revealed his love for his family and his testimony of the plan of salvation. "It is a dreadful blow to us all," he recorded in his journal. "I did not realize the seriousness of her illness although I knew she was sick. I fully expected to meet her again with the rest of the family within a few weeks, but the will of God be done. It is at such times that the hopes which the gospel present[s] to us are most welcome. We shall all meet again on the other side to enjoy the pleasures and blessings of each other's presence, where family ties will no more be broken, but where we shall all live to receive the blessings, and realize the tender mercies of our Father in heaven. May I always walk in the path of truth, and honor the name I bear, that the meetings with my kindred may be to me indeed most sweet and everlasting, is my humble prayer."[1]

Serving as an Apostle and later as President of the Church, President Joseph Fielding Smith repeatedly testified of the hope that comes through an understanding of the gospel. He taught, "We have the plan of salvation; we administer the gospel; and the gospel is the sole hope of the world, the one way that will bring peace on earth and right the wrongs that exist in all nations."[2]

Teachings of Joseph Fielding Smith

―――――――――― ∞∂) 1 (∂∞ ――――――――――

In the premortal spirit world, we rejoiced to learn of Heavenly Father's plan of salvation.

We are all members of the family of our Father in Heaven. We lived and dwelt with Him before the foundations of this earth were laid. We saw His face, felt His love, and heard His teachings, and He ordained the laws whereby we are able to advance and progress and gain eternal family units of our own.[3]

Our Father in heaven established a plan of salvation for his spirit children. This plan was designed to enable them to advance and progress until they obtain eternal life, which is the name of the kind of life our Father in Heaven lives. This plan is to enable the children of God to become like him and have the power and wisdom and knowledge which he possesses.[4]

We learn from the Pearl of Great Price, that there was a council held in heaven, when the Lord called before him the spirits of his children and presented to them a plan by which they should come down on this earth, partake of mortal life and physical bodies, pass through a probation of mortality and then go on to a higher exaltation through the resurrection which should be brought about through the atonement of his Only Begotten Son, Jesus Christ [see Moses 4:1–2; Abraham 3:22–28]. The thought of passing through mortality and partaking of all the vicissitudes of earth life in which they would gain experiences through suffering, pain, sorrow, temptation and affliction, as well as the pleasures of life in this mundane existence, and then, if faithful, passing on through the resurrection to eternal life in the kingdom of God, to be like him [see 1 John 3:2], filled them with the spirit of rejoicing, and they "shouted for joy." [See Job 38:4–7.] The experience and knowledge obtained in this mortal life, they could not get in any other way, and the receiving of a physical body was essential to their exaltation.[5]

The Fall of Adam and Eve "brought pain, it brought sorrow, it brought death; but . . . it brought blessings also."

2

The Fall of Adam and Eve was part of Heavenly Father's plan.

The plan of salvation, or code of laws, which is known as the gospel of Jesus Christ, was adopted in the heavens, before the foundation of the world was laid. It was appointed there that Adam our father should come to this earth and stand at the head of the whole human family. It was a part of this great plan, that he should partake of the forbidden fruit and fall, thus bringing suffering and death into the world, even for the ultimate good of his children.[6]

The Fall was an essential part of man's mortal probation. . . . Had Adam and Eve not partaken, the great gift of mortality would not have come to them. Moreover, they would have had no posterity, and the great commandment given to them by the Lord would not have been fulfilled.[7]

The fall of Adam brought to pass all of the vicissitudes of mortality. It brought pain, it brought sorrow, it brought death; but we must not lose sight of the fact that it brought blessings also. . . . It brought the blessing of knowledge and understanding and mortal life.[8]

3

Jesus Christ offered Himself as a sacrifice to save us from the Fall and from our sins.

Adam's transgression brought these two deaths, spiritual and temporal—man being banished from the presence of God, and becoming mortal and subject to all the ills of the flesh. In order that he should be brought back again, there had to be a reparation of the broken law. Justice demanded it.[9]

It is most natural and just that he who commits the wrong should pay the penalty—atone for his wrongdoing. Therefore, when Adam was the transgressor of the law, justice demanded that he, and none else, should answer for the sin and pay the penalty with his life. But Adam, in breaking the law, himself became subject to the curse, and being under the curse could not atone, or undo what he had done. Neither could his children, for they also were under the curse, and it required one who was not subject to the curse to atone for that original sin. Moreover, since we were all under the curse, we were also powerless to atone for our individual sins. It therefore became necessary for the Father to send his Only Begotten Son, who was free from sin, to atone for our sins as well as for Adam's transgression, which justice demanded should be done. He accordingly offered himself a sacrifice for sins, and through his death upon the cross took upon himself both Adam's transgression and our individual sins, thereby redeeming us from the fall, and from our sins, on condition of repentance.[10]

It is our duty to teach the mission of Jesus Christ. Why did he come? What did he do for us? How are we benefited? What did it cost him to do it? Why it cost his life, yes, more than his life! What did he do besides being nailed on the cross? Why was he nailed there? He was nailed there that his blood might be shed to redeem us from this most terrible penalty that could ever come, banishment from the presence of God. He died on the cross to bring us back again, to have our bodies and spirits reunited. He gave us that privilege. If we will only believe in him and keep his commandments, he died for us that we might receive a remission of our sins and not be called upon to pay penalty. He paid the price. . . .

. . . No man could do what he did for us. He did not have to die, he could have refused. He did it voluntarily. He did it because it was a commandment from his Father. He knew what the suffering was going to be; and yet, because of his love for us, he was willing to do it. . . .

The driving of the nails into his hands and into the Savior's feet was the least part of his suffering. We get into the habit, I think, of feeling, or thinking that his great suffering was being nailed to the cross and left to hang there. Well, that was a period in the world's history when thousands of men suffered that way. So his suffering, so far as that is concerned, was not any more than the suffering of other men who have been so crucified. What, then, was his great suffering? I wish we could impress this fact upon the minds of every member of this Church: His great suffering occurred before he ever went to the cross. It was in the Garden of Gethsemane, so the scriptures tell us, that blood oozed from every pore of his body; and in the extreme agony of his soul, he cried to his Father. It was not the nails driven into his hands and feet. Now do not ask me how that was done because I do not know. Nobody knows. All we know is that in some way he took upon himself that extreme penalty. He took upon him our transgressions, and paid a price, a price of torment.

Think of the Savior carrying the united burden of every individual—torment in some way which I say, I cannot understand; I just accept—which caused him to suffer an agony of pain, compared to which the driving of the nails in his hands and feet was very little. He cried in His anguish, to His Father, "If it be possible, let this cup pass!" and it could not pass [see Matthew 26:42; Mark 14:36; Luke 22:42]. Let me read you just a word or two here of what the Lord says in regard to that:

"For behold, I, God, have suffered these things for all, that they might not suffer if they would repent;

"But if they would not repent they must suffer even as I;

"Which suffering caused myself, even God, the greatest of all, to tremble because of the pain, and to bleed at every pore, and to suffer both body and spirit—and would that I might not drink the bitter cup, and shrink—

"Nevertheless, glory be to the Father, and I partook and finished my preparations unto the children of men." [D&C 19:16–19.]

When I read that it humbles me. His love for humanity, for the world, was so great that he was willing to carry a burden that no mortal man could carry, and pay an awful price that no other person ever could have paid, that we might escape.[11]

The Son of God [said]: "I'll go down and pay the price. I'll be the Redeemer and redeem men from Adam's transgression. I'll take upon me the sins of the world and redeem or save every soul from his own sins who will repent."[12]

Let us illustrate: A man walking along the road happens to fall into a pit so deep and dark that he cannot climb to the surface and regain his freedom. How can he save himself from his predicament? Not by any exertions on his own part, for there is no means of escape in the pit. He calls for help, and some kindly disposed soul, hearing his cries for relief, hastens to his assistance and by lowering a ladder, gives to him the means by which he may climb again to the surface of the earth. This was precisely the condition that Adam placed himself and his posterity in, when he partook of the forbidden fruit. All being together in the pit, none could gain the surface and relieve the others. The pit was banishment from the presence of the Lord and temporal death, the dissolution of the body. And all being subject to death, none could provide the means of escape.[13]

The Savior comes along, not subject to that pit, and lowers the ladder. He comes down into the pit and makes it possible for us to use the ladder to escape.[14]

In his infinite mercy, the Father heard the cries of his children and sent his Only Begotten Son, who was not subject to death nor to sin, to provide the means of escape. This he did through his infinite atonement and the everlasting gospel.[15]

The gratitude of our hearts should be filled to overflowing in love and obedience for [the Savior's] great and tender mercy. For what he has done we should never fail him. He bought us with a price, the price of his great suffering and the spilling of his blood in sacrifice on the cross.[16]

⟨⟨⟩⟩ **4** ⟨⟨⟩⟩

Building on the foundation of the Atonement of Jesus Christ, we work out our salvation during mortality.

Our Savior Jesus Christ is the central figure in this great plan of progression and salvation.[17]

Building on the foundation of the atonement, the plan of salvation consists of the following things:

First, we must have faith in the Lord Jesus Christ; we must accept him as the Son of God; we must put our trust in him, rely upon his word, and desire to gain the blessings which come by obedience to his laws.

Second, we must repent of our sins; we must forsake the world; we must determine in our hearts, without reservation, that we will live godly and upright lives.

Third, we must be baptized in water, under the hands of a legal administrator, who has power to bind on earth and seal in heaven; we must, through this sacred ordinance, enter into a covenant to serve the Lord and keep his commandments.

Fourth, we must receive the gift of the Holy Ghost; we must be born again; we must have sin and iniquity burned out of our souls as though by fire; we must gain a new creation by the power of the Holy Ghost.

Fifth, we must endure to the end; we must keep the commandments after baptism; we must work out our salvation with fear and trembling before the Lord; we must so live as to acquire the attributes of godliness and become the kind of people who can enjoy the glory and wonders of the celestial kingdom.[18]

Now I testify that these laws which men must obey to gain salvation, and which comprise the gospel of Jesus Christ, have been revealed in this day to prophets and apostles, and that they are now administered by his church, which he has again established upon the earth.[19]

We are, all of us here in this mortal world, on probation. We were sent here primarily to obtain tabernacles [bodies] for our eternal

*"Our Savior Jesus Christ is the central figure in this
great plan of progression and salvation."*

spirits; secondly, to be proved by trial, to have tribulation as well as
the abundant joy and happiness that can be obtained through a sacred covenant of obedience to the eternal principles of the gospel.
Mortality, as Lehi informed his children, is a "probationary state."
(2 Nephi 2:21.) It is here where we are to be tried and tested to see
if we will, when shut out of the presence of our Eternal Father but
still instructed in the way of eternal life, love and revere him and
be true to his Beloved Son, Jesus Christ.[20]

We came here to be tested and proved by coming in contact with
evil as well as the good. . . . The Father has permitted Satan and

his hosts to tempt us, but by the guidance of the Spirit of the Lord and the commandments given through revelation, we are prepared to make our choice. If we do evil, we have been promised that we will be punished; if we do good, we will receive the eternal reward of righteousness.[21]

This mortal probation [is] a brief period, just a short span linking the eternity past with the eternity future. Yet it [is] a period of tremendous importance. . . . This life is the most vital period in our eternal existence.[22]

5

All people will receive the blessing of resurrection through the Atonement of Jesus Christ.

We came into this world to die. That was understood before we came here. It is part of the plan, all discussed and arranged long before men were placed upon the earth. . . . We were ready and willing to make that journey from the presence of God in the spirit world to the mortal world, here to suffer all that pertains to this life, its pleasures and its sorrows, and to die; and death is just as essential as birth.[23]

Physical death, or the death of the mortal man, is not a permanent separation of the spirit and the tabernacle of flesh, notwithstanding the fact that the body returns again to the elements, but is only a temporary separation which shall cease at the resurrection day when the body shall be called forth from the dust to live again animated by spirit. This blessing comes to all men through the atonement of Christ, irrespective of their goodness or wickedness while in mortality. Paul said there should be a resurrection of both the just and the unjust (Acts 24:15), and the Savior said that all who were in their graves should hear his voice and should come forth "they that have done good, unto the resurrection of life; and they that have done evil, unto the resurrection of damnation" (John 5:29).[24]

Every fundamental part of every body will be restored to its proper place again in the resurrection, no matter what may become of the body in death. If it be burned by fire, eaten by sharks, no matter what. Every fundamental part of it will be restored to its own proper place.[25]

Spirits cannot be made perfect without the body of flesh and bones. This body and its spirit are brought to immortality and blessings of salvation through the resurrection. After the resurrection there can be no separation again, body and spirit become inseparably connected that man may receive a fulness of joy. In no other way, other than birth into this life and the resurrection, can spirits become like our eternal Father.[26]

—————————————— 6 ——————————————

The faithful will inherit eternal life with their families in the presence of Heavenly Father.

Some men inherit wealth through the industry of their fathers. Some men are through inheritance raised to worldly thrones, to power, and position, among their fellow men. Some seek for the inheritance of worldly knowledge and renown through the application of their own industry and perseverance; but there is one inheritance which is worth more than all, it is the inheritance of eternal exaltation.

The Scriptures say that eternal life—which is the life possessed by our Eternal Father and his Son, Jesus Christ,—is the greatest gift of God [see D&C 14:7]. Only those shall receive it who are cleansed from all sin. It is promised to those "who overcome by faith, and are sealed by the Holy Spirit of promise, which the Father sheds forth upon all those who are just and true. They are they who are the church of the Firstborn. They are they into whose hands the Father has given all things." [D&C 76:53–55; see also verse 52.][27]

This plan of salvation is family centered. . . . [It] is designed to enable us to create eternal family units of our own.[28]

Those who receive the exaltation in the celestial kingdom will have the "continuation of the seeds forever." They will live in the family relationship.[29]

We are taught in the gospel of Jesus Christ that the family organization will be, so far as celestial exaltation is concerned, one that is complete, an organization linked from father and mother and children of one generation to the father and mother and children of the next generation, and thus expanding and spreading out down to the end of time.[30]

These glorious blessings of eternal inheritance . . . do not come except through willingness to keep the commandments and even to suffer with Christ if need be. In other words, candidates for eternal life—the greatest gift of God—are expected to place all that they have on the altar, should it be required, for even then, and should they be required to lay down their lives for his cause, they could never pay him for the abundant blessings which are received and promised based on obedience to his laws and commandments.[31]

When we have come out of the world and have received the gospel in its fulness, we are candidates for celestial glory; nay, we are more than candidates, if we are faithful, for the Lord has given unto us the assurance that through our faithfulness, we shall enter into the celestial kingdom. . . .

. . . Let us live so that we will be assured of our place, and so we will know, through the lives we live, that we shall enter into His presence and dwell with Him, receiving the fulness of the blessings that have been promised. Who among the Latter-day Saints will be content with anything short of the fulness of salvation which is promised us? . . . It is necessary for us, in our humility, and in the spirit of repentance, to press on and on; keeping the commandments unto the end, for our hope and our goal is eternal life, and that is life in the presence of the Father and of the Son, "And this is life eternal," said the Lord," that they might know thee the only true God, and Jesus Christ whom thou hast sent." [John 17:3.][32]

I stand now, in what I might call the twilight of life, with the realization that in a not-far-distant day I shall be called upon to give an account of my mortal stewardship. . . .

I am sure that we all love the Lord. I know that he lives, and I look forward to that day when I shall see his face, and I hope to hear his voice say unto me: "Come, ye blessed of my Father, inherit the kingdom prepared for you from the foundation of the world." (Matt. 25:34.)

And I pray that this may be the happy lot of all of us, in our own due time.[33]

Suggestions for Study and Teaching

Questions

- As you read the journal entry in "From the Life of Joseph Fielding Smith," think of a time when you found comfort in your testimony of the plan of salvation. How might you help a family member or friend receive such comfort?

- How can President Smith's teachings about the council in heaven help us when we face trials? (See section 1.)

- President Smith taught that "we must not lose sight of the fact that [the Fall of Adam and Eve] brought blessings" (section 2). Why do you think it is important to remember this truth? What are some blessings you have received as a result of the Fall?

- In section 3, how does President Smith's example of a man falling into a pit relate to our lives? Reflect on how the Savior has rescued you through His Atonement.

- What do President Smith's words in section 4 suggest about the purpose of our life on the earth? What has the Lord given us to help us pass safely through this time of testing?

- How might you help someone understand President Smith's declaration in section 5 that "death is just as essential as birth"? How has the doctrine of resurrection influenced your life?

- In what ways is worldly wealth different from the "eternal inheritance" we can receive through the plan of salvation? (See section 6.) How can an understanding of these differences help us prepare for eternal life?

Related Scriptures

Job 38:4–7; 2 Nephi 2:15–29; 9:5–27; Alma 12:20–35; D&C 19:16–19; Moses 5:10–12

Teaching Help

"To help us teach from the scriptures and the words of latter-day prophets, the Church has produced lesson manuals and other materials. There is little need for commentaries or other reference material" (*Teaching, No Greater Call: A Resource Guide for Gospel Teaching* [1999], 52).

Notes

1. In Joseph Fielding Smith Jr. and John J. Stewart, *The Life of Joseph Fielding Smith* (1972), 117–18.

2. "To the Saints in Great Britain," *Ensign,* Sept. 1971, 4.

3. In "Pres. Smith Tells of Parents' Duty," *Church News,* Apr. 3, 1971, 10.

4. Address at the Logan Utah Institute of Religion, Jan. 10, 1971, 3; unpublished manuscript.

5. "Is Man Immortal?" *Improvement Era,* Feb. 1916, 318; see also *Doctrines of Salvation,* ed. Bruce R. McConkie, 3 vols. (1954–56), 1:58.

6. *Elijah the Prophet and His Mission* and *Salvation Universal* (1957), 65–66.

7. In Conference Report, Oct. 1966, 59.

8. "Principles of the Gospel: The Infinite Atonement—Redemption, Salvation, Exaltation," *Deseret News,* Church section, Apr. 22, 1959, 5; see also *Doctrines of Salvation,* 1:115.

9. "The Atonement," *Deseret News,* Church section, Mar. 2, 1935, 7; see also *Doctrines of Salvation,* 1:122.

10. *Elijah the Prophet and His Mission* and *Salvation Universal,* 79–80.

11. *Seek Ye Earnestly,* comp. Joseph Fielding Smith Jr. (1970), 118–20.

12. "Principles of the Gospel: The Infinite Atonement—Redemption, Salvation, Exaltation," 5; see also *Doctrines of Salvation,* 1:123.

13. *Elijah the Prophet and His Mission* and *Salvation Universal,* 80–81.

14. "Principles of the Gospel: The Infinite Atonement—Redemption, Salvation, Exaltation," 5; see also *Doctrines of Salvation,* 1:123.

15. *Elijah the Prophet and His Mission* and *Salvation Universal,* 81.

16. "Purpose and Value of Mortal Probation," *Deseret News,* Church section, June 12, 1949, 21; see also *Doctrines of Salvation,* 1:132.

17. Address at the Logan Utah Institute of Religion, Jan. 10, 1971, 3; unpublished manuscript.

18. "The Plan of Salvation," *Ensign,* Nov. 1971, 5.

19. "I Know That My Redeemer Liveth," *Ensign,* Dec. 1971, 26.

20. In Conference Report, Apr. 1965, 11.

21. In Conference Report, Apr. 1964, 107–8.

22. "Purpose and Value of Mortal Probation," 21; see also *Doctrines of Salvation,* 1:69.

23. In "Services for Miss Nell Sumsion," *Utah Genealogical and Historical Magazine,* Jan. 1938, 10–11.

24. "What Is Spiritual Death?" *Improvement Era,* Jan. 1918, 191–92; see also *Doctrines of Salvation,* 2:216–17.

25. *Answers to Gospel Questions,* comp. Joseph Fielding Smith Jr., 5 vols. (1957–66), 5:103; italics removed.

26. "The Law of Chastity," *Improvement Era,* Sept. 1931, 643; see also *Doctrines of Salvation,* 2:85–86.

27. *The Way to Perfection* (1931), 21–22.

28. *Sealing Power and Salvation,* Brigham Young University Speeches of the Year (Jan. 12, 1971), 2.

29. Personal correspondence, quoted in *Doctrines of Salvation,* 2:287; italics removed.

30. In Conference Report, Apr. 1942, 26; see also *Doctrines of Salvation,* 2:175.

31. *The Way to Perfection,* 23.

32. In Conference Report, Apr. 1922, 61–62.

33. "Let the Spirit of Oneness Prevail," *Ensign,* Dec. 1971, 136.

"The gospel is family centered; it must be lived in the family."

Strengthening and Preserving the Family

*"It is the will of the Lord to strengthen
and preserve the family unit."*

From the Life of Joseph Fielding Smith

President Joseph Fielding Smith declared, "The family is the most important organization in time or in eternity."[1] Nowhere did he teach this more clearly than in his own home, setting an example as a loving husband, father, and grandfather. Despite his busy schedule as an Apostle, he always made time for his family, "compensat[ing] for the days apart by heaping a double dose of affection upon them when home."[2]

President Smith's second wife, Ethel, was once asked, "Will you tell us something about the man you know?" Aware that many Church members saw her husband as overly stern, she responded:

"You ask me to tell you of the man I know. I have often thought when he is gone people will say, 'He is a very good man, sincere, orthodox, etc.' They will speak of him as the public knows him; but the man they have in mind is very different from the man I know. The man I know is a kind, loving husband and father whose greatest ambition in life is to make his family happy, entirely forgetful of self in his efforts to do this. He is the man that lulls to sleep the fretful child, who tells bedtime stories to the little ones, who is never too tired or too busy to sit up late at night or to get up early in the morning to help the older children solve perplexing school problems. When illness comes the man I know watches tenderly over the afflicted one and waits upon him. It is their father for whom they cry, feeling his presence a panacea for their ills. It is his hands that bind up the wounds, his arms that give courage to the sufferer, his voice that remonstrates with them gently when they err, until it becomes their happiness to do the thing that will make him happy. . . .

"The man I know is unselfish, uncomplaining, considerate, thoughtful, sympathetic, doing everything within his power to make life a supreme joy for his loved ones. That is the man I know."[3]

President Smith's children shared examples of his efforts to strengthen and preserve his family and "make life a supreme joy" for them. In a biography of Joseph Fielding Smith, coauthors Joseph Fielding Smith Jr. and John J. Stewart included the following recollection: "It was a happy day for his youngsters when they saw Dad don an apron and start a wholesale batch of pies. Mincemeat was one of his favorites. He made his own mincemeat filling. But he also ventured into other kinds of pies: apple, cherry, peach and pumpkin. His pie making efforts became a family project as youngsters were sent off in this direction and that to help gather in the necessary tools and ingredients. The savory, tantalizing aroma of pies baking in the big oven made a happy hour of anticipation. A watchful check was kept on them, that they did not come out either too soon or too late. Meanwhile Ethel stirred up a batch of homemade ice cream and the youngsters took turns cranking the ice cream freezer."[4]

Douglas A. Smith said that he and his father had a "great relationship." He shared examples of activities they enjoyed together: "We used to box once in a while, or at least feign the act of boxing. I had too much respect to hit him and he had too much love to hit me. . . . It was more or less shadowboxing. We used to play chess and I rejoiced when I could beat him. Now I look back and feel that maybe it was prearranged."[5]

Amelia Smith McConkie remembered: "It was almost fun to be sick as he gave us very special attention. . . . He entertained us by playing good music on the old Edison phonograph. To our delight he would dance to the music or march around the room, and even try to sing. . . . He brought us beautiful big, sweet oranges and sat on the bed to peel them, then gave us one segment at a time. He told us stories about his childhood, or how his father took care of him when he was sick. If the occasion warranted he would give us a blessing."[6] Amelia also revealed her father's method for disciplining his children: "If any of us needed to be corrected for some misbehavior he simply put his hands on our shoulders and looking into our eyes with a hurt look in his own, said, 'I wish my kiddies would be good.' No spanking or other punishment could ever have been more effective."[7]

President Smith's love for and attention to his children extended to his grandchildren. His grandson Hoyt W. Brewster Jr. told of a time when, as a missionary in the Netherlands, he was allowed to attend the dedication of the London England Temple in 1958. As he and other missionaries filed into the assembly room, his grandfather saw him. Hoyt later recalled: "Without a moment's hesitation, he jumped up from his chair and extended his arms, motioning me towards him. In that instance I did not see Joseph Fielding Smith, President of the Council of the Twelve Apostles . . . but a grandfather who saw one of his grandchildren for whom he had great love. I didn't hesitate to break ranks and rush to the stand where he embraced me and kissed me in front of that entire solemn assembly. That to me was one of the most sacred and memorable moments of my life."[8]

Teachings of Joseph Fielding Smith

1

The family is the most important organization in time or in eternity.

May I remind you of just how important the family unit is in the overall plan of our Father in heaven. In fact, the Church organization really exists to assist the family and its members in reaching exaltation.

Family unity and family commitment to the gospel are so important that the adversary has turned much of his attention to the destruction of families in our society. On every side there is an attack on the basic integrity of the family as the foundation of what is good and noble in life. . . . Liberalization of abortion laws throughout the world suggests the existing disregard for the sacredness of life. Families are torn apart by increasing use of illegal drugs and the abuse of legal drugs. Contempt for authority by more and more young people usually begins with disrespect and disobedience in homes. . . .

As the forces of evil attack the individual by tearing away at his family roots, it becomes critical for Latter-day Saint parents to maintain and strengthen the family. There may possibly be a few very strong individuals who can survive without the support of a family, but more of us need the love, teaching, and acceptance that come from those who care very deeply.[9]

There are certain old truths which will be truths as long as the world endures, and which no amount of progress can change. One of these is that the family (the organization consisting of father, mother, and children) is the foundation of all things in the Church; another, that sins against pure and healthy family life are those which, of all others, are sure in the end to be visited most heavily upon the nations in which they take place. . . .

Far more important than the question of occupation or wealth of people is the question of how their family life is conducted. All other things are of minor consequence, so long as there are real homes, and so long as those who make up these homes do their duty to each other.[10]

There is no substitute for a righteous home. That may not be so considered in the world, but it is and ought to be in the Church of Jesus Christ of Latter-day Saints. The family is the unit in the kingdom of God.[11]

The family is the most important organization in time or in eternity. . . . It is the will of the Lord to strengthen and preserve the family unit. We plead with fathers to take their rightful place as the head of the house. We ask mothers to sustain and support their husbands and to be lights to their children.[12]

The gospel is family centered; it must be lived in the family. It is here we receive our greatest and most important training as we seek to create for ourselves eternal family units patterned after the family of God our Father.[13]

*"The Church organization really exists to assist the
family and its members in reaching exaltation."*

2

The Lord instituted the family to endure eternally.

Marriage, we have learned, is an eternal principle ordained before the foundation of the world and instituted on this earth before death came into it. Our first parents were commanded to multiply and replenish the earth. It naturally follows that the family organization was also intended to be eternal. In the plan prepared for this earth the laws governing in the celestial world became the foundation. The great work and glory of the Lord is "to bring to pass the immortality and eternal life of man." [Moses 1:39.] The only way this can be done is through marriage and the family, in fact this is the eternal order among the exalted and has been worlds without end.[14]

The plan given in the Gospel for the government of man on this earth is typical of the law governing in the kingdom of God. Is it possible to imagine a greater source of sorrow than to be left in the eternal world without claim on father or mother or children? The thought of a nation without the family unit as its fundamental foundation, where all the citizens are comparatively strangers to each other and where natural affection is not found; where no family ties bind the groups together, is one of horror. Such a condition could lead to but one end—anarchy and dissolution. Is it not reasonable to believe the same thing true in relation to the kingdom of God? If in that kingdom, there were no family ties and all men and women were "angels" without the natural kinships, as many people believe, could it be a place of happiness—a heaven?[15]

In the temple of the Lord, a couple goes to be sealed or married for time and all eternity. Children born in that union will be the children of that father and mother not only in mortal life but in all eternity, and they become members of the family of God in heaven and on earth, as spoken of by Paul [see Ephesians 3:14–15], and that family order should never be broken. . . .

. . . Those children born to them have a right to the companionship of father and mother, and father and mother are under obligations before their Eternal Father to be true to each other and raise those children in light and truth, that they may in the eternities to come, be one—a family within the great family of God.[16]

We should remember, as Latter-day Saints, that outside of the celestial kingdom, there is no family organization [after death]. That organization is reserved for those who are willing to abide in every covenant and every obligation which we are called upon to receive while we sojourn here in this mortal life.[17]

The kingdom of God will be one great family. We call ourselves brothers and sisters. In very deed we become joint heirs with Jesus Christ through the gospel of Jesus Christ [see Romans 8:16–17], sons and daughters of God, and entitled to the fulness of the blessings of his kingdom if we will repent and keep [the] commandments.[18]

The hope of eternal life, including the reuniting of the members of the family when the resurrection comes, brings to the heart greater love and affection for each member of the family. With this hope, husbands are inclined to love their wives with a stronger and more holy love; and wives in like manner love their husbands. The tender feeling and solicitude on the part of parents for their children is increased, for the children become endeared to them with bands of love and happiness which cannot be broken.[19]

——————————— ⟨⟨⟩⟩ **3** ⟨⟨⟩⟩ ———————————

We strengthen and preserve our families as we spend time together, love each other, and live the gospel together.

The primary function of a Latter-day Saint home is to insure that every member of the family works to create the climate and conditions in which all can grow toward perfection. For parents, this requires a dedication of time and energy far beyond the mere providing of their children's physical needs. For children, this means controlling the natural tendency toward selfishness.

Do you spend as much time making your family and home successful as you do in pursuing social and professional success? Are you devoting your best creative energy to the most important unit in society—the family? Or is your relationship with your family merely a routine, unrewarding part of life? Parent and child must be willing to put family responsibilities first in order to achieve family exaltation.[20]

The home . . . is the workshop where human characters are built and the manner in which they are formed depends upon the relationship existing between parents and the children. The home cannot be what it should be unless these relationships are of the proper character. Whether they are so or not depends, it is true, upon both parents and children, but much more upon parents. They must do their best.[21]

"Oh, go away and leave me alone, I haven't time to be bothered," said a hurried, impatient mother to her little three-year-old daughter who was trying to help perform a certain household task. . . . The desire to help is born with every normal child and parents have no right to complain. There can be no such thing as household drudgery when all assist with the tasks, and through the association in the discharge of these duties comes the sweetest companionship that can be experienced.

If I had to suggest one thing which I think we as parents are most lacking, it would be a sympathetic understanding of our children. Live with the children; follow their paths. . . . Know everything that claims the interest of the children, be a good sport with them.[22]

We have been trying to impress upon parents the need of paying more attention to their children, having a little more of the spirit of the gospel in their homes, a little more unity and a little more faith; a little more responsibility religiously, spiritually on the part of the fathers; also, of the mothers; more of the teaching of the gospel in the home.[23]

To parents in the Church we say: Love each other with all your hearts. Keep the moral law and live the gospel. Bring up your children in light and truth; teach them the saving truths of the gospel; and make your home a heaven on earth, a place where the Spirit of the Lord may dwell and where righteousness may be enthroned in the heart of each member.[24]

I pray that our Heavenly Father will give all of us the strength to reach our true potential. I invoke his Spirit on the homes of the Church, that there may be love and harmony found there. May our Father preserve and exalt our families.[25]

Suggestions for Study and Teaching

Questions
- As you read the anecdotes in "From the Life of Joseph Fielding Smith," consider how President Smith's example can be a guide in your life. Think about ways you can personally improve to strengthen family relationships.

- Contemplate the importance of the family as outlined in section 1. What are you doing to fortify your family against the negative influences of the world?

- President Smith spoke of "the hope of eternal life, including the reuniting of the members of the family when the resurrection comes" (section 2). How does this hope influence your interaction with family members?

• In section 3, President Smith asks three soul-searching questions. Answer these questions in your mind. As you read this section, consider changes you can make in your life that can improve the feeling in your home.

Related Scriptures

Proverbs 22:6; 1 Nephi 8:37; D&C 88:119; 93:40–50; see also "The Family: A Proclamation to the World"

Teaching Help

"Ask participants to choose one section [of the chapter] and read it silently. Invite them to gather in groups of two or three people who chose the same section and discuss what they have learned" (from page vii of this book).

Notes

1. "Counsel to the Saints and to the World," *Ensign,* July 1972, 27.

2. Joseph Fielding Smith Jr. and John J. Stewart, *The Life of Joseph Fielding Smith* (1972), 14.

3. Ethel Smith, in Bryant S. Hinckley, "Joseph Fielding Smith," *Improvement Era,* June 1932, 459.

4. Joseph Fielding Smith Jr. and John J. Stewart, *The Life of Joseph Fielding Smith,* 228.

5. Douglas A. Smith, in D. Arthur Haycock, *Exemplary Manhood Award,* Brigham Young University Speeches of the Year (Apr. 18, 1972), 5.

6. Amelia Smith McConkie, "Joseph Fielding Smith," *Church News,* Oct. 30, 1993, 10.

7. Amelia Smith McConkie, "Joseph Fielding Smith," 10.

8. In Francis M. Gibbons, *Joseph Fielding Smith: Gospel Scholar, Prophet of God* (1992), 254.

9. In "Message from the First Presidency," *Ensign,* Jan. 1971, inside front cover and page 1.

10. "Our Children—'The Loveliest Flowers from God's Own Garden,'" *Relief Society Magazine,* Jan. 1969, 4.

11. In Conference Report, Oct. 1948, 152.

12. "Counsel to the Saints and to the World," 27.

13. "Mothers in Israel," *Relief Society Magazine,* Dec. 1970, 886.

14. *The Way to Perfection* (1931), 251.

15. "A Peculiar People," *Deseret News,* Church section, Apr. 2, 1932, 6; see also *Doctrines of Salvation,* ed. Bruce R. McConkie, 3 vols. (1954–56), 2:65–66.

16. In Conference Report, Apr. 1961, 49.

17. In Conference Report, Oct. 1948, 153.

18. In Conference Report, Apr. 1959, 24.

19. *The Way to Perfection,* 258.

20. In "Message from the First Presidency," *Ensign,* Jan. 1971, 1.

21. "Our Children—'The Loveliest Flowers from God's Own Garden,'" 6.

22. "Our Children—'The Loveliest Flowers from God's Own Garden,'" 6–7.

23. *Take Heed to Yourselves!* (1966), 354.

24. "Counsel to the Saints and to the World," 27.

25. In "Message from the First Presidency," *Ensign,* Jan. 1971, 1.

President Joseph Fielding Smith shared his reason for calling Latter-day Saints to repentance: "I love the members of the Church."

*"What we need in the Church, as well as out
of it, is repentance. We need more faith and
more determination to serve the Lord."*

From the Life of Joseph Fielding Smith

President Joseph Fielding Smith taught, "The forgiveness of sins comes through faith and sincere repentance."[1] He said that "it is necessary, not merely that we believe, but that we repent," and he also taught that when we perform good works in faith until the end, we will "receive the reward of the faithful and a place in the Celestial kingdom of God."[2] With a desire for all people to receive this reward, he testified of Jesus Christ and preached repentance throughout his ministry.

Early in his service as an Apostle, he said: "I have considered that it has been my mission, having been so impressed, I think, by the Spirit of the Lord in my travels in the stakes of Zion, to say unto the people that *now* is the day of repentance and to call upon the Latter-day Saints to remember their covenants, the promises they have made with the Lord, to keep his commandments, and follow the teachings and the instructions of the elders of Israel—the prophets of God—as they have been recorded in these holy scriptures. In all things we should walk humbly and circumspectly before the Lord that we might be blessed and guided by his Holy Spirit. I think this is the day of warning. It has been a time of warning from the day when the prophet first received the manifestation from the heavens that the gospel was to be restored."[3]

In a sacrament meeting one Sunday, President Smith told the congregation why he spoke with a warning voice. His son Joseph, who attended the meeting, later wrote: "I remember vividly some of the remarks [my father] made on that occasion. 'Who is your friend, or who loves you the most?' he asked the congregation. 'The person who tells you all is well in Zion, that prosperity is around the corner or the person who warns you of the calamities and difficulties that are promised unless the principles of the gospel are lived? I want you to know that I love the members of the Church, and I do not want one of them to point an accusing finger at me when we pass beyond the veil of mortal existence and say, "If you had only warned me I would not be in this predicament." And so I raise the warning voice in hopes that my brothers and sisters may be prepared for a kingdom of glory.'"[4]

Those who worked closely with President Smith saw that behind his stern warnings was a man with tender concern for people who struggled in sin. Elder Francis M. Gibbons, who served as a secretary to the First Presidency, was often present when President Smith considered matters of Church discipline. Elder Gibbons recalled: "His decisions were always made in kindness and love and with the widest latitude of mercy that the circumstances could justify. It was not uncommon for him to say on learning the circumstances of an aggravated case, 'Why don't people behave themselves?' This was not said accusingly or by way of condemnation but with sadness and regret."[5] President Spencer W. Kimball, who served with President Smith as a member of the Quorum of the Twelve Apostles, said, "Many times we have said that since the Twelve will be judges of Israel, any of us would be happy to fall into his hands, for his judgment would be kind, merciful, just, and holy."[6] When President Smith ordained bishops, he often counseled: "Remember, everyone has weaknesses, and there are at least two sides to every story. If you err in judgment, be sure you err on the side of love and mercy."[7]

Teachings of Joseph Fielding Smith

─────────── 1 ───────────

The first principle of the gospel is faith in the Lord Jesus Christ.

Our faith is centered in the Lord Jesus Christ, and through him in the Father. We believe in Christ, accept him as the Son of God, and have taken his name upon us in the waters of baptism.[8]

Let it be uppermost in your minds, now and at all times, that Jesus is the Christ, the Son of the living God, who came into the world to lay down his life that we might live. That is the truth, and is fundamental. Upon that our faith is built. It can not be destroyed. We must adhere to this teaching in spite of the teachings of the world, and the notions of men; for this is paramount, this is essential to our salvation. The Lord redeemed us with his blood, he gave us salvation, provided—and there is this condition which we must not forget—that we will keep his commandments, and always remember him. If we will do that then we shall be saved, while the ideas and the foolishness of men, shall perish from the earth.[9]

By faith we come to God. If we did not believe in the Lord Jesus Christ, if we had no faith in Him or in His atonement, we would not be inclined to pay any heed to His commandments. It is because we have that faith that we are brought into harmony with His truth and have a desire in our hearts to serve Him. . . .

. . . The first principle of the gospel is faith in the Lord Jesus Christ; and of course we are not going to have faith in the Lord Jesus Christ without having faith in His Father. Then if we have faith in God the Father and the Son and are guided, as we ought to be, by the Holy Ghost, we will have faith in the servants of the Lord through whom He has spoken.[10]

2

Faith means action.

"Faith is the moving cause of all action." [Lectures on Faith, lecture 1.] If you stop to consider that for a moment, I think you will agree that it is absolutely true in temporal things as well as in spiritual things. It is true with us in our own acts, as well as with the acts of God. . . .

"Faith without works is dead" [James 2:26]—in other words, it does not exist. I think James' meaning clearly is, "You show me your faith without your works, and nothing will result; but I will show you my faith with my works, and something will be accomplished." [See James 2:18.] Faith means action. . . . Faith, therefore, is stronger than belief. . . .

Faith is a gift of God. Every good thing is a gift of God. That is a teaching of the scriptures as found in the 11th chapter of Hebrews—which chapter is a very fine dissertation on faith—[and] in the revelations the Lord has given us in the Doctrine and Covenants, and in other scriptures. Faith cannot be obtained by inaction or through indifference or passive belief. The mere desire to obtain faith will not bring faith any more than the desire to be skilled in music or painting will bring proficiency in these things without intelligent action. There is where our trouble comes. We get a testimony of the Gospel, we believe in Joseph Smith, we believe in Jesus Christ, we believe in the principles of the Gospel, but how hard are we working at them?

. . . If we want to have a living, abiding faith, we must be active in the performance of every duty as members of this Church. . . .

Oh, if we had the faith manifested by Nephi! Read in the 17th chapter of 1 Nephi where his brothers were opposing him and making fun of him because he was going to build a ship, saying:

"Our brother is a fool, for he thinketh that he can build a ship; yea, and he also thinketh that he can cross these great waters." [1 Nephi 17:17.]

Nephi answered them:

"If God had commanded me to do all things I could do them. If he should command me that I should say unto this water, be thou earth, it should be earth; and if I should say it, it would be done." [1 Nephi 17:50.]

That was his faith.[11]

We are not walking now by sight, as we did before we came into this world, but the Lord expects that we shall walk by faith [see 2 Corinthians 5:7]; and walking by faith we shall receive the reward of the righteous, if we adhere unto those commandments which are given for our salvation.[12]

Unless a man will adhere to the doctrine and walk in faith, accepting the truth and observing the commandments as they have been given, it will be impossible for him to receive eternal life, no matter how much he may confess with his lips that Jesus is the

Christ, or believe that his Father sent him into the world for the redemption of man. So James is right when he says that the devils "believe and tremble," but they do not repent [see James 2:19].[13]

⟨ 3 ⟩

Repentance is the second principle of the gospel and is essential to our salvation and exaltation.

Repentance is the second fundamental principle of the gospel and the outgrowth of faith.[14]

What we need in the Church, as well as out of it, is repentance. We need more faith and more determination to serve the Lord.[15]

Is it true that some among us have an idea that it matters not that we sin so long as it is not a grievous sin, a deadly sin, that we will yet be saved in the kingdom of God? Nephi saw our day. He said that people would be saying that [see 2 Nephi 28:7–9]. But I say unto you, we cannot turn away from the path of truth and righteousness and retain the guidance of the Spirit of the Lord.[16]

There is no place in Zion for the wilful sinner. There is a place for the repentant sinner, for the man who turns away from iniquity and seeks for life eternal and the light of the Gospel. We should not look upon sin with the least degree of allowance, any more than the Lord can do so, but walk uprightly and perfectly before the Lord.[17]

Men can only be saved and exalted in the kingdom of God in righteousness; therefore, we must repent of our sins and walk in the light as Christ is in the light [see 1 John 1:7], that his blood may cleanse us from all sins and that we may have fellowship with the Lord and receive of his glory and exaltation.[18]

We need repentance, and we need to be told to repent.[19]

⟨ 4 ⟩

In the principle of repentance, the mercy of Heavenly Father and Jesus Christ is made manifest.

Repentance is one of the most comforting and glorious principles taught in the gospel. In this principle the mercy of our Heavenly Father and his Only Begotten Son, Jesus Christ, is made manifest perhaps more strongly than in any other principle. What a dreadful thing it would be if there were no forgiveness of sin and no

*"Repentance is one of the most comforting and
glorious principles taught in the gospel."*

means for the remission of sin for those who are humbly repentant!
We can only imagine in part the horror that would overtake us, if
we had to endure the punishment of our transgressions forever and
ever without the hope of any relief. How is that relief obtained? By
whom may it be obtained?

Our Lord has said:

"For God so loved the world, that he gave his only begotten
Son, that whosoever believeth in him should not perish, but have
everlasting life.

"For God sent not his Son into the world to condemn the world;
but that the world through him might be saved." [John 3:16–17; see
also verses 18–21.]

If the Father had not sent Jesus Christ into the world, then there
could have been no remission of sins and there could have been
no relief from sin through repentance.[20]

If we really understood and could feel even to a small degree, the love and gracious willingness on the part of Jesus Christ to suffer for our sins we would be willing to repent of all our transgressions and serve him.[21]

_____ ⟨∽⟩5⟨∾⟩ _____

Repentance includes sincere sorrow for sin and complete turning from sin.

The scriptures say:

"Thou shalt offer a sacrifice unto the Lord thy God in righteousness, even that of a broken heart and a contrite spirit." [D&C 59:8.]

That means repentance.

. . . Repentance, according to the definition given in the dictionary, is sincere sorrow for sin with self-condemnation, and complete turning from the sin. . . . There can be no true repentance without sorrow and the desire to be freed from sin.

Contrition is manifestation of a broken, or humbled, spirit because of sin and a sincere sense of the baseness of sin and realization of the mercy and grace of God granted to the repentant sinner. . . . For that reason the Lord says, as I have already quoted, we are to offer a sacrifice "in righteousness, even that of a broken heart and a contrite spirit." . . .

Repentance is a gift of God. . . . It is not so easy for some people to repent, but the gift of repentance and faith will be given to every man who will seek for it.[22]

I've learned from my own experience that when you want to change, really want to change, you can do it. Our conscience and the scriptures tell us what to live by—and they tell us what habits we should change for our eternal welfare and progress.[23]

_____ ⟨∽⟩6⟨∾⟩ _____

The time to repent is now.

God is not going to save every man and woman in the celestial kingdom. If you want to get there, and you have failings, if you are committing sins, if you are breaking the commandments of the Lord and you know it, it is a good time right now to repent and reform, and not get the idea that it is such a little thing that the Lord will forgive you, just a few stripes, just a little punishment and we will be forgiven; for you may find yourselves cast out, if you insist and persist in such a course.[24]

Procrastination, as it may be applied to gospel principles, is the thief of eternal life, which is life in the presence of the Father and the Son. There are many among us, even members of the Church, who feel that there is no need for haste in the observance of gospel principles and the keeping of the commandments. . . .

Do not let us forget the words of [Amulek]: "For behold, this life is the time for men to prepare to meet God; yea, behold the day of this life is the day for men to perform their labors.

"And now, as I said unto you before, as ye have had so many witnesses, therefore, I beseech of you that ye do not procrastinate the day of your repentance until the end; for after this day of life, which is given us to prepare for eternity, behold, if we do not improve our time while in this life, then cometh the night of darkness wherein there can be no labor performed.

"Ye cannot say, when ye are brought to that awful crisis, that I will repent, that I will return to my God. Nay, ye cannot say this; for that same spirit which doth possess your bodies at the time that ye go out of this life, that same spirit will have power to possess your body in the eternal world." [Alma 34:32–34.][25]

———————————— 7 ————————————

We owe it to the world to raise a voice of warning.

The Lord intends that men shall be happy—that is his purpose—but men refuse to be happy and make themselves miserable, because they think their ways are better than God's ways, and because of selfishness, greed, and the wickedness that is in their hearts; and that is the trouble with us today.[26]

From the observation that we make as we travel from one place to another and from what we read in the public press, we are of necessity forced to the conclusion that repentance from sin is extremely essential throughout the world today.[27]

Do not think that we have reached a condition where things could not be worse. Unless there is repentance they will be worse. And so I cry repentance to this people, to the Latter-day Saints, . . . and to the nations of the earth everywhere.[28]

We owe it to the world, to raise a voice of warning, and especially to the members of the Church [see D&C 88:81].[29]

It is our duty to look after each other, to protect each other, to warn each other of dangers, to teach each other the principles of the Gospel of the kingdom, and to stand together with a united front against the sins of the world.[30]

I know of nothing that is more important or necessary at this time than to cry repentance, even among the Latter-day Saints, and I call upon them as well as upon those who are not members of the Church, to heed these words of our Redeemer. Now he has stated definitely that no unclean thing can enter his presence. Only those who prove themselves faithful and have washed their garments in his blood through their faith and their repentance—none others shall find the kingdom of God.[31]

"Behold, all nations, kindreds, tongues and people shall dwell safely in the Holy One of Israel, if it so be that they will repent." [1 Nephi 22:28.] And I pray that they will repent. I want them to dwell safely. I want them to believe in the Holy One of Israel, who came into the world and atoned for our sins, for the sins of all mankind, who gave unto us redemption from death, who has promised unto us salvation and the remission of our sins on the condition of our repentance.

O, I wish all mankind would believe in him, would worship him and his Father, and would serve the Lord our God in the name of the Son, and then peace would come, then righteousness would prevail, then the Lord could establish his kingdom upon the earth.[32]

I plead with the world to repent and believe the truth, to let the light of Christ shine in their lives, to keep every good and true principle they have, and to add to these the further light and knowledge that has come by revelation in this day. I plead with them to join The Church of Jesus Christ of Latter-day Saints and reap the blessings of the gospel.

I plead with the members of the Church to do the works of righteousness, to keep the commandments, to seek the Spirit, to love the Lord, to put first in their lives the things of God's kingdom, and thereby work out their salvation with fear and trembling before the Lord [see Philippians 2:12].[33]

Suggestions for Study and Teaching

Questions

- In "From the Life of Joseph Fielding Smith," review President Smith's comments about why he wanted to "raise the warning voice." How is the call to repent an expression of love?

- What does it mean to you to center your faith in Heavenly Father and Jesus Christ? (See section 1.)

- Why does true faith always lead to action? (For some examples, see section 2.) What are some ways we can show our faith by our actions?

- How is repentance an "outgrowth of faith"? (See section 3.)

- Silently reflect on a time when you repented and felt the mercy and love of Heavenly Father and Jesus Christ (see section 4). What can you share about your gratitude for the Savior's Atonement?

- Why is repentance impossible "without sorrow and the desire to be freed from sin"? (See section 5.) How might the last two paragraphs in section 5 provide hope for someone who feels sorrow because of sin?

- In what ways is procrastination "the thief of eternal life"? (See section 6.) What are the dangers of procrastinating our repentance?

- As you review section 7, consider what it means to "raise a voice of warning." How can we be kind and loving in our efforts to warn others?

Related Scriptures

Hebrews 11:1–6; Mosiah 4:1–3; Alma 34:17; Ether 12:4; Moroni 7:33–34; D&C 18:10–16; Articles of Faith 1:4

Teaching Help

"It is the pupil who has to be put into action. When a teacher takes the spotlight, becomes the star of the show, does all the talking, and otherwise takes over all of the activity, it is almost certain that he is interfering with the learning of the class members" (Asahel D. Woodruff, *Teaching the Gospel* [1962], 37; in Virginia H. Pearce, "The Ordinary Classroom—A Powerful Place for Steady and Continued Growth," *Ensign,* Nov. 1996, 12).

Notes

1. *Answers to Gospel Questions,* comp. Joseph Fielding Smith Jr., 5 vols. (1957–66), 1:84.

2. "Faith and Works: The Clearing of a Seeming Conflict," *Improvement Era,* Oct. 1924, 1151; see also *Doctrines of Salvation,* comp. Bruce R. McConkie, 3 vols. (1954–56), 2:311.

3. In Conference Report, Oct. 1919, 88; italics in original.

4. Joseph Fielding Smith Jr., in *Take Heed to Yourselves!* (1966), v–vi.

5. Francis M. Gibbons, *Joseph Fielding Smith: Gospel Scholar, Prophet of God* (1992), viii.

6. Spencer W. Kimball, quoted by Bruce R. McConkie in "Joseph Fielding Smith: Apostle, Prophet, Father in Israel," *Ensign,* Aug. 1972, 28.

7. In Joseph Fielding Smith Jr. and John J. Stewart, *The Life of Joseph Fielding Smith* (1972), 10.

8. In Conference Report, Apr. 1970, 113.

9. In Conference Report, Oct. 1921, 186; see also *Doctrines of Salvation,* 2:302.

10. "Redemption of Little Children," *Deseret News,* Apr. 29, 1939, Church section, 3; see also *Doctrines of Salvation,* 2:302–3.

11. "Faith," *Deseret News,* Mar. 16, 1935, Church section, 3, 7.

12. In Conference Report, Apr. 1923, 139.

13. "Faith and Works: The Clearing of a Seeming Conflict," 1151; see also *Doctrines of Salvation,* 2:311.

14. *The Restoration of All Things* (1945), 196.

15. "The Pearl of Great Price," *Utah Genealogical and Historical Magazine,* July 1930, 104; see also *Doctrines of Salvation,* 2:48.

16. In Conference Report, Oct. 1950, 13.

17. In Conference Report, Apr. 1915, 120.

18. In Conference Report, Oct. 1969, 109.

19. "A Warning Cry for Repentance," *Deseret News,* May 4, 1935, Church section, 6; see also *Doctrines of Salvation,* 3:44.

20. *The Restoration of All Things,* 196–97.

21. *The Restoration of All Things,* 199.

22. "Repentance and Baptism," *Deseret News,* Mar. 30, 1935, Church section, 6.

23. "My Dear Young Fellow Workers," *New Era,* Jan. 1971, 5.

24. "Relief Society Conference Minutes," *Relief Society Magazine,* Aug. 1919, 473; see also *Doctrines of Salvation,* 2:17.

25. In Conference Report, Apr. 1969, 121, 123.

26. "A Warning Cry for Repentance," 6; see also *Doctrines of Salvation,* 3:35.

27. In Conference Report, Oct. 1966, 58.

28. In Conference Report, Oct. 1932, 91–92; see also *Doctrines of Salvation,* 3:31–32.

29. In Conference Report, Apr. 1937, 59; see also *Doctrines of Salvation,* 3:49.

30. In Conference Report, Apr. 1915, 120.

31. In Conference Report, Oct. 1960, 51.

32. In Conference Report, Oct. 1919, 92.

33. In Conference Report, Oct. 1970, 7–8.

"This do in remembrance of me" (Luke 22:19).

The Significance of the Sacrament

"The partaking of these emblems constitutes one of the most holy and sacred ordinances in the Church."

From the Life of Joseph Fielding Smith

On October 5, 1929, after 19 years of service as an Apostle, Elder Joseph Fielding Smith stood in the Salt Lake Tabernacle to deliver his 39th general conference address. He said, "There are one or two thoughts that I desire to present in relation to the question of the sacrament, more particularly in regard to the meetings that have been set apart in the Church by revelation, by commandment of the Lord, for the partaking of these emblems representing the body and the blood of Jesus Christ." As an introduction to this topic, he shared his feelings about the sacrament:

"In my judgment the sacrament meeting is the most sacred, the most holy, of all the meetings of the Church. When I reflect upon the gathering of the Savior and his apostles on that memorable night when he introduced the sacrament; when I think of that solemn occasion my heart is filled with wonderment and my feelings are touched. I consider that gathering one of the most solemn and wonderful since the beginning of time.

"There the Savior taught them of his coming sacrifice, which in their bewilderment they could not understand. He plainly told them of his death and that his blood should be shed, and this was said in the very hour of his agony for the sins of the world. It was a very solemn occasion; there the sacrament was instituted, and the disciples were commanded to meet together often and commemorate the death and sufferings of Jesus Christ, for his sacrifice was for the redemption of the world.

"He was about to take upon him the responsibility of paying the debt brought upon the world through the fall, that men might be redeemed from death and from hell. He had taught the people that he was to be lifted up that he might draw all men unto him, and that all who would repent and believe in him, keeping his commandments, should not suffer, for he would take upon himself their sins."[1]

Teachings of Joseph Fielding Smith

1

The Lord has commanded us to meet often to partake of the sacrament.

The partaking of these emblems [the bread and water] constitutes one of the most holy and sacred ordinances in the Church, an ordinance which has replaced the slaying and eating of the paschal lamb which [symbolized] the sacrifice upon the cross of our Redeemer. . . . From the time of the exodus from Egypt to the crucifixion of our Redeemer, the Israelites were commanded to observe the passover at a certain time each year. On the solemn night before the crucifixion the Lord changed this ordinance and gave in its stead the sacrament. We have been commanded to meet often, not merely once each year, and go to the house of prayer and there remember our Redeemer and make covenant with Him in partaking oft of this holy ordinance.[2]

The person who absents himself from a sacrament meeting week after week and month after month, and nothing prevents him from coming, is not loyal to the truth. He does not love it. If he did, he would be present to partake of these emblems—just a little piece of bread, a little cup of water. He would want to do that to show his love for the truth and his loyal service to the Son of God.[3]

We have been called upon to commemorate this great event [the Atonement of Jesus Christ] and to keep it in mind constantly. For this purpose we are called together once each week to partake of these emblems, witnessing that we do remember our Lord, that we are willing to take upon us his name and that we will keep his commandments. This covenant we are called upon to renew each week, and we cannot retain the Spirit of the Lord if we do not consistently comply with this commandment. If we love the Lord we will be present at these meetings in the spirit of worship and prayer, remembering the Lord and the covenant we are to renew each week through this sacrament as he has required it of us.[4]

2

We partake of the sacrament in remembrance of the Atonement of Jesus Christ.

It's the duty of the members of the Church to walk humbly and faithfully in the knowledge and understanding of the atonement of Jesus Christ. . . . I have the feeling, I'd like to be wrong but I don't think I am, that a very, very large percentage of the members of the Church do not realize what it means to eat a little morsel of bread, drink a little cup of water in remembrance of the shedding of the blood of our Savior, Jesus Christ, and his sacrifice upon the cross.

Let me call attention to the blessing [on the bread]. I am going to read it humbly so we'll understand what's in it:

"O God, the Eternal Father, we ask thee in the name of thy Son, Jesus Christ, to bless and sanctify this bread to the souls of all those who partake of it, that they may eat in remembrance of the body of thy Son, and witness unto thee, O God, the Eternal Father, that they are willing to take upon them the name of thy Son, and always remember him and keep his commandments which he has given them; that they may always have his Spirit to be with them. Amen." [D&C 20:77.] . . .

To eat in remembrance of him. Does that mean that I would just remember that nearly 2,000 years ago wicked men took him, hung him on the cross, drove nails in his hands and feet and left him there to die? To me it has a far deeper meaning than that. To remember him—why was he on the cross? What benefit comes to [me] because he was on the cross? What suffering did he go through on the cross that I might be redeemed or relieved of my sins?

Well, naturally a person would think: He had nails driven in his hands and his feet and he hung there until he died. . . . What else did he suffer? This is a thing I think that most of us overlook. I am convinced that his greatest suffering was not the driving of nails in his hands and in his feet and hanging on the cross, as excruciating and as terrible as that was. He was carrying another load that was far more significant and penetrating. How? We do not understand clearly, but I get a glimpse of it.[5]

There isn't one of us I take it that hasn't done something wrong and then been sorry and wished we hadn't. Then our consciences strike us and we have been very, very miserable. Have you gone through that experience? I have. . . . But here we have the Son of God carrying the burden of my transgressions and your transgressions. . . . His greatest torment was not the nails in his hands or in his feet, as bad as they were, but the torment of mind in some way that is not clear to me. But he carried the burden—our burden. I added something to it; so did you. So did everybody else. He took it upon himself to pay the price that I might escape—that you might escape—the punishment on the conditions that we will receive his gospel and be true and faithful in it.

Now that's what I'm trying to think about. That's what I'm remembering—the excruciating agony when he was crying in his prayer to his Father to let the cup pass. He's not pleading just for relief from driving nails in his hand[s] or in his feet, he had a more severe torment than all of that, in some way that I do not understand.[6]

It is impossible for weak mortals, and we are all weak, to fully comprehend the extent of the suffering of the Son of God. We cannot realize the price He had to pay. To the Prophet Joseph Smith He said:

"For behold, I, God, have suffered these things for all, that they might not suffer if they would repent; but if they would not repent, they must suffer even as I; which suffering caused myself, even God, the greatest of all, to tremble because of pain, and to bleed at every pore, and to suffer both body and spirit; and would that I might not drink the bitter cup and shrink—nevertheless, glory be to the Father, and I partook and finished my preparations unto the children of men." [D&C 19:16–19.]

It is, however, within our grasp to know and realize that this excruciating agony of His sacrifice has brought to us the greatest blessing that could possibly be given. Moreover, we are able to

"I wish we could get the members of the Church to understand more clearly the covenants they make when they partake of the sacrament."

realize that this extreme suffering—which was beyond the power of mortal man either to accomplish or endure—was undertaken because of the great love which the Father and the Son had for mankind. . . .

. . . If we fully appreciated the many blessings which are ours through the redemption made for us, there is nothing that the Lord could ask of us that we would not anxiously and willingly do.[7]

I am sure if we could picture before us—as I have tried many times to do—the solemn occasion when the Savior met with his apostles; if we could see them there assembled, the Lord in his sadness, sorrowing for the sins of the world, sorrowing for one of his apostles who was to betray him, yet teaching these eleven men who loved him and making covenant with them, I am sure we would feel in our hearts that we would never forsake him. If we could see them there assembled and could realize the weight of the burden which was upon our Lord; and after their supper and the singing of an hymn, their going forth, the Lord to be betrayed, mocked and scorned, the disciples to forsake him in the deepest hour of his trial—if we could understand all this, feebly though it be, and feebly it must be, I am sure, my brethren and sisters, we would forever more want to walk in the light of truth. If we could see the Savior of men suffering in the garden and upon the cross and could fully realize all that it meant to us, we would desire to keep his commandments and we would love the Lord our God with all our heart, with all our might, mind and strength, and in the name of Jesus Christ would serve him.[8]

———————— 3 ————————

It is our duty to thoughtfully consider the covenant we make when we partake of the sacrament.

I wish we could get the members of the Church to understand more clearly the covenants they make when they partake of the sacrament at our sacrament meetings.[9]

I have seen two members of the Church sitting together [in sacrament meeting], enter into a conversation, stop long enough for the blessing to be asked on the water or on the bread, then start again on their conversation. . . . That is shocking to me, and I am sure it is to the Lord.[10]

It is our duty to carefully and thoughtfully consider the nature of [the sacrament] prayers when we hear them offered in our meetings. There are four very important things we covenant to do each time we partake of these emblems, and in partaking, there is the token that we subscribe fully to the obligations, and thus they become binding upon us. These are as follows:

1. We eat in remembrance of the body of Jesus Christ, promising that we will always remember His wounded body slain upon the cross.

2. We drink in remembrance of the blood which was shed for the sins of the world, which atoned for the transgression of Adam, and which frees us from our own sins on condition of our true repentance.

"It is our duty to carefully and thoughtfully consider the nature of [the sacrament] prayers when we hear them offered."

3. We covenant that we will be willing to take upon us the *name* of the Son and always remember Him. In keeping this covenant we promise that we will be called by His name and never do anything that would bring shame or reproach upon that name.

4. We covenant that we will keep His commandments which He has given us; not one commandment, but that we will be willing to "live by every word that proceedeth forth from the mouth of God." [D&C 84:44.]

If we will do these things then we are promised the continual guidance of the Holy Ghost, and if we will not do these things we will not have that guidance.[11]

I want to ask you a few questions, and I speak, of course, to all the members of the Church. Do you think a man who comes into the sacrament service in the spirit of prayer, humility, and worship, and who partakes of these emblems representing the body and blood of Jesus Christ, will knowingly break the commandments of the Lord? If a man fully realizes what it means when he partakes of the sacrament, that he covenants to take upon him the name of Jesus Christ and to always remember him and keep his commandments, and this vow is renewed week by week—do you think such a man will fail to pay his tithing? Do you think such a man will break the Sabbath day or disregard the Word of Wisdom? Do you think he will fail to be prayerful, and that he will not attend his quorum duties and other duties in the Church? It seems to me that such a thing as a violation of these sacred principles and duties is impossible when a man knows what it means to make such vows week by week unto the Lord and before the saints.[12]

Suggestions for Study and Teaching

Questions

- In "From the Life of Joseph Fielding Smith," President Smith shares his thoughts about the time when the Savior instituted the sacrament. Why is this event significant to you?

- As you study section 1, consider the importance of attending sacrament meeting each week. How can you prepare yourself for sacrament meeting? What can parents do to help their children prepare?

- What impresses you about President Smith's thoughts when he partook of the sacrament? (See section 2.) What can we do to remember the Savior and His Atonement when we partake of the sacrament?

- Give attention to the covenants listed in section 3. Silently ponder how you feel about these covenants. How do these covenants influence your life?

Related Scriptures

Matthew 26:26–29; 1 Corinthians 11:23–29; 3 Nephi 18:1–13; Mormon 9:29; Moroni 4–5; D&C 20:75–79; 59:9–12

Teaching Help

"Assign participants to read selected questions at the end of the chapter (either individually or in small groups). Ask them to look for teachings in the chapter that relate to the questions. Then invite them to share their thoughts and insights with the rest of the group" (from page vii in this book).

Notes

1. In Conference Report, Oct. 1929, 60–61; see also *Doctrines of Salvation,* ed. Bruce R. McConkie, 3 vols. (1954–56), 2:340–41.

2. "Importance of the Sacrament Meeting," *Relief Society Magazine,* Oct. 1943, 590; see also *Doctrines of Salvation,* 2:339–40.

3. *Seek Ye Earnestly,* comp. Joseph Fielding Smith Jr. (1972), 99.

4. In Conference Report, Oct. 1929, 61; see also *Doctrines of Salvation,* 2:341.

5. "Fall-Atonement-Resurrection-Sacrament," address delivered at the Salt Lake City Utah University Institute of Religion, Jan. 14, 1961, 7–8.

6. "Fall-Atonement-Resurrection-Sacrament," 8.

7. "Importance of the Sacrament Meeting," 591–92.

8. In Conference Report, Oct. 1929, 63; see also *Doctrines of Salvation,* 2:347.

9. "Fall-Atonement-Resurrection-Sacrament," 7.

10. *Seek Ye Earnestly,* 122.

11. "Importance of the Sacrament Meeting," 591.

12. In Conference Report, Oct. 1929, 62–63; see also *Doctrines of Salvation,* 2:346.

*Joseph and Hyrum Smith: "In life they were not divided,
and in death they were not separated!" (D&C 135:3).*

Joseph and Hyrum Smith, Witnesses for Jesus Christ

"We raise our voices in thanksgiving for the lives and ministries of the Prophet Joseph Smith, of Hyrum Smith the Patriarch, and of the prophets and apostles and righteous men and women who have built on the foundation they laid."

From the Life of Joseph Fielding Smith

From the time he was very young, Joseph Fielding Smith knew that his family had a special connection to the Prophet Joseph Smith. He was inspired by the example of his grandfather Hyrum Smith, an older brother and loyal friend to the Prophet Joseph. Hyrum served faithfully at his brother's side as a leader in the Church. He also helped with the publication of the Book of Mormon and was called to be one of the Eight Witnesses of the book. On June 27, 1844, Joseph and Hyrum were martyred in Carthage, Illinois, sealing their testimonies of the Savior and His gospel. "In life they were not divided, and in death they were not separated!" (D&C 135:3).

Joseph Fielding Smith never knew his Smith grandparents. Long before he was born, his grandfather Hyrum was martyred. Hyrum's wife Mary Fielding Smith also died young. Joseph Fielding Smith said: "I never knew my Grandmother Smith. I have always regretted that, because she was one of the most noble women who ever lived, but I did know her good sister, my Aunt Mercy Thompson, and as a boy I used to go and visit her in her home and sit at her knee, where she told me stories about the Prophet Joseph Smith, and, oh, how grateful I am for that experience."[1]

Joseph Fielding Smith also learned from the example of his father, Joseph F. Smith, who had known the Prophet Joseph Smith personally. Of his father, Joseph Fielding Smith said: "There was no element of doubt or uncertainty in his testimony. Especially was this so when he spoke of the divinity of our Savior or the mission of the prophet Joseph Smith."[2]

These examples and teachings led Joseph Fielding Smith to have a testimony of the restored gospel in his childhood. "I do not remember the time when I did not believe in the mission of our Lord and Savior Jesus Christ nor in the mission of the Prophet Joseph Smith,"[3] he later said. When he taught the gospel, he sometimes expressed his testimony in familial terms: "Do I love the Prophet Joseph Smith? Yes, I do, as my father did before me. I love him because he was the servant of God and because of the restoration of the gospel and because of the benefits and blessings that have come to me and mine, and to you and yours, through the blessings that were bestowed upon this man and those who were associated with him."[4]

Although President Smith was grateful for the teachings and heritage of his family, his testimony was his own. He said, "I have always been very grateful for the testimony coming to me through the Spirit of the Lord that Joseph Smith, the Prophet of God, was called to stand at the head of the Dispensation of the Fulness of Times."[5] On another occasion he testified: "It is my knowledge, by the gift of God, that Joseph Smith in the year 1820 did see the Father and the Son; that the Father introduced his Son; that the Son spoke to him, asked him what he wanted to know, and gave him counsel; told him what to do, with the promise that eventually other light would come and the fulness of the gospel, which was not then upon the face of the earth, would be restored." Then he shared an assurance that all people could receive the same testimony: "Every soul upon the face of the earth who has a desire to know it has the privilege, for every soul that will humble himself, and in the depths of humility and faith, with a contrite spirit, go before the Lord, will receive that knowledge just as surely as he lives."[6]

Teachings of Joseph Fielding Smith

1

Two themes stand out uppermost: that Jesus Christ is the Son of God and that Joseph Smith was a prophet.

We link the names of Jesus Christ and of Joseph Smith. Christ is the Lord; he worked out the atoning sacrifice; he is the resurrection and the life; through him all men are raised in immortality, while those who believe and obey his laws shall also gain eternal life.

Joseph Smith was a prophet, called in these last days to receive by revelation the saving truths of the gospel and to stand as a legal administrator, having power from on high, to administer the ordinances of the gospel.

Since these truths revealed through him are the ones which shall go forth to every nation before the Second Coming, it is little wonder that we find Moroni saying to Joseph Smith that his "name should be had for good and evil among all nations, kindreds, and tongues, or that it should be both good and evil spoken of among all people." [Joseph Smith—History 1:33.]

Nor is it any wonder when we later find the Lord saying to the Prophet: "The ends of the earth shall inquire after thy name, and fools shall have thee in derision, and hell shall rage against thee;

"While the pure in heart, and the wise, and the noble, and the virtuous, shall seek counsel, and authority, and blessings constantly from under thy hand." (D&C 122:1–2.)

The ends of the earth are now beginning to inquire after the name of Joseph Smith, and many people in many nations are rejoicing in the gospel restored through his instrumentality.

Since the beginning of this dispensation, the testimony of Jesus, as revealed to Joseph Smith, has been preached in the United States, Canada, Great Britain, most of Europe, and the islands of the Pacific.

In recent years there has been an almost unbelievable expansion of the work in Mexico, in the Central American countries, and in South America.

And Asia is now [in 1971] being opened to the message of the gospel in a way that surpasses anything of the past. The Church is becoming established in Japan and Korea, in Taiwan and Hong Kong, and we are getting started in Thailand, Singapore, and Indonesia.

And the day will come, in the providence of the Lord, when other nations, now closed to the message of truth, shall have their doors opened to us, and the elders of Israel will go in to tell the honest in heart in those nations about Christ and the gospel of his kingdom that has come upon the earth in this day through the Prophet Joseph Smith.[7]

Joseph Smith is the revealer of the knowledge of Christ and of salvation to the world for this day and generation.[8]

Two themes stand out uppermost always in my mind. That Jesus Christ is the Son of God, who was crucified for the sins of the world, and that Joseph Smith was a prophet called and appointed to usher in the dispensation of the fulness of times. That is my message to the world.[9]

_____ ⟨◯⟩ 2 ⟨◯⟩ _____

The Lord called Joseph Smith to stand at the head of this glorious dispensation.

Joseph Smith . . . came and under direction of holy messengers laid the foundation for the kingdom of God and of this marvelous work and a wonder that the world might be prepared for the coming of the Lord.[10]

I know that he [Joseph Smith] was called, appointed by our Father in heaven; that he received revelation and guidance from the Son of God that would be of benefit and a blessing to all men if they would receive it.[11]

There is no doubt in my mind that the Lord raised the Prophet Joseph Smith up and gave him revelation, commandment, opened the heavens to him, and called upon him to stand at the head of this glorious dispensation. I am perfectly satisfied in my mind that in his youth, when he went out to pray, he beheld and stood in the actual presence of God the Father and his Son Jesus Christ; in

"Joseph Smith was a prophet called and appointed to usher in the dispensation of the fulness of times."

my mind there is no doubt—I know this to be true. I know that he later received visitations from Moroni, the Aaronic Priesthood under the hands of John the Baptist, the Melchizedek Priesthood under the hands of Peter, James, and John, and that The Church of Jesus Christ of Latter-day Saints was organized on the sixth day of April 1830, by divine command.[12]

In choosing a representative to stand at the head of this "great and marvelous work about to come forth unto the children of men," [see D&C 4:1] the Lord did not select one who was versed in the learning and traditions of the world. His ways are not the ways of man, neither are his thoughts like the thoughts of men [see Isaiah 55:8]. One taught in the learning of the world would have had too much to unlearn of the traditions and philosophy of men. In his great wisdom the Lord chose an unsophisticated child—a boy fourteen years of age. Unto this youth the Lord revealed the fulness of the gospel, which the world would not receive because of unbelief. Through years of heavenly guidance—for he was instructed by messengers from the presence of the Lord—this young man, Joseph Smith, was prepared to direct the work of the restoration of the Gospel and the building of the Kingdom of God.[13]

3

The Lord said that this generation would have His word through the Prophet Joseph Smith.

In every age when the gospel is on earth, it must be revealed to the Lord's prophets, and they must be called to stand as legal administrators to perform and to direct the performance of the ordinances of salvation for their fellowmen.

Joseph Smith is the prophet whom the Lord called in this day to restore the truths of salvation and to receive the keys and powers to administer these saving truths.

To him the Lord said: ". . . this generation shall have my word through you." (D&C 5:10.) And then, referring to the gospel restored through Joseph Smith, the Lord said: "This Gospel of the Kingdom shall be preached in all the world, for a witness unto all nations, and then shall the end come, or the destruction of the wicked." [Joseph Smith—Matthew 1:31.][14]

I now say—

That Joseph Smith is the one to whom all men must look in this day to learn the truth about Christ and his gospel;

That in due course the name of this prophet shall be known in every corner of the earth and among all people;

That the honest in heart will accept him as a prophet and will worship that Lord whom he revealed;

That the church that he organized by divine command prospers because it follows the revelations that came through him;

And that all who believe the teachings of Joseph Smith and labor in the course set by him shall come to a knowledge that Jesus Christ is the Son of God who was crucified for the sins of the world.

In the same way that I know Jesus is the Christ—and that is by revelation from the Holy Spirit—I know that Joseph Smith is and was and everlastingly shall be a prophet of God. . . .

In a spirit of testimony and thanksgiving, I [share] these inspired words from the Doctrine and Covenants: "Joseph Smith, the Prophet and Seer of the Lord, has done more, save Jesus only, for the salvation of men in this world, than any other man that ever lived in it." (D&C 135:3.)[15]

4

Joseph Smith and his brother Hyrum were united in life and in death.

I am thankful for the restoration of eternal truth in this final gospel dispensation; for the mission and ministry of Joseph Smith, the Prophet, and my grandfather, Hyrum Smith, the Patriarch, and for the fact that the keys of the kingdom of God have been committed again to man on the earth.[16]

"And again, verily I say unto you, blessed is my servant Hyrum Smith, for I, the Lord, love him because of the integrity of his heart, and because he loveth that which is right before me, saith the Lord." [D&C 124:15.]

Who would not be happy to have such a tribute of confidence and praise given him, and coming from the Lord? Hyrum Smith was among the first baptized in this dispensation. Through his life he stood by the side of his brother Joseph and strengthened him by encouragement, faith and devoted love. Hyrum was a man of wonderful tenderness of heart. He possessed deep humility and loved his brother better than he loved his own life. This is shown in his death through which he obtained a martyr's crown. He was fearless in his defense of truth. Verily he "loved that which is right."

Hyrum Smith was born on the ninth day of February, 1800, and was nearly six years the senior of the Prophet. No honor came to Joseph Smith that was not shared by Hyrum who rejoiced with his brother in all the blessings the Lord bestowed upon him. This same quality of brotherly love was shown by the Prophet Joseph for his brother Hyrum. They passed through the same sorrows and joys together. The same persecutions descended upon them both. They

Together, Joseph and Hyrum Smith sealed their testimonies with their blood.

shared the same dungeons for the Gospel's sake, and when the time came for the sealing of their testimony, they shared together the crown of martyrdom. "In life they were not divided, and in death they were not separated." [D&C 135:3.] . . .

This is a merited tribute from the Prophet: "Brother Hyrum, what a faithful heart you have got! Oh may the Eternal Jehovah crown eternal blessings upon your head, as a reward for the care you have had for my soul! Oh how many are the sorrows we have shared together; and again we find ourselves shackled with the unrelenting hand of oppression. Hyrum, thy name shall be written in the book of the Law of the Lord, for those who come after thee to look upon, that they may pattern after thy works."

Again the Prophet said: "I could pray in my heart that all my brethren were like unto my beloved brother Hyrum, who possesses the mildness of a lamb, and the integrity of a Job, and in short, the meekness and humility of Christ and I love him with that love that is stronger than death, for I never had occasion to rebuke him, nor he me." [17]

5
Joseph and Hyrum Smith sealed
their testimonies with their blood.

My grandfather, the Patriarch Hyrum Smith, was called to hold the keys of this dispensation jointly with the Prophet Joseph, his younger brother. The Lord has said that in the mouths of two witnesses shall all things be established [see 2 Corinthians 13:1]. . . .

Joseph Smith could not have stood alone, else his work would have failed, just as the work of the Savior required the confirmation of another witness, and who could testify for Christ other than his Father? [See John 8:12–18.] And so the Lord called another man to stand with Joseph Smith and to hold the keys of salvation in this dispensation as a witness with him. . . .

. . . Not only was [Hyrum] called to become the Patriarch of the Church, which was his birthright, but at the same time the Lord said to him:

"And from this time forth I appoint unto him that he may be a prophet, and a seer, and a revelator unto my church, as well as my servant Joseph;

"That he may act in concert also with my servant Joseph; and that he shall receive counsel from my servant Joseph, who shall show unto him the keys whereby he may ask and receive, and be crowned with the same blessing, and glory, and honor, and priesthood, and gifts of the priesthood, that once were put upon him that was my servant Oliver Cowdery;

"That my servant Hyrum may bear record of the things which I shall show unto him, that his name may be had in honorable remembrance from generation to generation, forever and ever." [D&C 124:94–96.]

In accord with this calling and commandment, the Prophet Joseph Smith conferred upon Hyrum Smith all the keys, authority and gifts of the priesthood which he, the Prophet, held, and which were formerly held by Oliver Cowdery. The Lord also revealed to Hyrum Smith all that was necessary to make him completely and to the full degree, a witness with his brother Joseph, as a prophet, seer, revelator and president of the Church, and to stand through

113

all time and all eternity at the head of this dispensation with his brother Joseph, a witness for Jesus Christ.[18]

With his brother, my grandfather, Patriarch Hyrum Smith, he [Joseph Smith] sealed his testimony with his blood in Carthage Jail. And I, for one, want to be an instrument in the Lord's hands of letting the ends of the earth know that salvation is again available because the Lord raised up a mighty seer in this day to reestablish his kingdom on earth.[19]

We raise our voices in thanksgiving for the lives and ministries of the Prophet Joseph Smith, of Hyrum Smith the Patriarch, and of the prophets and apostles and righteous men and women who have built on the foundation they laid.[20]

Suggestions for Study and Teaching

Questions

- President Smith told of family members who helped nurture his childhood testimony of Joseph Smith's mission (see "From the Life of Joseph Fielding Smith"). What can we do to help children gain a testimony of the mission of the Prophet Joseph Smith?

- In what ways are the names of Jesus Christ and Joseph Smith linked? (See section 1.) How has the ministry of the Prophet Joseph Smith influenced your testimony of the Savior and His gospel?

- Ponder President Smith's observations about the Lord calling Joseph Smith rather than "one who was versed in the learning and traditions of the world" (section 2). How can this understanding help us when we feel inadequate to fulfill our responsibilities?

- In section 3, President Smith quotes Doctrine and Covenants 5:10 and 135:3. How might you explain these verses to someone who is unfamiliar with the mission of Joseph Smith?

- What can you learn from the relationship between Joseph Smith and his brother Hyrum? (See section 4.)

- What are your feelings as you think about Joseph and Hyrum Smith sealing their testimonies with their blood? (See section 5.) In what ways can we honor their sacrifice?

Related Scriptures

Joseph Smith Translation, Genesis 50:30–31; 2 Nephi 3:5–15; D&C 11:11–26; 76:22–24; 135

Teaching Help

One way to encourage diligent learning is to listen carefully when someone asks a question or makes a comment. "Listening is an expression of love. It often requires sacrifice. When we truly listen to others, we often give up what we want to say so they can express themselves" (*Teaching, No Greater Call* [1999], 66).

Notes

1. In Conference Report, Apr. 1962, 44.

2. In Bryant S. Hinckley, "Joseph Fielding Smith," *Improvement Era,* June 1932, 459.

3. In Conference Report, Apr. 1962, 44.

4. In Conference Report, Apr. 1960, 73.

5. In Conference Report, Apr. 1962, 45.

6. In Conference Report, Oct. 1949, 88–89.

7. In Conference Report, Oct. 1970, 6.

8. "The First Prophet of the Last Dispensation," *Ensign,* Aug. 1971, 7.

9. In Conference Report, Apr. 1920, 108–9.

10. In Conference Report, Apr. 1920, 107.

11. In Conference Report, Oct. 1949, 88.

12. "To Know for Ourselves," *Improvement Era,* Mar. 1970, 3.

13. *Essentials in Church History* (1950), 20–21.

14. In Conference Report, Oct. 1970, 6.

15. "The First Prophet of the Last Dispensation," 7.

16. "A Prophet's Blessing," *Ensign,* July 1972, 130.

17. "Hyrum Smith: A Tribute by Joseph Fielding Smith," *Improvement Era,* Feb. 1933, 201; italics removed from original; see also *Teachings of Presidents of the Church: Joseph Smith* (2007), 461.

18. In Conference Report, Apr. 1930, 91–93; see also *Doctrines of Salvation,* ed. Bruce R. McConkie, 3 vols. (1954–56), 1:216–19.

19. "The First Prophet of the Last Dispensation," 7.

20. "Ogden Temple Dedicatory Prayer," *Ensign,* Mar. 1972, 9.

President Joseph Fielding Smith, a dedicated servant in the Lord's kingdom

The Church and Kingdom of God

"Let all men know assuredly that this is the Lord's Church and he is directing its affairs. What a privilege it is to have membership in such a divine institution!"

From the Life of Joseph Fielding Smith

Joseph Fielding Smith's service as President of the Church, from January 23, 1970, to July 2, 1972, was the culmination of a lifetime of dedication in the Lord's kingdom. He joked that his first Church assignment came when he was a baby. When he was nine months old, he and his father, President Joseph F. Smith, accompanied President Brigham Young to St. George, Utah, to attend the dedication of the St. George Temple.[1]

As a young man, Joseph Fielding Smith served a full time mission and was later called to be president in a priesthood quorum and a member of the general board of the Young Men's Mutual Improvement Association (the forerunner to today's Young Men organization). He also worked as a clerk in the Church Historian's office, and he quietly helped his father as an unofficial secretary when his father was President of the Church. Through these service opportunities, Joseph Fielding Smith came to appreciate the Church's inspired organization and its role in leading individuals and families to eternal life.

Joseph Fielding Smith was ordained an Apostle of the Lord Jesus Christ on April 7, 1910. He served as a member of the Quorum of the Twelve Apostles for almost 60 years, including almost 20 years as President of that Quorum. As an Apostle, he helped direct the Church throughout the world. He participated in many aspects of the Church's mission, serving as Church Historian, president of the

Salt Lake Temple, president of the Utah Genealogical Society, and a Counselor in the First Presidency.

A simple and unassuming man, Joseph Fielding Smith never sought these positions. But when the Lord called him to serve, he willingly and enthusiastically obeyed. He quietly exhibited this dedication one day when, at age 89, he went to a meeting. Walking from his home, he slipped and fell down a flight of steps. Although he hurt his leg, he walked about a quarter of a mile—"limping like an old man," he said—so he could fulfill his responsibilities. After the meeting, he walked back home, where he finally allowed a doctor to examine him. The doctor found that President Smith's leg was fractured in multiple places. President Smith later commented on the experience. "The meeting got a little long," he said. "But then, most meetings do."[2]

In a message to Latter-day Saint youth, President Smith shared his reason for being so dedicated to the work of the Church:

"I know that God lives. I know that Jesus Christ is the Only Begotten Son in the flesh of our Father. I have perfect faith in the mission of the Prophet Joseph Smith and those who have succeeded him.

"I know that we have the truth of the everlasting gospel of Jesus Christ, just as well as I know that I live. If I did not know it, I wouldn't want to be here or have anything to do with this work. But I know it in every fiber of my body. God has revealed it to me."[3]

Teachings of Joseph Fielding Smith

―――――――――― ⚬⚭⚬ **1** ⚬⚭⚬ ――――――――――

After centuries of spiritual darkness and apostasy, the Lord has restored His gospel and organized His Church on the earth.

The Lord [has] restored the gospel and organized again his Church upon the earth. The reason for such organization and restoration is the fact that for centuries the world had been in spiritual darkness, without the authority, and without the understanding; they knew not how to worship the living God. . . .

The everlasting covenant had been broken; the correct understanding of gospel principles had disappeared through apostasy; the right to officiate in the ordinances of the gospel had ceased among men. It became necessary that all this might be restored, and that faith might increase among the people through an opening of the heavens and a restoration of the gospel.

So the Lord sent his messengers from his presence, with the fulness of the gospel, and with power, and the authority of the priesthood to bestow upon men, and gave them commandments . . . because the Lord knew the calamities which were to come upon the world, and it was his will that a proper warning, and the opportunity to receive the gospel be given unto men that they might repent and turn from their evil ways and serve the Lord [see D&C 1:17 23].[4]

We announce that The Church of Jesus Christ of Latter-day Saints is the kingdom of God on earth, the only place where men may come to learn the true doctrines of salvation and find the authority of the holy priesthood.[5]

My beloved brethren and sisters: I am grateful beyond any measure of expression for the blessings the Lord has given to me, and to the faithful members of his church in the various nations of the earth, and to all his children everywhere.

I thank him every day of my life that he has restored in these last days his everlasting gospel for the salvation of all who will believe and obey its laws.[6]

--------------------- 2 ---------------------

The Lord Himself directs the work of the Church, and it is our privilege to have membership in it.

The Church of Jesus Christ of Latter-day Saints is in literal reality the kingdom of God on earth.[7]

I desire to say that no man of himself can lead this church. It is the Church of the Lord Jesus Christ; he is at the head. The church bears his name, has his priesthood, administers his gospel, preaches his doctrine, and does his work.

He chooses men and calls them to be instruments in his hands to accomplish his purposes, and he guides and directs them in their labors. But men are only instruments in the Lord's hands, and the honor and glory for all that his servants accomplish is and should be ascribed unto him forever.

If this were the work of man, it would fail, but it is the work of the Lord, and he does not fail. And we have the assurance that if we keep the commandments and are valiant in the testimony of Jesus and are true to every trust, the Lord will guide and direct us and his church in the paths of righteousness, for the accomplishment of all his purposes.[8]

To all members of the Church throughout the world I would like to say that this church has a divinely appointed mission to perform under the direction and leadership of Jesus Christ, our Savior, and that nothing will stop his plans pertaining to it. It will fulfill the designs of our Father in heaven. I hope the Saints throughout the world daily thank the Lord for being members of his church and for the mission of the Prophet Joseph Smith in restoring the gospel for our joy and happiness.[9]

To the honest in heart in all nations we say: The Lord loves you. He wants you to receive the full blessings of the gospel. He is now inviting you to believe the Book of Mormon, to accept Joseph Smith as a prophet, and to come into his earthly kingdom and thereby become heirs of eternal life in his heavenly kingdom.[10]

There never was a time since the organization of the Church when a man led the Church. It was not so in the days of Joseph Smith nor Brigham Young; it has not been so since. It is the Lord's work, and do not forget that it is the Almighty who is going to do this work, and not man.[11]

I know that The Church of Jesus Christ of Latter-day Saints is the kingdom of God on earth, and that as now constituted and officered it has the Lord's approval and is moving in the course so directed.

Let all men know assuredly that this is the Lord's Church and he is directing its affairs. What a privilege it is to have membership in such a divine institution![12]

———————————— 3 ————————————

The Church is organized to help members find joy and happiness in this life and eternal life in the life to come.

The Lord has established all things in order and has given us a perfect system. Men cannot improve upon it. If we would carry out that which the Lord has revealed, as he has revealed it, then all things would be perfect, for the organization is a perfect organization; the theory of it—the plan of it—is without flaw.[13]

The Lord has set up in his church a priesthood organization headed by apostles and prophets. And he has also given other organizations . . . to aid and assist in the priesthood.

In every gospel dispensation there are special needs to be met, problems to be solved, and help that must be given to assist and aid the members of the Church in working out their salvation "with fear and trembling" before the Lord. (See Phil. 2:12.) Hence we have auxiliary organizations [Relief Society, Young Men, Young Women, Primary, and Sunday School] to aid and assist the priesthood. They are so organized as to meet the needs of the people in whatever social conditions may exist. They are part of the government of God and are set up to help members of the Church perfect their lives and do those things which assure them of joy and happiness in this life and eternal life in the life to come. . . .

The Church and its agencies constitute in effect a service organization to help the family and the individual. Home teachers, priesthood leaders, and bishops are appointed to lead those with whom they labor to eternal life in our Father's kingdom, and the auxiliary organizations are appointed to aid and assist in this great work of salvation.

We cannot stress too strongly the great need to utilize all of these programs for the benefit and blessing of all our Father's children. . . .

If all of us do all of the things we should in carrying forward the programs of the Church, the Lord will bless and prosper us so fully that success shall attend our labors, and out of it all peace and joy will be our lot here and eternal glory hereafter.[14]

*"Your able service does not go unnoticed by that God whom
you serve and in whose work you are engaged."*

―――――――――――― 4 ――――――――――――

**Our service in the Church expresses love for others
and appreciation for the Lord's infinite service.**

The Lord is with the Church. He is guiding us. His spirit is resting
upon this people. What he requires of us is that we serve him in
humility and with a oneness of heart and soul.[15]

Our Savior came into the world to teach us love for each other,
and as that great lesson was made manifest through his great suffering and death that we might live, should we not express our love
for our fellowmen by service rendered in their behalf? Should we
not show our appreciation for the infinite service he rendered us,
by giving service in his cause?

The man who does only those things in the Church which concern himself alone will never reach exaltation. For instance, the man who is willing to pray, to pay his tithes and offerings, and to attend to the ordinary duties which concern his own personal life, and nothing more, will never reach the goal of perfection.[16]

Never refuse to serve. When a presiding officer asks your help, be glad to accept and give the best you have to that labor. The Lord expects this of us, and we are under covenant to do so. This course brings joy and peace, and at the same time those who serve receive the greatest blessing. The teacher gains more than the one taught; the blessing returned to us when we accept a call to work in the Church is far greater than the blessing we can impart to others. He who refuses to perform any labor or shirks responsibility when it is given him in the Church is in grave danger of losing the guidance of the Spirit. Eventually he becomes lukewarm and indifferent to all duties, and, like the plant that is not cultivated and watered, he shrivels up and dies a spiritual death.[17]

Your able service does not go unnoticed by that God whom you serve and in whose work you are engaged.[18]

It is my prayer that all of us, working together as true brothers and sisters in the Lord's kingdom, may so labor as to accomplish the great work that lies ahead.[19]

———————————— 5 ————————————

In this dispensation, the kingdom of God and the work of the Lord will spread throughout the world.

A dispensation of the Gospel is defined as the granting to divinely chosen officers, by a commission from God of power and authority to dispense the word of God, and to administer in all the ordinances thereof. . . .

There have been times when the Gospel has been taken from men because of their transgression. Such was the case in the days of Noah. Israel turned from the Lord and was left in darkness for many generations preceding the advent of Jesus Christ, and when he came among men he restored the fulness of the Gospel. He sent his disciples to proclaim his message in all the world, but not many centuries had passed before the people had again fallen into error and lost the authority to act in the name of the Lord. This made it necessary for the opening of the heavens and the introduction of a new dispensation to make ready for the second coming of our Lord in the clouds of heaven to reign upon the earth in glory for a thousand years, which event is near, even at our doors.[20]

The gospel itself has been the same in all dispensations; the plan of salvation is the same for all our Father's children in every age. From time to time it has been lost by apostasy, but whenever the Lord has had a people on earth, they have been offered the same laws and truths of salvation that he has revealed to us.

But there is one great added thing we have received in this age that has never been had before. In this dispensation the Lord has decreed that the Church shall never again be led astray; this time the gospel is here to stay. This time the revealed truth is destined to prepare a people for the second coming of the Son of Man, and the Church will be established in all parts of the earth when the Lord comes to usher in the millennial era of peace and righteousness.[21]

We are members of a world church, a church that has the plan of life and salvation, a church set up by the Lord himself in these last days to carry his message of salvation to all his children in all the earth. . . .

We have attained the stature and strength that are enabling us to fulfill the commission given us by the Lord through the Prophet Joseph Smith that we should carry the glad tidings of the restoration to every nation and to all people.

And not only shall we preach the gospel in every nation before the second coming of the Son of Man, but we shall make converts and establish congregations of Saints among them.[22]

The kingdom of God and the work of the Lord will spread more and more; it will progress more rapidly in the world in the future than it has done in the past. The Lord has said it, and the Spirit beareth record; and I bear testimony to this, for I do know that it is true. The kingdom of God is here to grow, to spread abroad, to take root in the earth, and to abide where the Lord has planted it by his own power and by his own word, never more to be destroyed, but to continue until the purposes of the Almighty shall be accomplished—every principle that has been spoken of by the prophets since the world began. It is God's work, which he himself, by his own wisdom and not by the wisdom of man, has restored to the earth in the latter days.[23]

The gospel is for all men, and the Church shall be established everywhere, in all nations, even to the ends of the earth, before the second coming of the Son of Man.[24]

I know and testify that the Lord's purposes on earth shall prevail. The Church of Jesus Christ of Latter-day Saints is here to stay. The Lord's work shall triumph. No power on earth can prevent the spread of truth and the preaching of the gospel in every nation.[25]

I leave my blessing with you and my assurance that God is with his people, and that the work in which we are engaged shall triumph and roll forth until the eternal purposes of the Lord are fulfilled.[26]

Suggestions for Study and Teaching

Questions

- How can we follow President Smith's example in our Church service? (See "From the Life of Joseph Fielding Smith.")

- Ponder President Smith's teachings about the Restoration of the gospel (see section 1). What are your feelings when you think about living at a time when the Lord's Church has been restored to the earth?

- President Smith testified that Jesus Christ is at the head of the Church (see section 2). How might you share your testimony of this truth with someone who is not a member of the Church?

- How have the organizations and programs of the Church helped you receive the blessings mentioned in section 3? How have they helped your family?

- President Smith said, "Our Savior came into the world to teach us love for each other" (section 4). In what ways can we follow the Savior's example of love when we serve as home teachers or visiting teachers?

- As you review section 5, notice how this dispensation is different from others. How can this understanding influence our service in the Church? What are your feelings as you think about preparing the world for the Savior's Second Coming?

Related Scriptures

Mosiah 18:17–29; D&C 1:30; 65:1–6; 115:4; 128:19–22

Teaching Help

"When you use a variety of learning activities, learners tend to understand gospel principles better and retain more. A carefully selected method can make a principle clearer, more interesting, and more memorable" (*Teaching, No Greater Call* [1999], 89).

Notes

1. See Joseph Fielding Smith Jr. and John J. Stewart, *The Life of Joseph Fielding Smith* (1972), 16.

2. In *The Life of Joseph Fielding Smith,* 4.

3. "My Dear Young Fellow Workers," *New Era,* Jan. 1971, 5.

4. In Conference Report, Oct. 1944, 140–41.

5. "Out of the Darkness," *Ensign,* June 1971, 4.

6. In Conference Report, Apr. 1970, 4.

7. "Use the Programs of the Church," *Improvement Era,* Oct. 1970, 3.

8. In Conference Report, Apr. 1970, 113.

9. "For Thus Shall My Church Be Called," *Improvement Era,* Apr. 1970, 3.

10. "Counsel to the Saints and to the World," *Ensign,* July 1972, 27.

11. In Conference Report, Oct. 1968, 123.

12. In Conference Report, Oct. 1970, 8.

13. "The One Fundamental Teaching," *Improvement Era,* May 1970, 3.

14. "Use the Programs of the Church," 2–3.

15. "The One Fundamental Teaching," 3.

16. In Conference Report, Apr. 1968, 12.

17. In Conference Report, Apr. 1966, 102.

18. In Conference Report, Apr. 1970, 59.

19. In Conference Report, Apr. 1970, 114.

20. "A Peculiar People: Gospel Dispensations," *Deseret News,* Dec. 5, 1931, Church section, 6.

21. "A Call to Serve," *New Era,* Nov. 1971, 5.

22. In Conference Report, British Area General Conference 1971, 5.

23. In Conference Report, Oct. 1968, 123.

24. In Conference Report, British Area General Conference 1971, 176.

25. "Counsel to the Saints and to the World," 28.

26. In Conference Report, Apr. 1970, 148–49.

Witnesses of the Book of Mormon

"It seems to me that any member of this Church would never be satisfied until he or she had read the Book of Mormon time and time again and thoroughly considered it so that he or she could bear witness that it is in very deed a record with the inspiration of the Almighty upon it."

From the Life of Joseph Fielding Smith

President Joseph Fielding Smith served as the Church Historian and Recorder from March 1921 to February 1970. In this position, he was instrumental in procuring original documents of historical significance to the Church. One of these documents was a handwritten testimony signed by David Whitmer, one of the three special witnesses of the Book of Mormon. President Smith was also privileged to handle a handwritten testimony of Oliver Cowdery, another of the Three Witnesses of the Book of Mormon. After copying these two documents by hand, President Smith read them in at least two public discourses—once in March 1939 and again in the October 1956 general conference of the Church.

Although President Smith felt these written testimonies were significant enough to share, he spoke more frequently of another testimony of the Book of Mormon: his own, which he received long before he ever worked in the Church Historian's Office. He said, "I started to read the Book of Mormon before I was old enough to be a deacon, and I have been reading it ever since, and I know that it is true."[1] "I have read it many, many times," he told the Latter-day Saints. "I have not read it enough. It still contains truths that I still may seek and find, for I have not mastered it, but I know it is true."[2]

An angel showed the gold plates to Oliver Cowdery and David Whitmer, two of the Three Witnesses, with Joseph Smith present. The angel later showed the plates to Martin Harris, the third witness.

In sharing these testimonies of the Book of Mormon, President Smith's purpose was to encourage others to receive their own testimonies. He declared, "I bear witness to you that the Lord has made it very clear to me by revelation which I have received, and many of you who are here present can bear witness likewise, that these things are true, and that is the privilege of any sincere person who will endeavor to read with a prayerful spirit and a desire to know whether the book is true or not; and he will receive that testimony according to the promise that was made by Moroni, who sealed the record to come forth in the Dispensation of the Fulness of Times."[3]

Teachings of Joseph Fielding Smith

1

The Book of Mormon is a sacred record that contains the everlasting gospel and bears witness of Jesus Christ.

The Book of Mormon is the sacred history of the ancient inhabitants of the American continent, and contains the predictions of their prophets, the commandments of the Lord to them, and the history and destiny of those ancient peoples. It is the American volume of scripture, and is just as sacred and inspired as is the Bible, which contains the sacred records of the Hebrew race on the eastern hemisphere.[4]

The Nephite prophets in prayer earnestly sought that their writings should be preserved to come forth and to speak as from the dead, to bear witness to the remnant of Lehi, and also to Jew and Gentile, that God had revealed to them the fulness of the Gospel. Their anxiety was that in these last days men might be brought to repentance and faith in God through the testimony given many centuries before to these Nephite prophets. In fact, we learn from the Book of Mormon that this is the main object of the Book of Mormon, as stated in many of its passages. . . .

. . . The Lord made it very clear to the Nephite prophets that their history and prophecies would be preserved to come forth in the latter days as a witness for Jesus Christ and to establish among the people his Gospel. Nephi prophesied to the Gentiles and the Jews of our day and left for them his testimony in a most emphatic and telling manner. (2 Nephi 33.) Moroni did the same. (Moroni 10:24–34.)[5]

Nephi, one of the earliest prophets of the Israelitish colony, predicted nearly six hundred years before the Christian era, that when the records containing the history of his people should be revealed from the dust, it would be in a day when the people would "deny the power of God, the Holy One of Israel," and they would say: "Hearken unto us, and hear ye our precept; for behold there is no God today, for the Lord and the Redeemer hath done His work, and He hath given His power unto men." [2 Nephi 28:5.] Again, many among them would say when presented with a new volume of scripture containing the history of the people of this western world: "A Bible! A Bible! We have got a Bible, and there cannot be any more Bible." [2 Nephi 29:3.]

. . . This new volume of scripture was to be a witness, not only for Christ and to contain the everlasting Gospel, but was also to be a witness for the Jewish scriptures—the Bible; and these two records—according to the prophesying of Nephi, his father, and also Joseph, son of Israel—were to grow together bearing testimony of the everlasting gospel [see 2 Nephi 3:11–13; 29:10–14]. As such a witness these records stand today testifying of the truth to the condemnation of all who reject their teachings.[6]

I know that Joseph Smith translated the Book of Mormon by the gift and power of God, and that it has come forth "to the convincing of the Jew and Gentile that Jesus is the Christ, the Eternal God, manifesting himself unto all nations." [Title page of the Book of Mormon.][7]

―――――――――――― 2 ――――――――――――

In accordance with the law of witnesses, the Lord called special witnesses to testify of the Book of Mormon.

There is a law definitely stated in the scriptures governing testimony and the appointment of witnesses. This law the Lord has always followed in granting new revelation to the people.[8]

All down through the ages this law [the law of witnesses] has been a fixed and definite one. If we had perfect records of all ages, we would find that whenever the Lord has established a dispensation, there has been more than one witness to testify for him. Paul in writing to the Corinthians said: "In the mouth of two or three witnesses shall every word be established." [2 Corinthians 13:1.][9]

In regard to the coming forth of the Book of Mormon, the Lord said that he would choose witnesses. There should be three special witnesses that should bear record to the world, and said he:

"And there is none other which shall view it, save it be a few according to the will of God, to bear testimony of his word unto the children of men; for the Lord God hath said that the words of the faithful should speak as if it were from the dead.

"Wherefore, the Lord God will proceed to bring forth the words of the book; and in the mouth of as many witnesses as seemeth him good will he establish his word; and wo be unto him that rejecteth the word of God!" (2 Ne. 27.13–14.)[10]

The three men called to serve as special witnesses of the coming forth of the Book of Mormon by the power of God, are Oliver Cowdery, David Whitmer, and Martin Harris. . . . They were associated with Joseph Smith in the establishing of this marvelous work in this dispensation. . . .

Their testimony is that they received a visitation of an angel from the presence of the Lord, who laid before them the golden record from whence the Book of Mormon was translated and instructed them. They beheld the engravings upon the plates as the leaves were turned one by one before them, and the voice of God was heard by them declaring from the heavens that the translation was by the gift and power of God, and commanding them to bear record of it to all the world. These three witnesses, through adversity, persecution, and all the vicissitudes of life, always remained true to their testimony that they beheld the plates in the presence of an angel and heard the voice of God speaking to them from the heavens.

There were eight other witnesses who also beheld the plates, handled them, examined carefully the engravings upon them as they were shown them by Joseph Smith. Their testimony is also given to the world and appears in each issue of the Book of

Joseph Smith showed the gold plates to the Eight Witnesses.

Mormon. All of these eight men remained true to this testimony until death.

These twelve witnesses [including Joseph Smith], four of whom beheld angels and had heavenly visions, and eight who beheld the record as it was shown to them by Joseph Smith, are all, it appears, that the Lord deemed necessary to establish the truth of the Book of Mormon, as he promised through Nephi that he would do. "And wo be unto him that rejecteth the word of God!" The testimonies of these men more than satisfy the law.[11]

Joseph Smith . . . was alone in the first vision, alone when Moroni brought the message to him, alone when he received the plates; but after that he was not alone. The Lord called other witnesses. Grandmother Smith [Joseph Smith's mother, Lucy Mack Smith] in her history says that the Prophet came home weeping for joy after the witnesses had beheld the plates under the direction of an angel of God, because, he said, "The load has been lifted and I am no longer alone." [12]

3

The Three Witnesses remained faithful to their testimonies of the Book of Mormon.

All three [special] witnesses became estranged and left the Church. Oliver Cowdery and Martin Harris came back humbly seeking membership in the Church and both died in full fellowship. David Whitmer remained out of the Church; however, all three of these men remained faithful to the testimony they gave to the world which is found in each copy of the Book of Mormon. [13]

This is a testimony of David Whitmer, given in Richmond, Missouri, March 19, 1881—copied from the original document, which was published in the Richmond *Conservator* on that date.

"Unto all nations, kindreds, tongues and people unto whom these presence shall come—

"It having been represented by one John Murphy of Polo [Caldwell County], Missouri, that I had in a conversation with him last summer, denied my testimony as one of the three witnesses to the Book of Mormon—

"To the end thereof, that he may understand me now if he did not then, and that the world may know the truth, I wish now, standing as it were, in the very sunset of life, and in the fear of God, once for all to make this public statement:

"That I have never at any time, denied that testimony or any part thereof, which has so long since been published with that book, as one of the three witnesses.

"Those who know me best, will know that I have always adhered to that testimony—And that no man may be misled or doubt my present views in regard to the same, I do now again affirm the truth of all my statements as then made and published."[14]

Now let me say something about Martin Harris. . . . While continuing true to his testimony of the Book of Mormon he was for many years disgruntled with the Church. But some time after the saints came to Utah some of our good brethren went after him, found him and warmed him up, and brought him back. He came out here [to Utah], was re-baptized, and lived here for a number of years, bearing witness of his testimony among the settlements. He died here and was buried [in Clarkston, Utah].

Now we come to Oliver Cowdery. What about Oliver Cowdery, the most important of the three, who was with Joseph Smith so many times at the appearing of angels and the restoration of keys? What about him? He left the Church and became extremely bitter, but never denied the testimony. Some people have said he did, but he did not. Always he was true to that testimony. . . .

. . . After the saints were driven from Nauvoo and were out on the plains and everything looked the darkest (Sidney Rigdon said they had gone to their destruction and there was no hope for them, and the newspapers said they could not survive!), under those conditions, Oliver Cowdery . . . asked to come back to the Church. . . . He was received back, and was preparing to take a mission to Great Britain when he was taken ill and died. He died at the home of David Whitmer, bearing testimony to the truth.[15]

—————— 〰4〰 ——————

Each member of the Church can be a witness of the Book of Mormon.

These are not all the witnesses who can speak of the divine mission of Joseph Smith, or of the truth of the Book of Mormon. The promise is made in the Book of Mormon that all who desire to know whether it is true and contains the word of the Lord may know that it is true if they will ask with a sincere heart, with real intent, having faith in Christ, for he will reveal it to them by the power of the Holy Ghost [see Moroni 10:3–5]. There are hundreds of thousands who have put this promise to the test and can in all sincerity say that they have received that knowledge.[16]

"There is an inspiration and feeling of peaceful joy and satisfaction which accompany the sincere and prayerful reading of this book."

I am just as firmly convinced that this Book of Mormon from which I have read is the word of God and was revealed, as Joseph Smith declared it was revealed, as I am that I stand here looking into your faces. Every soul on the face of the earth who has intelligence enough to understand may know that truth. How can he know it? All he has to do is to follow the formula that was given by the Lord himself when he declared to the Jews that they who would do the will of his Father should know of the doctrine, whether it was of God or whether he spoke of himself [see John 7:17]. My witness to all the world is that this book is true. . . .

I know that the testimony of these [three] witnesses recorded in each copy of the Book of Mormon is true, that they stood in the presence of an angel of God who declared unto them that the record as it was translated was correct, that their testimony that God spoke to them from the heavens calling upon them to bear witness of that fact is true, and there is not a soul who cannot receive that testimony if he desires to receive it, by reading this book prayerfully and faithfully, with a desire to know the truth as Moroni has declared by revelation. He shall know the truth regarding the restoration of this scripture given to the ancient inhabitants of this continent.[17]

It seems to me that any member of this Church would never be satisfied until he or she had read the Book of Mormon time and time again, and thoroughly considered it so that he or she could bear witness that it is in very deed a record with the inspiration of the Almighty upon it, and that its history is true. . . .

. . . No member of this Church can stand approved in the presence of God who has not seriously and carefully read the Book of Mormon.[18]

When you read the Book of Mormon you know you are reading the truth. Why? Because God directed men to write events as they occurred and He gave them the wisdom and inspiration to do this. Thus records were written by men who believed in God. These records never fell into the hands of apostates; but the historians wrote and spoke as they were moved upon by the Holy Ghost, and we know that what they wrote is true because the Lord has put His stamp of approval upon it [see D&C 17:6].[19]

—————————————— ⟨⟨⟨ 5 ⟩⟩⟩ ——————————————

As we continue to read the Book of Mormon sincerely and prayerfully, it endears itself to us more and more.

All who have sincerely read the Book of Mormon have been impressed with the inspired contents of its pages. . . . There is an inspiration and feeling of peaceful joy and satisfaction which accompany the sincere and prayerful reading of this book.[20]

As I read [the Book of Mormon] I am impressed more and more with its sacredness, with the message which it contains in defense of the mission of the Lord Jesus Christ, and the gospel which has been restored in the dispensation of the fulness of times for the salvation of souls. This record endears itself to me more and more day by day as I see unfolded the fulfillment of prophecies uttered by these prophets who now speak from the dead, and from the dust to the nations of the earth, crying unto them repentance, and calling upon them to believe in Christ.[21]

Suggestions for Study and Teaching

Questions

- President Smith said that he had not read the Book of Mormon enough (see "From the Life of Joseph Fielding Smith"). What can we learn from this observation?

- In this chapter, section 1 includes some of President Smith's teachings about the purposes of the Book of Mormon. How have these purposes been fulfilled in your life?

- Although Oliver Cowdery, Martin Harris, and David Whitmer left the Church, not one of them ever denied his testimony of the Book of Mormon (see sections 2 and 3). Why is this fact significant as we consider their testimonies?

- President Smith said that all people can be witnesses of the Book of Mormon (see section 4). How have you gained a testimony of the book? What can you do to share this witness?

- Of the Book of Mormon, President Smith said, "This record endears itself to me more and more day by day" (section 5). How have you seen this to be true for you? What can a person do to strengthen his or her testimony of the Book of Mormon?

Related Scriptures

1 Nephi 6:3–5; 2 Nephi 29:7–8; Jacob 4:1–4; Enos 1.13; D&C 20:8–12

Teaching Help

"Testify whenever the Spirit prompts you to do so, not just at the end of each lesson. Provide opportunities for those you teach to bear their testimonies" (*Teaching, No Greater Call* [1999], 45).

Notes

1. In Conference Report, Oct. 1961, 18.
2. In Conference Report, Oct. 1949, 89; see also *Doctrines of Salvation,* ed. Bruce R. McConkie, 3 vols. (1954–56), 3:231.
3. In Conference Report, Oct. 1956, 20; see also Moroni 10:3–5.
4. "Origin of the First Vision," *Improvement Era,* Apr. 1920, 503; see also *Doctrines of Salvation,* 3:209.
5. *Church History and Modern Revelation* (1953), 1:31–32.
6. "Predictions in the Bible Concerning the Book of Mormon," *Improvement Era,* Sept. 1923, 958–59; see also *Doctrines of Salvation,* 3:228–29.
7. In Conference Report, Oct. 1970, 8.
8. "Testimonies of the Witnesses to the Book of Mormon," *Improvement Era,* Sept. 1927, 950; see also *Doctrines of Salvation,* rev. ed., 1:203.

9. *Doctrines of Salvation,* rev. ed., 1:203; italics deleted from original.

10. In Conference Report, Oct. 1956, 19–20.

11. "Testimonies of the Witnesses to the Book of Mormon," 952–53; see also *Doctrines of Salvation,* 3:229–30.

12. *Doctrines of Salvation,* rev. ed., 1:210–11.

13. "Testimonies of the Witnesses to the Book of Mormon," 952; see also *Doctrines of Salvation,* 3:229–30.

14. In Conference Report, Oct. 1956, 20.

15. *Doctrines of Salvation,* rev. ed., 1:226–28.

16. "Testimonies of the Witnesses to the Book of Mormon," 953; see also *Doctrines of Salvation,* 3:231.

17. In Conference Report, Oct. 1949, 89; see also *Doctrines of Salvation,* 3:231–32.

18. In Conference Report, Oct. 1961, 18.

19. "History and History Recorders," *Utah Genealogical and Historical Magazine,* Apr. 1925, 55; see also *Doctrines of Salvation,* 2:202.

20. "Origin of the First Vision," 503.

21. In Conference Report, Apr. 1925, 73.

Our Search for Truth

*"It is a requirement that is made of us, as members
of this Church, to make ourselves familiar
with that which the Lord has revealed, that we
may not be led astray. . . . How are we going
to walk in the truth if we do not know it?"*

From the Life of Joseph Fielding Smith

When Joseph Fielding Smith was eight years old, his father gave
him a copy of the Book of Mormon and asked him to read it. "I
received this Nephite record with thanksgiving," he later recalled,
"and applied myself to the task which had been assigned to me."
His love for the book motivated him to get his chores done quickly
and sometimes even leave baseball games early so he could find
quiet places to read. In less than two years after receiving the gift
from his father, he read the book twice. Of that early study, he later
said, "There are certain passages that have been stamped upon my
mind and I have never forgotten them."[1] He also read other books.
"I used to read the books that were prepared for the Primary children and for the Sunday School children in those early days," he
said, "and I usually had a book in my hands when I was home. . . .
Later I read the History of the Church as recorded in the *Millennial
Star.* I also read the Bible, the Book of Mormon, the Pearl of Great
Price, the Doctrine and Covenants, and other literature that fell into
my hands."[2]

President Smith maintained this thirst for gospel knowledge
throughout his life. As he learned the truths of the gospel, he shared
them and, when necessary, defended them. Three years after he
was ordained an Apostle, he received a priesthood blessing that
included the following counsel: "You have been blessed with ability
to comprehend, to analyze, and defend the principles of truth above

Elder Joseph Fielding Smith of the Quorum of the Twelve
Apostles and President Joseph F. Smith, 1914

many of your fellows, and the time will come when the accumulative evidence that you have gathered will stand as a wall of defense against those who are seeking and will seek to destroy the evidence of the divinity of the mission of the Prophet Joseph; and in this defense you will never be confounded, and the light of the Spirit will shed its rays upon your heart as gently as the dews that fall from heaven, and it will unfold to your understanding many truths concerning this work."[3] He lived true to these prophetic words. As a gospel scholar, teacher, and writer, he worked diligently to explain and defend the doctrines of salvation. President Heber J. Grant once called him the "best posted man on the scriptures" among all the General Authorities.[4]

Toward the end of his life, President Smith often reflected on the blessings he had received through his study of the gospel:

"All my life I have studied and pondered the principles of the gospel and sought to live the laws of the Lord. As a result there has come into my heart a great love for him and for his work and for all those who seek to further his purposes in the earth."[5]

"All my days I have studied the scriptures and have sought the guidance of the Spirit of the Lord in coming to an understanding of their true meaning. The Lord has been good to me, and I rejoice in the knowledge he has given me and in the privilege that has been and is mine to teach his saving principles."[6]

Teachings of Joseph Fielding Smith

―――――――――― ∞ 1 ∞ ――――――――――

We should seek truth in many fields, but the most important knowledge is gospel knowledge.

We believe in education. As a people we have always sought learning in every field, and as a Church we have spent great sums and made considerable sacrifice to make education opportunities available to the Church members. And particularly in this day of scientific research and development. We think our young people should get as much education and technical training as in wisdom is necessary.

But we think this pursuit of worldly learning should be tempered with a like pursuit of spiritual understanding. It is more important, a thousand times over, to have a knowledge of God and his laws, so that we can do the things which bring salvation, than it is to have all the worldly knowledge that can be obtained.[7]

Everyone should learn something new every day. You all have inquiring minds and are seeking truth in many fields. I sincerely hope your greatest search is in the realm of spiritual things, because it is there that we are able to gain salvation and make the progress that leads to eternal life in our Father's kingdom.

The most important knowledge in the world is gospel knowledge. It is a knowledge of God and his laws, of those things that men must do to work out their salvation with fear and trembling before the Lord [see Philippians 2:12; Mormon 9:27].[8]

Not all truth is of the same value or importance. Some truths are greater than others. The greatest truth, or the greatest truths, we find in the fundamentals of the gospel of Jesus Christ. First of all, that Jesus Christ is the Son of God, the Redeemer of the world, who came into this world to die that men might live. That truth we should know. It is far more important to know that Jesus Christ is our Redeemer, that he has given unto us the principles of eternal life, than it is to know all that can be obtained in secular education.[9]

So far as the philosophy and wisdom of the world are concerned, they mean nothing unless they conform to the revealed word of God. Any doctrine, whether it comes in the name of religion, science, philosophy, or whatever it may be, if it is in conflict with the revealed word of the Lord, will fail. It may appear plausible. It may be put before you in language that appeals and which you may not be able to answer. It may appear to be established by evidence that you cannot controvert, but all you need to do is to abide your time. Time will level all things. You will find that every doctrine, every principle, no matter how universally believed, if it is not in accord with the divine word of the Lord to his servants, will perish. Nor is it necessary for us to try to stretch the word of the Lord in a vain attempt to make it conform to these theories and teachings. The word of the Lord shall not pass away unfulfilled, but these false

"Ye shall know the truth, and the truth shall make you free" (John 8:32).

doctrines and theories will all fail. Truth, and only truth, will remain when all else has perished.[10]

—————— 2 ——————

The Lord has commanded us to search the scriptures.

The Lord has commanded the members of the Church in this day to seek him by prayer, by faith and study. We have been commanded to study the commandments he has given us in the Doctrine and Covenants, in the Book of Mormon and in all the scriptures, with the promise that "Whatever principle of intelligence we attain unto in this life, it will rise with us in the resurrection. And if a person gains more knowledge and intelligence in this life through his diligence and obedience than another, he will have so much the advantage in the world to come." [D&C 130:18–19.] . . . The Savior said to the Jews: "Search the scriptures; for in them ye think ye have eternal life: and they are they which testify of me." [John 5:39.] How many members of the Church *think* likewise, but fail to prepare themselves by study and by faith?[11]

It seems to me that a member of this Church would not be able to rest in peace and comfort and have a clear conscience without having knowledge by study and by faith of the standard works of the Church. These records are priceless. The world mocks at them, but through their teachings we are permitted to come nearer unto God, get a better understanding of our Heavenly Father and his Son Jesus Christ, become closer acquainted with them and to know more in regard to the wonderful plan of salvation which they have given unto us and unto the world.[12]

Ancient prophets, who saw our times, have spoken, not particularly for the benefit of the people of their day, but for the benefit of the people living in the days of which these prophecies speak.[13]

I say to you, my brethren and sisters, you cannot keep the commandments of the Lord and walk in righteousness unless you know what they are. The Lord has commanded us to search the scriptures, for the things which they contain are true and shall be fulfilled [see D&C 1:37]. . . . Search the scriptures; make yourselves familiar with that which the Lord has revealed for your salvation, the salvation of your house, and of the world.[14]

―――――――――――― 3 ――――――――――――

We have a great responsibility to hearken to the message of truth that the Lord is now revealing to His servants.

If we will hearken unto the words of the Lord and search for ourselves and obtain knowledge from the Book of Mormon, from the Bible, from the Doctrine and Covenants, from the Pearl of Great Price, and from the instruction given us from time to time by the authorities of the Church, and seek to do the will of the Lord, remembering our prayers and our covenants before him, we will not go astray.[15]

In the ninth Article of Faith we declare that "We believe all that God has revealed, all that He does now reveal, and we believe that He will yet reveal many great and important things pertaining to the Kingdom of God." This being true, it becomes necessary for us to understand all that He has revealed, and that which He is now revealing; otherwise we are not in touch with His work and cannot know His will concerning us, for we do not comprehend it.[16]

The Latter-day Saints should put their trust in their leaders, and follow the teachings of the authorities of the Church, for they speak unto them with the voice of prophecy and inspiration. The Lord has declared in the very first section in the Doctrine and Covenants, that whether he speak by his own voice or through the voice of his servants, it is the same [see D&C 1:38]. Therefore, we are under just as great responsibility and obligation to hearken unto the voice of the one who stands at the head to teach the people, or to listen unto the voice of the elders of Israel, as they carry among the people the message of truth, as we are [if] the Lord should send from his presence an angel or should come himself to declare these things unto us.[17]

We can know gospel truth by study, faith, and obedience and through the guidance of the Holy Ghost.

It would be well if we would follow the counsel the Lord has given us, which is: "And whoso treasureth up my word, shall not be deceived." [Joseph Smith—Matthew 1:37.] Treasuring up his word is far more than merely reading it. To treasure it one must not only read and study, but seek in humility and obedience to do the commandments given, and gain the inspiration which the Holy Spirit will impart.[18]

We sometimes hear the complaint, "I haven't time." But we all have time to read and study which is our solemn duty. Can we not arrange to find at least fifteen minutes in each day to devote to systematic reading and reflection? This would be but a trifling amount of time, yet it would be one hour and forty-five minutes in a week; seven and one-half hours in a month of thirty days, and ninety-one hours and a quarter in the year. . . .

. . . Very few among us read too much; most of us read too little. The Lord has said: "And as all have not faith, seek ye diligently and teach one another words of wisdom; yea, seek ye out of the best books words of wisdom, seek learning even by study and also by faith." [D&C 88:118; 109:7.][19]

We are expected to study and learn all we can by research and analysis. But there are limits to our learning abilities in the realms of reason and study. The things of God can be known only by the Spirit of God. We must gain knowledge by faith.[20]

Men may search, they may study, they may learn, of course, a great many things; they may lay up a great fund of information, but they will never be able to come to the fulness of truth . . . unless they are guided by the Spirit of truth, the Holy Ghost, and keep the commandments of God.[21]

True faith accompanied by the spirit of humility will lead men to a knowledge of the truth. There is no good reason why men everywhere may not know the truth which makes men free. There is no good reason why all men cannot discover the light of truth and know whether or not the Lord has spoken again in these latter days. Paul declared that men should "seek the Lord, if haply they might feel after him, and find him, though he is not far from every one of us." [Acts 17:27.] Even in the midst of the spiritual darkness and lack of faith, which covers the earth, the arm of the Lord is not shortened. He will hear the earnest plea of the honest seeker after truth; and none need walk without the knowledge of divine truth and where to find the Church of Jesus Christ. All a person needs is humble faith and a contrite spirit with the determination to walk in the light, and the Lord will reveal it unto him.[22]

We may all know the truth; we are not helpless. The Lord has made it possible for every man to know by the observance of [His] laws, and through the guidance of His Holy Spirit, who is sent purposely to teach us when we comply with the law, so that we may know that truth which makes us free [see John 8:32].[23]

—————————— 5 ——————————

**As we put our lives in harmony with the truth,
the Lord increases our light and understanding.**

It is a requirement that is made of us, as members of this Church, to make ourselves familiar with that which the Lord has revealed, that we may not be led astray. . . . How are we going to walk in the truth if we do not know it?[24]

"Let us search [the] scriptures, let us know what the Lord has revealed, let us put our lives in harmony with His truth."

Our sole objective where the truths of salvation are concerned should be to find out what the Lord has revealed and then to believe and act accordingly.[25]

If we will follow the spirit of light, the spirit of truth, the spirit that is set forth in the revelations of the Lord; if we will, through the spirit of prayer and humility, seek for the guidance of the Holy Ghost, the Lord will increase our light and our understanding; so that we shall have the spirit of discernment, we shall understand the truth, we shall know falsehood when we see it, and we shall not be deceived.

Who is it that is deceived in this Church? Not the man who has been faithful in the discharge of duty; not the man who has made himself acquainted with the word of the Lord; not the man who has practiced the commandments given in these revelations; but the man who is not acquainted with the truth, the man who is in spiritual darkness, the man who does not comprehend and understand the principles of the Gospel. Such a man will be deceived, and when these false spirits come among us he may not understand or be able to distinguish between light and darkness.

But if we will walk in the light of the revelations of the Lord, if we will hearken to the counsels that are given by those who stand in the councils of the Church, empowered to give the instructions, we will not go astray.[26]

Let us search [the] scriptures, let us know what the Lord has revealed, let us put our lives in harmony with His truth. Then we will not be deceived, but we will have power to resist evil and temptation. Our minds will be quickened and we will be able to comprehend truth and segregate it from error.[27]

If there is any doctrine or principle connected with the teachings of the Church that we do not understand, then let us get on our knees. Let us go before the Lord in the spirit of prayer, of humility, and ask that our minds might be enlightened that we may understand.[28]

"That which is of God is light, and he that receiveth light and continueth in God"—that is the key to the situation—"receiveth more light, and that light groweth brighter and brighter until the perfect day." [D&C 50:24.]

So we understand from this that the man who seeks God and [is] guided by the Spirit of truth, or the Comforter, and continues in God, will grow in knowledge, in light, in truth, until eventually there will come to him the perfect day of light and truth.

Now, we will not get all that in this life. It is impossible for a man to reach that goal in the few years of mortal existence. But what we learn here, that which is eternal, that which is inspired by the Spirit of truth, will continue with us beyond the grave and then we shall go on, if still continuing in God, to receive light and truth until eventually we shall come to that perfect day.[29]

The promise has been made to all those who will receive the light of truth and through their research and obedience endeavor to acquaint themselves with the Gospel, that they shall receive line upon line, precept by precept, here a little and there a little, until the fulness of truth shall be their portion; even the hidden mysteries of the kingdom shall be made known unto them; "for every one that asketh receiveth; and he that seeketh findeth; and to him that knocketh it shall be opened." [Matthew 7:8; 3 Nephi 14:8; see also Isaiah 28:10; D&C 76:1–10; 98:11–12.] All these are heirs of salvation and they shall be crowned with glory, immortality, and eternal life, as sons and daughters of God, with an exaltation in His celestial kingdom.[30]

Suggestions for Study and Teaching

Questions

- As you read about President Smith's efforts to learn the gospel (see "From the Life of Joseph Fielding Smith"), reflect on your own efforts. What blessings have come to you as you have studied the scriptures and other gospel teachings?

- What can we learn from section 1 about the balance between spiritual learning and secular learning? How can we help family members and others to give priority to spiritual knowledge as they pursue educational goals?

- How have the scriptures helped you "become closer acquainted" with Heavenly Father and Jesus Christ? (See section 2.) Think about what you can do to improve your study of the scriptures

- After reading section 3, think about the blessings you have received as you have followed the counsel of Church leaders. How can we share the teachings of living prophets with our families and others?

- What does it mean to you to treasure up the word of the Lord? (For some ideas, see section 4.) In what ways might "at least fifteen minutes in each day to devote to systematic reading and reflection" influence our lives?

- Ponder how the counsel in section 5 applies in your life. As false information becomes more aggressive and accessible, how can we "distinguish between light and darkness"? What can we do to help children and youth?

Related Scriptures

Psalm 119:105; John 7:17; 2 Timothy 3:15–17; 2 Nephi 4:15; 32:3; Helaman 3:29–30; D&C 19:23; 84:85; 88:77–80

Teaching Help

"Even when you teach many people at the same time, you can reach out to individuals. For example, you reach out to individuals when you greet each person warmly at the beginning of class. . . . You also reach out when you make participation inviting and safe" (*Teaching, No Greater Call* [1999], 35).

Notes

1. See Joseph Fielding Smith Jr. and John J. Stewart, *The Life of Joseph Fielding Smith* (1972), 57.

2. *The Life of Joseph Fielding Smith,* v.

3. In *The Life of Joseph Fielding Smith,* 195.

4. Heber J. Grant, in Richard O. Cowan, "Advice from a Prophet: Take Time Out," *Brigham Young University Studies,* spring 1976, 416.

5. "I Know That My Redeemer Liveth," *Ensign,* Dec. 1971, 27.

6. In Conference Report, Oct. 1970, 5.

7. Address at the Logan Utah Institute of Religion, Jan. 10, 1971, 1–2, Church History Library; unpublished manuscript.

8. "The Most Important Knowledge," *Ensign,* May 1971, 2.

9. In Conference Report, Apr. 1955, 51.

10. In Conference Report, Oct. 1952, 60.

11. *Answers to Gospel Questions,* comp. Joseph Fielding Smith Jr., 5 vols. (1957–66), 1:xiv; italics in original.

12. In Conference Report, Oct. 1961, 18.

13. In Conference Report, Oct. 1927, 142.

14. In Conference Report, Oct. 1920, 58–59.

15. In Conference Report, Oct. 1918, 56–57.

16. "Search the Scriptures," *Young Woman's Journal,* Nov. 1917, 592.

17. In Conference Report, Oct. 1916, 73.

18. "The Resurrection," *Improvement Era,* Dec. 1942, 780; see also *Doctrines of Salvation,* ed. Bruce R. McConkie, 3 vols. (1954–56), 1:305.

19. "How and What to Read," *Improvement Era,* Aug. 1913, 1004–5; see also *Doctrines of Salvation,* 3:207.

20. "Pres. Smith Stresses Value of Education," *Church News,* June 12, 1971, 3.

21. "And the Truth Shall Make You Free," *Deseret News,* Mar. 30, 1940, Church section, 4; see also *Doctrines of Salvation,* 1:299.

22. *The Restoration of All Things* (1945), 195.

23. "Evidences of Eternal Life," *Deseret News,* June 3, 1933, Church section, 5; see also *Doctrines of Salvation,* 1:295–96.

24. In Conference Report, Oct. 1934, 65; see also *Doctrines of Salvation,* 1:302.

25. "Out of the Darkness," *Ensign,* June 1971, 2.

26. In Conference Report, Apr. 1931, 71; see also *Doctrines of Salvation,* 1:285–86.

27. "The New and Everlasting Covenant," *Deseret News,* May 6, 1939, Church section, 8; see also *Doctrines of Salvation,* 1:301.

28. In Conference Report, Oct. 1959, 20.

29. "And the Truth Shall Make You Free," 4; punctuation and capitalization standardized.

30. "Search the Scriptures," 591–92; see also *Doctrines of Salvation,* 1:303.

Honoring the Priesthood Keys Restored through Joseph Smith

*"May I now say—very plainly and very emphatically—
that we have the holy priesthood and that the keys of
the kingdom of God are here. They are found only
in The Church of Jesus Christ of Latter-day Saints."*

From the Life of Joseph Fielding Smith

President Joseph Fielding Smith declared: "I have a perfect knowledge of the divine mission of the Prophet Joseph Smith. There is no doubt in my mind that the Lord raised him up and gave him revelation, commandment, opened the heavens to him, and called upon him to stand at the head of this glorious dispensation."[1] President Smith coupled this "perfect knowledge" with a respectful reverence for the priesthood keys restored through the Prophet Joseph. He always honored and supported those who held the keys, and he counseled all Church members to have that same respect. He said, "Every man who is properly chosen to preside in any capacity in the Church should be honored in his calling."[2]

At one point in Joseph Fielding Smith's service as an Apostle, the First Presidency and Quorum of the Twelve Apostles were engaged in an ongoing discussion about a difficult question. Elder Smith had expressed a strong opinion about the issue. One day President Heber J. Grant, who was then the President of the Church, came to Elder Smith's office. President Grant explained that after prayerfully considering the issue, he had felt impressed to recommend an action that differed from Elder Smith's views. Immediately Elder Smith voiced his support for President Grant's decision. He later declared, "So far as I am concerned, when the President of the Church says

When Peter, James, and John conferred the Melchizedek Priesthood on Joseph Smith and Oliver Cowdery, they also bestowed priesthood keys.

the Lord has manifested to him or inspired him to do anything, I would support him fully in that action."[3]

Joseph Fielding Smith gave such support to all his priesthood leaders, not just the President of the Church. For example, Nathan Eldon Tanner was called to serve as a member of the Quorum of the Twelve in October 1962. One year later, he was called as a Counselor in the First Presidency, thus placing him in a presiding position over President Smith, who was the President of the Quorum of the Twelve. President Tanner later expressed his gratitude for President Smith's support: "When I was called to the First Presidency, though he was the senior member of the Twelve and had been in office for over fifty years, he showed great respect for me in that position and gave me full support and confidence."[4]

President Smith also honored the priesthood leaders in his ward. When he was serving as a member of the Quorum of the Twelve Apostles, he said: "I have no right . . . to baptize one of my own children without first going to the bishop in the ward where I live and getting his consent, because he holds the keys for that ward to which I belong as a member. I have never baptized any of my children . . . except I have gone to the bishop and got his sanction to perform that ordinance and to confirm them members of the Church."[5]

Teachings of Joseph Fielding Smith

_____ ⟨⟨⟩⟩ **1** ⟨⟨⟩⟩ _____

Priesthood keys are the power and authority to direct the Lord's work on the earth.

There is a difference between receiving an office in the priesthood and in receiving the keys of the priesthood. This we should clearly understand. . . .

. . . While all men hold the priesthood who are ordained to any office, yet there are special, or directing, authorities, bestowed upon those who are called to preside. These authorities are called keys.[6]

[Priesthood] keys are the right of presidency; they are the power and authority to govern and direct all of the Lord's affairs on earth. Those who hold them have power to govern and control the manner in which all others may serve in the priesthood.[7]

When men are commissioned by the one who holds these keys, then their acts are valid. That which they do is sealed and ratified in the Church both on earth and in the heavens.[8]

--------- 2 ---------

The Lord has sent holy messengers from His presence to restore the keys of the priesthood.

We believe that following a long night of darkness, unbelief, and departure from the truths of pure and perfect Christianity, the Lord in his infinite wisdom has again restored to earth the fullness of the everlasting gospel.

We know Joseph Smith is a prophet; that the Father and the Son appeared to him in the spring of 1820 to usher in this final gospel dispensation; that he translated the Book of Mormon by the gift and power of God; that he received keys and authority from angels sent for this very purpose; and that the Lord revealed to him the doctrines of salvation.[9]

The Lord does not recognize any ordinance or ceremony, even though it be made or performed in his name, unless it is in accordance with his will and done by one who is recognized as his authorized servant. It was for that reason that he sent from his presence holy messengers to Joseph Smith and others, to restore that which had been taken from the earth, even the fullness of the gospel, and the fullness and the keys of priesthood.[10]

The keys of priesthood had to be restored. It was not sufficient that John the Baptist came with the keys of the Aaronic Priesthood, and Peter, James, and John with the keys of the Melchizedek Priesthood, by virtue of which the Church was organized, but there had to be an opening of the heavens and a restoration of keys held by all the prophets who have headed dispensations from the days of Adam down to the days of Peter, James, and John. These prophets came in their turn and each bestowed the authority which he held.[11]

All the keys of all dispensations had to be brought in order to fulfil the words of the prophets and the purposes of the Lord in bringing to pass a complete restoration of all things. Therefore the father of the human family, the first man on the earth, Adam, had to come, and he came with his power. Moses came, and others. All who had keys came and bestowed their authorities. . . . We have not the dates when some of these authorities were made manifest, but the Prophet Joseph Smith in writing to the Saints in Nauvoo in regard to the salvation of the dead declared, as we have it recorded in section 128 of the Doctrine and Covenants [verses 17–21], that all these prophets came with their keys in the dispensation in which we live.[12]

After the organization of the Church the Lord commanded His Saints that they build a house unto His name. The Saints hardly realized the importance of it, and they did not go to work at once to build that house, so the Lord rebuked them [see D&C 95:1–4]. After the rebuke they went to with their might and in their poverty built the Kirtland Temple. What was it built for? As a holy sanctuary where Jesus Christ could come, where He could send His servants, the prophets, with their keys of authority. . . . We know that three of the great prophets of old who held important keys did come upon the 3rd day of April in the year 1836.

First came Moses [see D&C 110:11]. He gave unto Joseph Smith and Oliver Cowdery the keys of the gathering of Israel. . . . He gathered Israel, and while he was not privileged to place them in possession of the land, nevertheless the keys were in his hands for the gathering. He came to Peter, James, and John on the mount at the transfiguration and there bestowed upon them the same keys for the gathering of Israel in the day in which they lived. He was sent to the Prophet Joseph Smith and Oliver Cowdery to bestow the keys for the gathering of Israel in the dispensation of the fulness of times. . . .

Elias came after Moses had conferred his keys and brought the gospel of the dispensation in which Abraham lived [see D&C 110:12]. Everything that pertains to that dispensation, the blessings that were conferred upon Abraham, the promises that were given to his posterity, all had to be restored, and Elias, who held the keys of that dispensation, came.

Then Elijah, the last of the prophets who held the keys of the sealing power in old Israel, came and bestowed that power, the power of sealing [see D&C 110:13–16]. Some members of the Church have been confused in thinking that Elijah came with

155

*In the Kirtland Temple, Elijah appeared to Joseph Smith and
Oliver Cowdery and bestowed the keys of sealing.*

the keys of baptism for the dead or of salvation for the dead. Elijah's
keys were greater than that. They were keys of sealing, and those
keys of sealing pertain to the living and embrace the dead who are
willing to repent.[13]

Elijah the prophet . . . bestowed upon them [Joseph Smith and
Oliver Cowdery] the sealing power, the power to use the priesthood
to bind on earth and seal in heaven.[14]

[The] sealing power puts the stamp of approval upon every ordinance that is done in this Church and more particularly those that are performed in the temples of the Lord.[15]

Brethren and sisters, this is a glorious dispensation. All other dispensations flow into it. All authorities, all powers, are centered in this dispensation in which we live. We are privileged to partake of these blessings through our faithfulness.[16]

May I now say—very plainly and very emphatically—that we have the holy priesthood and that the keys of the kingdom of God are here. They are found only in The Church of Jesus Christ of Latter-day Saints.[17]

3

The President of the Church holds the keys over all the Church.

A short time before his martyrdom, the Prophet [Joseph Smith] bestowed upon the Twelve Apostles—who constitute the second quorum in the Church—all the keys and all the ordinances and priesthood necessary for them to hold in order to carry on this great and glorious work of universal salvation.[18]

This priesthood and these keys . . . have been given to each man who has been set apart as a member of the Council of the Twelve. But since they are the right of presidency, they can only be exercised in full by the senior apostle of God on earth, who is the president of the Church.[19]

The President of the Church holds the keys over all the Church. . . . In him is concentrated the power of the Priesthood. He holds all the keys of every nature, pertaining to the dispensation of the Fulness of Times. All the keys of former dispensations which have been revealed, are vested in him.[20]

4

We should honor those to whom the President of the Church has delegated keys of authority.

[The President of the Church] has the right to delegate authority and to withdraw authority as he sees fit and receives inspiration so to do.[21]

Remember there is only one on the face of the earth who holds the sealing power of the priesthood, and he can delegate that power unto others, that they may act and they may seal on earth and it is valid, it is binding, so long as he sanctions it; if he withdraws it, no man can exercise that power.[22]

No man can officiate in and confer the blessings of the temple without the authority to do so being delegated to him by the President of the Church. No man can officiate in any capacity in this Church without the virtue accompanying him in that act, as it is obtained through the power and keys held by the President of the Church. . . . If by virtue of his keys he should say that certain privileges should be withdrawn from the people, then no man would have authority to officiate in conferring those particular privileges. Should anyone attempt to do so, the act would be invalid, and the one so attempting to officiate would have to answer before the bar of God, if not before the Church, and would be found in transgression. . . .

. . . When the apostles or other brethren visit the stakes of Zion and are appointed to set in order anything requiring attention there, they do it by virtue of the commission, or authority, delegated to them by the President of the Church. This same principle applies in the lesser degree in stakes and in wards.[23]

Every man who is properly chosen to preside in any capacity in the Church should be honored in his calling. When a man is ordained to the office of a bishop, he is given the keys of presidency over the ward in which he resides and should be honored in his calling by every member of the ward, no matter what office any man may hold. The same is true of the president of the stake, the president of a quorum, or whatever it may be. To illustrate what this means we are taught that no father has the right, although he may hold the Melchizedek Priesthood, to baptize one of his own children without first obtaining the sanction of his bishop. When the sanction is obtained, the father is authorized to perform that ordinance for his child. Should any father take it upon himself to perform a baptism, or to ordain his son, without first obtaining the sanction of the presiding officer in the ward or stake, as the case may be, who holds the keys of authority, he would be in transgression. This applies to an apostle as well as to the elder in a ward. Even the President of the Church would never think to act in any matter of this kind without first recognizing the bishop of his ward or the president of his stake and the authority which had been delegated to the bishop or the president of the stake.[24]

—————————————— 5 ——————————————

The united voice of those who hold the keys of the kingdom will always guide us where the Lord wants us to be.

I think there is one thing which we should have exceedingly clear in our minds. Neither the President of the Church, nor the First Presidency, nor the united voice of the First Presidency and the Twelve will ever lead the Saints astray or send forth counsel to the world that is contrary to the mind and will of the Lord.

An individual may fall by the wayside, or have views, or give counsel which falls short of what the Lord intends. But the voice of the First Presidency and the united voice of those others who hold with them the keys of the kingdom shall always guide the Saints and the world in those paths where the Lord wants them to be. . . .

I testify that if we shall look to the First Presidency and follow their counsel and direction, no power on earth can stay or change our course as a church, and as individuals we shall gain peace in this life and be inheritors of eternal glory in the world to come [see D&C 59:23].[25]

Suggestions for Study and Teaching

Questions
- In what ways can we follow President Smith's example as we sustain those who hold priesthood keys? (See "From the Life of Joseph Fielding Smith.")

- How does section 1 help you understand the difference between holding an office in the priesthood and holding priesthood keys? Why do you think this is an important distinction?

- In what ways have you been blessed because priesthood keys have been restored to the earth? (See section 2.)

- How do you think the Church is strengthened by the organization described in sections 3 and 4? How are individual Church members strengthened?

- What are your feelings as you consider President Smith's words about the unity among the First Presidency and the Quorum of the Twelve Apostles? When have you received guidance through their "united voice"? (See section 5.)

Related Scriptures

Matthew 16:13–19; Acts 3:21; D&C 21:4–6; 27:5–13; 65:2; 128:8–21; 132:7

Teaching Help

"There may . . . be times when you do not know the answer to a question. If this happens, simply say that you do not know. You may want to say that you will try to find the answer. Or you may want to invite learners to find the answer, giving them time in another lesson to report on what they have learned" (*Teaching, No Greater Call* [1999], 64).

Notes

1. In Conference Report, Apr. 1951, 58.

2. *Answers to Gospel Questions,* comp. Joseph Fielding Smith Jr., 5 vols. (1957–66), 2:40.

3. In Francis M. Gibbons, *Joseph Fielding Smith: Gospel Scholar, Prophet of God* (1992), 342.

4. N. Eldon Tanner, "A Man without Guile," *Ensign,* Aug. 1972, 33.

5. "Principles of the Gospel: The New and Everlasting Covenant," *Deseret News,* May 6, 1939, Church section, 5; see also *Doctrines of Salvation,* ed. Bruce R. McConkie, 3 vols. (1954–56), 3:136–37.

6. In Conference Report, Apr. 1967, 98.

7. "Eternal Keys and the Right to Preside," *Ensign,* July 1972, 87.

8. In Conference Report, Apr. 1967, 99.

9. "Out of the Darkness," *Ensign,* June 1971, 4.

10. "The Coming of Elijah," *Ensign,* Jan. 1972, 5.

11. "The Keys of the Priesthood Restored," *Utah Genealogical and Historical Magazine,* July 1936, 98–99.

12. "The Keys of the Priesthood Restored," 101.

13. "The Keys of the Priesthood Restored," 99–100.

14. In Conference Report, Apr. 1970, 58.

15. In Conference Report, Apr. 1948, 135; see also *Doctrines of Salvation,* 3:129.

16. "The Keys of the Priesthood Restored," 101.

17. "Eternal Keys and the Right to Preside," 87–88.

18. *Doctrines of Salvation,* 3:154.

19. "Eternal Keys and the Right to Preside," 87.

20. "Priesthood—Restoration of Keys," *Deseret News,* Sept. 16, 1933; Church section, 4; see also *Doctrines of Salvation,* 3:135.

21. "The Keys of the Priesthood Restored," 101; see also *Doctrines of Salvation,* 3:135.

22. *Elijah the Prophet and His Mission* and *Salvation Universal* (1957), 50; see also *Doctrines of Salvation,* 3:136.

23. In Conference Report, Apr. 1967, 98–99.

24. *Answers to Gospel Questions,* 2:40–41.

25. "Eternal Keys and the Right to Preside," 88.

The Oath and Covenant of the Priesthood

*"The blessings of the Lord are offered to the Saints
and to the world through the ministrations of those
who hold his holy priesthood, who represent him."*

From the Life of Joseph Fielding Smith

On April 9, 1951, after serving for 41 years as an Apostle, Joseph Fielding Smith was sustained as President of the Quorum of the Twelve. Not long after the sustaining vote, President Smith addressed the congregation. He briefly shared his feelings about his calling:

"I realize the position I have been called to fulfil is one of great importance. It makes me humble. . . .

"I thank the Lord for the gospel of Jesus Christ, for my membership in the Church, for the opportunity which has come to me to give service. I have only one desire, weak as I am, and that is to magnify to the best of my ability the calling which is mine."[1]

President Smith frequently exhorted priesthood holders to magnify their callings. Although he publicly shared his own desire to magnify his callings in the priesthood,[2] he rarely told about his efforts to do so. However, he once reflected on the priesthood service he had given with his friend George F. Richards, who had preceded him as President of the Quorum of the Twelve:

"For forty years I sat in council, attended conferences, and served in various ways with President George F. Richards. . . .

"We have traveled together from one end of the stakes of Zion to the other. In the early days, we, the brethren of the general authorities, went two by two in the visits to the stakes of Zion. Where

President Joseph Fielding Smith, speaking at the British Area Conference, August 1971. Seated, left to right: Elders Marion G. Romney, Richard L. Evans, and Howard W. Hunter.

railroads did not take us, and such places were numerous, we usually traveled in what were known as 'whitetops,' which were light spring wagons. Distant trips usually meant appointments to two stakes, frequently to three or four.

"On such trips meetings were held daily between stake conferences in the various settlements, or wards, of the stakes. Such trips were over bumpy roads, sometimes merely trails, through heavy dust in the summer and the biting cold of the winter, frequently through heavy mud or heavy snows."[3]

Elder Francis M. Gibbons, who served as a secretary to the First Presidency, shared an insight about the way President Smith magnified his callings in the priesthood: "While [he] was fully conscious of his authority, he was always meek and mild mannered in exercising it. His character was devoid of arrogance, posturing, or self-importance. He never put on airs, never flaunted the prerogatives of his office."[4]

As President of the Church, Joseph Fielding Smith spoke in five priesthood sessions of general conference, encouraging brethren to magnify their callings in the priesthood. The teachings in this chapter are taken from four of those sermons, giving special attention to an address President Smith gave on October 3, 1970. Because the sermons were delivered in priesthood meetings, the words in this chapter are directed to men. However, these words include an understanding that the power of the priesthood is a great blessing for all members of the Church. In one of the sermons, President Smith said: "I think we all know that the blessings of the priesthood are not confined to men alone. These blessings are also poured out upon our wives and daughters and upon all the faithful women of the Church. These good sisters can prepare themselves, by keeping the commandments and by serving in the Church, for the blessings of the house of the Lord. The Lord offers to his daughters every spiritual gift and blessing that can be obtained by his sons, for neither is the man without the woman, nor the woman without the man in the Lord [see 1 Corinthians 11:11]."[5]

Teachings of Joseph Fielding Smith

————— ⟨∞⟩ 1 ⟨∞⟩ —————

Men should have a clear understanding of the covenant they make when they receive offices in the priesthood.

I desire to call your attention to the oath and covenant of the Melchizedek Priesthood. I think if we have a clear understanding of the covenant we make when we receive offices in the priesthood, and of the promise the Lord gives if we magnify our callings, then we shall have a greater incentive to do all the things we must do to gain eternal life.

May I say further that everything connected with this higher priesthood is designed and intended to prepare us to gain eternal life in the kingdom of God.

In the revelation on priesthood, given to Joseph Smith in September 1832, the Lord says that the Melchizedek Priesthood is everlasting; that it administers the gospel, is found in the true church in all generations, and holds the keys of the knowledge of God. He says that it enables the Lord's people to be sanctified, to see the face of God, and to enter into the rest of the Lord, "which rest is the fulness of his glory." (See D&C 84:17–24.)

Then, speaking of both the Aaronic and Melchizedek priesthoods, the Lord says: "For whoso is faithful unto the obtaining these two priesthoods of which I have spoken, and the magnifying their calling, are sanctified by the Spirit unto the renewing of their bodies.

"They become the sons of Moses and of Aaron and the seed of Abraham, and the church and kingdom, and the elect of God.

"And also all they who receive this priesthood receive me, saith the Lord;

"For he that receiveth my servants receiveth me;

"And he that receiveth me receiveth my Father;

"And he that receiveth my Father receiveth my Father's kingdom; therefore all that my Father hath shall be given unto him.

"And this is according to the oath and covenant which belongeth to the priesthood.

"Therefore, all those who receive the priesthood, receive this oath and covenant of my Father, which he cannot break, neither can it be moved."

The penalty for breaking the covenant and altogether turning therefrom is then given, together with this commandment: ". . . beware concerning yourselves, to give diligent heed to the words of eternal life.

"For you shall live by every word that proceedeth forth from the mouth of God." (D&C 84:33–44.)[6]

Those of you who hold the Aaronic Priesthood have not yet received this oath and covenant which belongs to the Higher Priesthood, but you do have great power and authority given you from the Lord. The Aaronic Priesthood is a preparatory priesthood that schools and trains us to be worthy of these other great blessings that come later.

If you serve faithfully as a deacon, as a teacher, and as a priest, you gain the experience and acquire the abilities and capacities which enable you to receive the Melchizedek Priesthood and to magnify your calling in it.[7]

―――――――――― 2 ――――――――――

Priesthood holders promise to magnify their callings in the priesthood and live by every word that proceeds from the mouth of God.

As all of us know, a covenant is a contract and an agreement between at least two parties. In the case of gospel covenants, the parties are the Lord in heaven and men on earth. Men agree to keep the commandments and the Lord promises to reward them accordingly. The gospel itself is the new and everlasting covenant and embraces all of the agreements, promises, and rewards which the Lord offers to his people.

And so when we receive the Melchizedek Priesthood we do so by covenant. We solemnly promise to receive the priesthood, to magnify our callings in it, and to live by every word that proceedeth forth from the mouth of God. The Lord on his part promises us that if we keep the covenant, we shall receive all that the Father hath, which is life eternal. Can any of us conceive of a greater or more glorious agreement than this?

Sometimes we speak loosely of magnifying our priesthood, but what the revelations speak of is magnifying our callings in the priesthood, as elders, seventies, high priests, patriarchs, and apostles.

The priesthood held by man is the power and authority of God delegated to man on earth to act in all things for the salvation of mankind. Priesthood offices or callings are ministerial assignments to perform specially assigned service in the priesthood. And the way to magnify these callings is to do the work designed to be performed by those who hold the particular office involved.

It does not matter what office we hold as long as we are true and faithful to our obligations. One office is not greater than another, although for administrative reasons one priesthood holder may be called to preside over and direct the labors of another.

My father, President Joseph F. Smith, said: "There is no office growing out of this priesthood that is or can be greater than the priesthood itself. It is from the priesthood that the office derives its authority and power. No office gives authority to the priesthood. No office adds to the power of the priesthood. But all offices in the Church derive their power, their virtue, their authority, *from* the priesthood."

We are called upon to magnify our callings in the priesthood and to do the work which goes with the office we receive. And so the Lord says, in the revelation on priesthood: "Therefore let every man stand in his own office, and labor in his own calling; . . . that the system may be kept perfect." (D&C 84:109–10.)

This is one of the great goals toward which we are working in the priesthood program of the Church, to have elders do the work of elders, seventies the work of seventies, high priests the work of high priests, and so on, so that all priesthood holders may magnify their own callings and reap the rich blessings promised from such a course.[8]

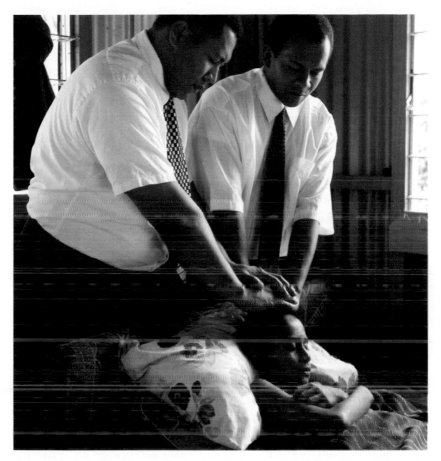

"The priesthood . . . is the power and authority of God delegated to man on earth to act in all things for the salvation of mankind."

We are ambassadors of the Lord Jesus Christ. Our commission is to represent him. We are directed to preach his gospel, to perform the ordinances of salvation, to bless mankind, to heal the sick and perhaps perform miracles, to do what he would do if he were personally present—and all this because we hold the holy priesthood.

As the Lord's agents we are bound by his law to do what he wants us to do regardless of personal feelings or worldly enticements. Of ourselves we have no message of salvation, no doctrine that must be accepted, no power to baptize or ordain or marry for eternity. All these things come from the Lord, and anything we do with reference to them is the result of delegated authority.[9]

_◦◦◦) 3 (◦◦◦_

The promise of exaltation is offered to every Melchizedek Priesthood holder who is true to the oath and covenant of the priesthood.

Now may I say a few words about the oath which accompanies the reception of the Melchizedek Priesthood.

To swear with an oath is the most solemn and binding form of speech known to the human tongue; and it was this type of language which the Father chose to have used in the great Messianic prophecy about Christ and the priesthood. Of him it says: "The Lord hath sworn, and will not repent, Thou are a priest for ever after the order of Melchizedek." (Ps. 110:4.)

In explaining this Messianic prophecy, Paul says that Jesus had "an unchangeable priesthood," and that through it came "the power of an endless life." (See Heb. 7:24, 16.) Joseph Smith said that "all those who are ordained unto this priesthood are made like unto the Son of God, abiding a priest continually," that is, if they are faithful and true [see Joseph Smith Translation, Hebrews 7:3].

And so Christ is the great prototype where priesthood is concerned, as he is with reference to baptism and all other things. And so, even as the Father swears with an oath that his Son shall inherit all things through the priesthood, so he swears with an oath that all of us who magnify our callings in that same priesthood shall receive all that the Father hath.

This is the promise of exaltation offered to every man who holds the Melchizedek Priesthood, but it is a conditional promise, a promise conditioned upon our magnifying our callings in the priesthood and living by every word that proceedeth forth from the mouth of God.

It is perfectly clear that there are no more glorious promises that have or could be made than those that came to us when we accepted the privilege and assumed the responsibility of holding the holy priesthood and of standing as ministers of Christ.

The Aaronic Priesthood is a preparatory priesthood to qualify us to make the covenant and receive the oath that attends this higher priesthood.[10]

-------------------------- 4 --------------------------

The blessings of the Lord are offered to all people through the ministrations of those who hold His holy priesthood.

There is nothing in all this world as important to each of us as putting first in our lives the things of God's kingdom, as keeping the commandments, as magnifying our callings in the priesthood, as going to the house of the Lord and being offered the fullness of the blessings of our Father's kingdom.[11]

The blessings of the Lord are offered to the Saints and to the world through the ministrations of those who hold his holy priesthood, who represent him, who are in fact his servants and agents and are willing to serve him and keep his commandments.[12]

It is my prayer that all of us who have been called to represent the Lord and hold his authority may remember who we are and act accordingly.

. . . I have sought all my days to magnify my calling in [the] priesthood and hope to endure to the end in this life and to enjoy the fellowship of the faithful saints in the life to come.[13]

My feelings are to bless those, both young and old, who are magnifying their callings in the priesthood, and to ask the Lord to pour out upon them the good things of his Spirit in this life and assure them of the riches of eternity in the life to come. . . .

What a glorious thing it is to know that the Lord has offered to each of us the fullness of the priesthood, and has promised us that if we will receive this priesthood and magnify our callings, we shall gain an everlasting inheritance with him in his kingdom![14]

Suggestions for Study and Teaching

Questions

- President Smith taught that through the priesthood, "the Lord offers to his daughters every spiritual gift and blessing that can be obtained by his sons" ("From the Life of Joseph Fielding Smith"). What are your thoughts as you ponder this statement?

- President Smith said that priesthood holders have a greater incentive to strive for eternal life when they understand their covenants and the Lord's promises (see section 1). How is this true for all members of the Church?

• How does President Smith's explanation of magnifying a calling (see section 2) differ from other uses of the word *magnify?* How have you been blessed through the service of Church members who have magnified their callings?

• President Smith taught, "Christ is the great prototype where priesthood is concerned" (section 3). What can we do to follow the example of Jesus Christ in our service to others?

• In section 4, review President Smith's words about the blessings offered in the temple. How can parents help their children prepare for the blessings of the priesthood available in the temple?

Related Scriptures

Hebrews 5:4; Alma 13:1–2, 6; D&C 20:38–60; 84:19–22; 107:99–100; Articles of Faith 1:5

Teaching Help

"A skilled teacher doesn't think, 'What shall I do in class today?' but asks, 'What will my students do in class today?'; not, 'What will I teach today?' but rather, 'How will I help my students discover what they need to know?'" (Virginia H. Pearce, "The Ordinary Classroom—A Powerful Place for Steady and Continued Growth," *Ensign,* Nov. 1992, 12; see also *Teaching, No Greater Call* [1999], 61).

Notes

1. In Conference Report, Apr. 1951, 152.

2. See Conference Report, Apr. 1951, 152; Conference Report, Oct. 1970, 92.

3. "President George F. Richards: A Tribute," *Relief Society Magazine,* Oct. 1950, 661.

4. Francis M. Gibbons, *Joseph Fielding Smith: Gospel Scholar, Prophet of God* (1992), 352.

5. In Conference Report, Apr. 1970, 59.

6. In Conference Report, Oct. 1970, 90–91.

7. In Conference Report, Apr. 1970, 59.

8. In Conference Report, Oct. 1970, 91–92; see also Joseph F. Smith, in Conference Report, Oct. 1903, 87.

9. "Our Responsibilities as Priesthood Holders," *Ensign,* June 1971, 49.

10. In Conference Report, Oct. 1970, 92.

11. In Conference Report, Apr. 1970, 59.

12. "Blessings of the Priesthood," *Ensign,* Dec. 1971, 98.

13. In Conference Report, Oct. 1970, 92.

14. In Conference Report, Apr. 1970, 58.

Baptism

"Baptism is literally . . . a transplanting, or resurrection from one life to another—the life of sin to the life of spiritual life."

From the Life of Joseph Fielding Smith

In the April 1951 general conference, President Joseph Fielding Smith spoke about his experience 67 years earlier when he was baptized at the age of 8. On the day of his baptism, he said, he felt that he "stood pure, clean, before the Lord." But he learned that he would have to put forth effort throughout his life to keep himself in that condition. He recalled: "I had a sister who was very kind, as all my sisters were, who impressed upon my mind the need of keeping myself unspotted from the world. Her teachings to me the day I was baptized have stayed with me all the days of my life."[1]

True to his sister's teachings, President Smith encouraged members of the Church to keep their baptismal covenant—to stay "within [the] spiritual life" they received when they were baptized.[2] He declared:

"There is no more important counsel that can be given to any member of the Church than to keep the commandments after baptism. The Lord offers us salvation on condition of repentance and faithfulness to his laws."[3]

Teachings of Joseph Fielding Smith

1

Baptism by immersion is in the similitude of birth, death, and resurrection.

Baptism, the third principle and first ordinance of the Gospel, is essential to salvation and exaltation in the kingdom of God. Baptism

*This painting depicts a man being baptized
in the Dnieper River near Kyiv, Ukraine.*

is, first, the means by which the repentant individual obtains remission of sins. Second, it is the gateway into the kingdom of God. The Lord, talking with Nicodemus, tells us so in John 3:1–11. . . .

. . . Baptism is by immersion in water. . . . Baptism cannot be by any other means than immersion of the entire body in water, for the following reasons:

(1) It is in the similitude of the death, burial and resurrection of Jesus Christ, and of all others who received the resurrection.

(2) Baptism is also a birth and in the similitude of the birth of a child into this world.

(3) Baptism is literally, as well as a figure of the resurrection, a transplanting, or resurrection from one life to another—the life of sin to the life of spiritual life.

I want to take up the second reason: Baptism is also a birth and in the similitude of the birth of a child into this world. . . . In Moses 6:58–60 we read:

"Therefore I give unto you a commandment, to teach these things freely unto your children, saying:

"That by reason of transgression cometh the fall, which fall bringeth death, and inasmuch as ye were born into the world by water, and blood, and the spirit, which I have made, and so became of dust a living soul, even so ye must be born again into the kingdom of heaven, of water, and of the Spirit, and be cleansed by blood, even the blood of mine Only Begotten; that ye might be sanctified from all sin, and enjoy the words of eternal life in this world, and eternal life in the world to come, even immortal glory;

"For by the water ye keep the commandment; by the Spirit ye are justified, and by the blood ye are sanctified." . . .

. . . Every child that comes into this world is carried in water, born in water, and of blood and of the spirit. So when we are born into the kingdom of God we must be born in the same way: by baptism born of the water; through the shedding of the blood of Christ cleansed and sanctified; and justified through the Spirit of God, for baptism is not complete without the baptism of the Holy

Ghost. You see the parallel between birth into the world and birth into the kingdom of God. . . .

Coming to the third reason: Baptism is literally, as well as a figure of the resurrection, a transplanting, or resurrection from one life to another—the life of sin to the life of spiritual life. . . .

. . . All men and women . . . need repentance. . . . They are in spiritual death. How are they going to get back? By being buried in the water. They are dead, and are buried in the water and come forth in the resurrection of the spirit back into spiritual life. That is what baptism is.[4]

◯◯◯ 2 ◯◯◯

Little children who have not reached the years of accountability do not need baptism because they are redeemed through the Atonement of Jesus Christ.

I know that little children who have not reached years of accountability, and hence are not guilty of sin, are . . . redeemed through the blood of Christ, and it is solemn mockery to contend that they need baptism, denying the justice and mercy of God [see Moroni 8:20–23].[5]

In the 29th Section of the Doctrine and Covenants the Lord says this (verses 46–47):

"But, behold, I say unto you, that little children are redeemed from the foundation of the world through mine Only Begotten;

"Wherefore, they cannot sin, for power is not given unto Satan to tempt little children, until they begin to become accountable before me."

Now that sounds good. "Little children are redeemed from the foundation of the world." What does He mean by that? It means that before the foundation of this earth was laid, this plan of redemption, the plan of salvation which we are supposed to follow in this mortal life, was all prepared, and God, knowing the end from the beginning, made provisions for the redemption of little children through the atonement of Jesus Christ. . . .

. . . When you look into the face of a little babe and he looks up and smiles at you, can you believe that that little child is tainted with any kind of sin that will deprive it of the presence of God should it die? . . .

I remember when I was in the mission field in England, there was an American family there. . . . When [the husband] heard the Elders preaching on the streets he invited them to his home because they were his countrymen. He was not interested in the gospel; he was interested in them because they also came from the United States. Well, I happened to be laboring there. I was not the first he heard preach, but later I was invited to his home. . . .

We thought we would go to his home and talk baseball and football and other things, and compare things in the United States with things in Great Britain—things that he was interested in. That is what we did, and at first we did not say a word about religion. We went back several times, and he thought we were pretty good fellows because we were not trying to crowd our religion down his throat. But after a while they began to ask questions—we knew they would—and one evening as we sat in their home the man's wife turned to me and said: "Elder Smith, I want to ask you a question." Before she could ask her question she began to cry. I did not know what the matter was. She sobbed, and when she had composed herself enough to ask the question she told me this story:

When they went over to England they had the misfortune of losing a little baby. . . . They went to the minister [of the church they were attending] and wanted to have that baby laid away with a Christian burial. . . . The minister said to her: "We can't give your child a Christian burial because it was not christened. Your baby is lost." That was a rather blunt way to put it, but that is the way she told the story, and that woman's heart had been aching and aching for two or three years. So she asked the question of me: "Is my baby lost? Will I never see it again?" I turned and read to her from the Book of Mormon the words of Mormon to his son Moroni [see Moroni 8]. I said: "Your baby is not lost. No baby is lost. Every baby is saved in the kingdom of God when it dies."

. . . "And I also beheld that all children who die before they arrive at the years of accountability, are saved in the Celestial Kingdom of heaven." [D&C 137:10.] That is what the Lord said to the Prophet Joseph Smith in a revelation or a vision that he had in the Kirtland

Temple. Does not that sound good? Is it not just? Is it not right? . . . [A baby] is not responsible for original sin, it is not responsible for any sin, and the mercy of God claims it and it is redeemed.

But how is it with you and me? Here we are, capable of understanding, and the Lord says: "Whoso having knowledge, have I not commanded to repent?" [D&C 29:49.] We are commanded to repent, we are commanded to be baptized, we are commanded to have our sins washed away in the waters of baptism, because we are capable of understanding and we have all sinned. But I have not been baptized and you have not been baptized for anything that Adam did. I have been baptized that I might be cleansed from that which I have done myself, and so with you, and that I might come into the kingdom of God.

. . . The Lord has made provisions for those who are without law, and little children are not subject to the law of repentance. How could you teach a little child to repent? It has not anything to repent of.

The Lord has placed—and that in His own judgment—the age of accountability at eight years. After we get to be eight years of age we are supposed to have understanding sufficient that we should be baptized. The Lord takes care of those who are under that age.[6]

3

Every person baptized into the Church has made a covenant with the Lord.

Each person, as he enters the waters of baptism, takes upon himself a covenant.

"And again, by way of commandment to the church concerning the manner of baptism—All those who humble themselves before God, and desire to be baptized, and come forth with broken hearts and contrite spirits, and witness before the church that they have truly repented of all their sins, and are willing to take upon them the name of Jesus Christ, having a determination to serve him to the end, and truly manifest by their works that they have received of the Spirit of Christ unto the remission of their sins, shall be received by baptism into his church." (D&C 20:37.)[7]

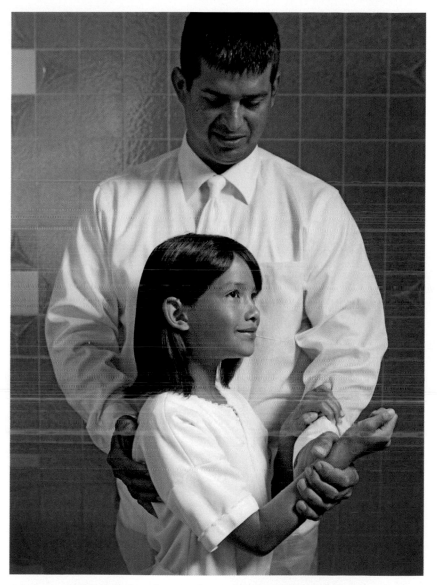

*"Every person baptized into this Church has made a
covenant with the Lord to keep His commandments."*

I am going to read from the 59th section of the Doctrine and
Covenants:

"Wherefore I give unto them [meaning the members of the
Church] a commandment, saying thus: Thou shalt love the Lord thy

God with all thy heart, with all thy might, mind, and strength; and in the name of Jesus Christ thou shalt serve Him.

"Thou shalt love thy neighbor as thyself. Thou shalt not steal; neither commit adultery, nor kill, nor do anything like unto it.

"Thou shalt thank the Lord thy God in all things." [D&C 59:5–7.]

Every person baptized into this Church has made a covenant with the Lord to keep His commandments, and in this commandment, reiterated in the dispensation in which we live, we are told that we are to serve the Lord with all the heart and all the mind, and with all the strength that we have, and that too in the name of Jesus Christ. Everything that we do should be done in the name of Jesus Christ.

In the waters of baptism we covenanted that we would keep these commandments; that we would serve the Lord; that we would keep this first and greatest of all the commandments, and love the Lord our God; that we would keep the next great commandment, we would love our neighbor as ourselves; and with all the might that we have, with all the strength, with all our hearts we would prove to Him that we would "live by every word that proceedeth forth from the mouth of God;" [D&C 84:44] that we would be obedient and humble, diligent in His service, willing to obey, to hearken to the counsels of those who preside over us and do all things with an eye single to the glory of God.

We should not forget these things, for this commandment is binding upon us as members of the Church.[8]

4

To gain the full blessings of the gospel, we must continue to be humble, repentant, and obedient after we are baptized.

One of the great purposes of the true church is to teach men what they must do after baptism to gain the full blessings of the gospel.[9]

Every soul baptized, truly baptized, has humbled himself; his heart is broken; his spirit is contrite; he has made a covenant before God that he will keep his commandments, and he has forsaken all his sins. Then after he gets into the Church, is it his privilege to sin after he is in? Can he let down? Can he indulge in some of the things which the Lord has said he should avoid? No. It is just as necessary that he have that contrite spirit, that broken heart, after he is baptized as it is before.[10]

I have heard some of our young men, and some not so young, talking on baptism. They say they do not know why it is, since baptism is for the remission of sins, that a man does not have to be baptized every time he commits a sin. Do you see the reason? As long as a man sins and stays within spiritual life he is alive, he can repent and be forgiven. He does not need to be baptized to be brought back to where he already is.[11]

Who, among Latter-day Saints, is seeking a place in the telestial kingdom? Who, among the Latter-day Saints, is seeking a place in the terrestrial kingdom? With those kingdoms we should want nothing to do; it is not the intention of the man who is baptized into the Church, or ought not to be, to so live that he will not find a place in the celestial kingdom of God; for baptism, itself, is the way into that kingdom. Baptism is of two-fold nature; primarily for the remission of sins, and then, entrance into the kingdom of God, not the telestial kingdom, not into the terrestrial kingdom, but entrance into the celestial kingdom, where God dwells. That is what baptism is for; that is what the gift of the Holy Ghost, by the laying on of hands, is for—to prepare us that we may, through obedience, continue on and on, keeping the commandments of the Lord, until we shall receive the fulness in the celestial kingdom.[12]

Suggestions for Study and Teaching

Questions

- As you read President Smith's memories in "From the Life of Joseph Fielding Smith," reflect on your baptism. How has your understanding of baptism grown since them? How can we help family members or friends who are preparing to be baptized?

- What insights about baptism do you gain from President Smith's teachings in section 1? How can his teachings about the symbolism of baptism increase our understanding of the baptismal covenant?

- What does the account in section 2 teach about Heavenly Father's love for His children? Think about people you know who might benefit from learning the doctrine taught in this account.

- Ponder your efforts to keep the baptismal covenant (see section 3). How does this covenant influence your interactions with family members and others?

- Consider President Smith's statement at the beginning of section 4. What do you think people need to be taught after they have been baptized? How can we help each other keep the baptismal covenant?

Related Scriptures

Matthew 3:13–17; 2 Nephi 31:5–13; Mosiah 18:8–13; 3 Nephi 11:31–39; D&C 68:25–27; Articles of Faith 1:4

Teaching Help

"You can help those you teach feel more confident about their ability to participate in a discussion if you respond positively to every sincere comment. For example, you might say, 'Thank you for your answer. That was very thoughtful' . . . or 'That is a good example' or 'I appreciate all that you have said today'" (*Teaching, No Greater Call* [1999], 64).

Notes

1. In Conference Report, Apr. 1951, 57–58.

2. "Repentance and Baptism," *Deseret News,* Mar. 30, 1935, Church section, 8; see also *Doctrines of Salvation,* ed. Bruce R. McConkie, 3 vols. (1954–56), 2:326.

3. In Conference Report, Oct. 1970, 7.

4. "Repentance and Baptism," 6, 8; see also *Doctrines of Salvation,* 2:323–26.

5. "Testimony of Elder Joseph F. Smith Jr.," *Liahona: The Elder's Journal,* Mar. 30, 1915, 629.

6. "Redemption of Little Children," *Deseret News,* Apr. 29, 1939, Church section, 7.

7. "Seek Ye Earnestly the Best Gifts," *Ensign,* June 1972, 2.

8. In Conference Report, Apr. 1940, 95; see also *Doctrines of Salvation,* 2:328.

9. "The Plan of Salvation," *Ensign,* Nov. 1971, 5.

10. In Conference Report, Oct. 1950, 12; see also *Doctrines of Salvation,* 2:329.

11. "Repentance and Baptism," 8; see also *Doctrines of Salvation,* 2:326.

12. In Conference Report, Apr. 1922, 60–61.

The Gift of the Holy Ghost

"We may after baptism and confirmation
become companions of the Holy Ghost who
will teach us the ways of the Lord, quicken our
minds and help us to understand the truth."

From the Life of Joseph Fielding Smith

President Joseph Fielding Smith taught that every faithful member of the Church "has a right to receive the revelations that are expedient and necessary for his [or her] guidance individually."[1] He always sought this personal guidance, especially in his efforts to teach and safeguard his sons and daughters. Elder Francis M. Gibbons, who served as a secretary to the First Presidency, related the following experience, as it was told to him by President Smith's son Reynolds (nicknamed Reyn).

"Reyn confided that he had had a cigarette in his mouth only once in his life, and then for only a fleeting moment. It occurred when he was a student at the Roosevelt Junior High School in Salt Lake City. [The school's] entrance was on a quiet side street that had very little vehicular traffic. On this day, Reyn had just walked out of the front entrance of the school with a friend who smoked who urged him, as he had often done, to 'just try one.' On this occasion, the friend succeeded. Reyn took one of the cigarettes and lit up. A few puffs later, who should pull up at the curb in his car but Reyn's father. Rolling down the window, Elder Smith said to his astounded son, 'Reynolds, I want to talk to you tonight after dinner' and drove off. Reyn reported, 'When my father called me Reynolds, I knew he meant business.' Elder Smith let Reyn stew in his guilt the rest of the afternoon and during the evening meal, when he had surprisingly little to say. Afterward, seated uncomfortably in his father's study, . . . Reynolds faced judgment. What he received

*"And when Paul had laid his hands upon them,
the Holy Ghost came on them" (Acts 19:6).*

was merely a kindly, loving lecture about the evils of 'that filthy habit' and a reminder of who he was and how his conduct reflected on the whole family. It ended with the request that Reyn promise he would never again put a cigarette in his mouth. Reyn took the pledge. 'It never happened again,' he said. Through all the intervening years, including a stint in the United States Navy during World War II where smoking was endemic, he honored the commitment made to his father."

Reflecting on this experience, Elder Gibbons observed: "The odds against Joseph Fielding Smith appearing on that out-of-the-way street at the very moment his young son lit up his one and only cigarette are astronomical. Although he did not say it, Reyn's manner and tone implied that the incident convinced him of the extraordinary depth and power of his father's spiritual sensitivity, especially as it related to the welfare of his family."[2]

Teachings of Joseph Fielding Smith

1

The mission of the Holy Ghost is to bear witness of the Father and the Son and of all truth.

The Holy Ghost is the third member of the Godhead. He is a Spirit, in the form of a man. The Father and the Son are personages of tabernacle, they have bodies of flesh and bones. The Holy Ghost is a personage of Spirit, and has a spirit body only [see D&C 130:22]. His mission is to bear witness of the Father and the Son and of all truth [see 2 Nephi 31:18; Moroni 10:5].[3]

He partakes of the things of the Father and the Son and reveals them to those who serve the Lord in faithfulness. It was through the teachings of the Comforter, or Holy Ghost, that the teachings of Jesus Christ were recalled by the apostles [see John 14:26]. It is through the teachings of the Holy Spirit that prophecy comes [see 2 Peter 1:21].[4]

The Spirit of God speaking to the spirit of man has power to impart truth with greater effect and understanding than the truth can be imparted by personal contact even with heavenly beings.

Through the Holy Ghost the truth is woven into the very fibre and sinews of the body so that it cannot be forgotten.[5]

2

The Holy Ghost manifests the truth to honest people everywhere.

We believe the Holy Ghost is a revelator and that he will bear testimony to honest people everywhere that Jesus Christ is the Son of God, that Joseph Smith is a prophet, and that this church is "the only true and living church upon the face of the whole earth." (D&C 1:30.)

There is no need for anyone to remain in darkness; the light of the everlasting gospel is here; and every sincere investigator on earth can gain a personal witness from the Holy Spirit of the truth and divine nature of the Lord's work.

Peter said: ". . . God is no respecter of persons; but in every nation he that feareth him, and worketh righteousness, is accepted" by him (Acts 10:34–35), which means that the Lord will pour out his Spirit upon the faithful so they will know of themselves of the truths of this religion.[6]

The Holy Ghost will manifest himself to any individual who asks for the truth, just as He did to Cornelius [see Acts 10]. We have this statement in the Book of Mormon by Moroni, as he was just closing his record, chapter 10, verse 4:

"And when ye shall receive these things, I would exhort you that ye would ask God, the Eternal Father, in the name of Christ, if these things are not true; and if ye shall ask with a sincere heart, with real intent, having faith in Christ, he will manifest the truth of it unto you, by the power of the Holy Ghost."

Every man can receive a manifestation of the Holy Ghost, even when he is out of the Church, if he is earnestly seeking for the light and for the truth. The Holy Ghost will come and give the man the testimony he is seeking, and then withdraw.[7]

∽3∼

Following baptism, the gift of the Holy Ghost is given by the laying on of hands.

The promise was made in the days of the primitive church of Jesus Christ that all who would repent, be baptized for the remission of sins and would be faithful, should receive the gift of the Holy Ghost by the laying on of hands. That same promise has been made to all who will accept the Gospel in this dispensation, for the Lord says:

"And whoso having faith you shall confirm in my church, by the laying on of hands, and I will bestow the gift of the Holy Ghost upon them." [D&C 33:15.][8]

You cannot get the gift of the Holy Ghost by praying for it, by paying your tithing, by keeping the Word of Wisdom—not even by being baptized in water for the remission of sins. You must complete that baptism with the baptism of the Spirit. The Prophet said on one occasion that you might as well baptize a bag of sand as not confirm a man and give him the gift of the Holy Ghost, by the laying on of hands. You cannot get it any other way.[9]

I believe in the doctrine of laying on of hands for the gift of the Holy Ghost, by which we are brought into communion with our Father in heaven and learn of His ways, that we may walk in His paths.[10]

∽4∼

Through the gift of the Holy Ghost, members of the Church can have the Holy Ghost as a constant companion.

The Holy Ghost is the Messenger, or Comforter, which the Savior promised to send to his disciples after he was crucified. This Comforter is, by his influence, to be a constant companion to every baptized person, and to administer unto the members of the Church by revelation and guidance, knowledge of the truth that they may walk in its light. It is the Holy Ghost who enlightens the mind of the truly baptized member. It is through him that individual revelation comes, and the light of truth is established in our hearts.[11]

After we are baptized, we are confirmed. What is that confirmation for? To make us companions with the Holy Ghost; to give us the privilege of the guidance of the third member of the Godhead—companionship, that our minds might be enlightened, that we might be quickened by the Holy Spirit to seek for knowledge and understanding concerning all that pertains to our exaltation.[12]

We may after baptism and confirmation become companions of the Holy Ghost who will teach us the ways of the Lord, quicken our minds and help us to understand the truth.[13]

We are promised that when we are baptized, if we are true and faithful, we will have the guidance of the Holy Ghost. What is the purpose of it? To teach us, to direct us, to bear witness to us of the saving principles of the gospel of Jesus Christ. Every child old enough to be baptized, and who is baptized, is entitled to the guidance of the Holy Ghost. I have heard people say that a little child eight years of age could not understand. I know better than that. I had a testimony of this truth when I was eight years old, coming through the Holy Ghost. I have had it ever since.[14]

What a glorious privilege this is to be guided constantly by the Holy Ghost and to have the mysteries of the kingdom of God made manifest.[15]

5

The companionship of the Holy Ghost is available only to those who prepare themselves to receive it.

It is my judgment that there are many members of this Church who have been baptized for the remission of their sins, and who have had hands laid upon their heads for the gift of the Holy Ghost, but who have never received that gift—that is, the manifestations of it. Why? Because they have never put themselves in order to receive these manifestations. They have never humbled themselves. They have never taken the steps that would prepare them for the companionship of the Holy Ghost. Therefore, they go through life without that knowledge; they are lacking in understanding. When those who are cunning and crafty in their deceit come to them criticizing the authorities of the Church and the doctrines of the Church, these weak members do not have understanding enough,

"It is a commandment from the Lord that members of the Church should be diligent in their activities and study of the fundamental truths of the gospel."

information enough, and enough of the guidance of the Spirit of the Lord to resist false doctrines and teachings. They listen and think that perhaps they have made a mistake, and the first thing you know they find their way out of the Church, because they do not have understanding.[16]

It is a commandment from the Lord that members of the Church should be diligent in their activities and study of the fundamental truths of the gospel as it has been revealed. The Spirit of the Lord will not continue to strive with the indifferent, with the wayward and the rebellious who fail to live within the light of divine truth. It is the privilege of every baptized person to have an abiding testimony of the restoration of the gospel, but this testimony will grow dim and eventually disappear unless we are constantly receiving spiritual good through study, obedience, and diligent seeking to know and understand the truth.[17]

We have the right to the guidance of the Holy Ghost, but we can't have that guidance if we willfully refuse to consider the revelations that have been given to help us to understand and to guide us in the light and truth of the everlasting gospel. We can't hope to have that guidance when we refuse to consider these great revelations which mean so much to us both temporally and spiritually. Now if we find ourselves in this condition of unbelief or unwillingness to seek for the light and the knowledge which the Lord has placed within our reach, then we are liable or in danger of being deceived by evil spirits, the doctrines of devils, and the teachings of men [see D&C 46:7]. And when these false influences are presented before us, we will not have the distinguishing understanding by which we can segregate them and know that they are not of the Lord. And so we may become prey unto the ungodly, to the vicious, to the cunning, to the craftiness of men.[18]

The Spirit of the Lord will not dwell in unclean tabernacles, and when a person turns from the truth through wickedness, that Spirit does not follow him and departs, and in the stead thereof comes the spirit of error, the spirit of disobedience, the spirit of wickedness, the spirit of eternal destruction.[19]

―――――――――――――――― 6 ――――――――――――――――

As we remain faithful, the Holy Ghost will give us revelations to lead and direct us throughout our lives.

The Lord has made the promise to all who will repent and remain faithful, exercising a spirit of humility and diligence, that they will be entitled to the guidance of the Spirit of God. This Spirit will lead them and direct them throughout their lives.[20]

Every member of the Church has had hands laid upon his head for the gift of the Holy Ghost. He has a right to receive the revelations that are expedient and necessary for his guidance individually; not for the Church, but for himself. He has a right through his obedience, through his humility, to receive light and truth as it shall be revealed through the Spirit of Truth, and he who will hearken to that Spirit and seek for the gift of the Spirit in humility and faith shall not be deceived.[21]

We must walk in holiness of life in the light and in the truth with proper understanding which comes through the gift and power of the Holy Ghost which is promised to all who will believe unto repentance and receive the words of eternal life. If we are in fellowship with this Spirit then we walk in the light and have fellowship with God.[22]

It is the privilege of every member of the Church to know the truth, to speak by the truth, to have the inspiration of the Holy Ghost; it is our privilege, individually, . . . to receive the light and to walk in the light; and if we continue in God, that is, keep all of His commandments, we shall receive more light until eventually there shall come to us the perfect day of knowledge. [See D&C 50:24.][23]

We come back into the presence of God our Father, at last, through the guidance of the Holy Ghost.[24]

Suggestions for Study and Teaching

Questions

- What does the account in "From the Life of Joseph Fielding Smith" teach about the Holy Ghost? When has the Spirit prompted you to help someone?

- President Smith referred to "the Spirit of God speaking to the spirit of man" (section 1). In what ways is communication to our spirits different from communication to our ears or our eyes? How is it more powerful?

- What are some differences between receiving a manifestation of the Spirit, as Cornelius did, and receiving the gift of the Holy Ghost? (See section 2.)

- President Smith taught that baptism is incomplete without the gift of the Holy Ghost (see section 3). In what ways would your life be incomplete without the gift of the Holy Ghost?

- Ponder President Smith's teachings in section 4 about what it means to have the constant companionship of the Holy Ghost. In what ways have you been blessed through this companionship?

- What can we do to prepare to receive the companionship of the Holy Ghost? (For some examples, see section 5.)

- As you review section 6, give attention to the guidance we can receive through the Holy Ghost. How can parents teach their children to recognize and receive this guidance?

Related Scriptures

John 16:13; Acts 19:1–6; 1 Corinthians 12:3; 1 Nephi 10:17–19; 2 Nephi 31:15–20; 3 Nephi 19:9; D&C 46:13; Articles of Faith 1:4

Teaching Help

"Do not be concerned if learners are silent for a few seconds after you have asked a question. Do not answer your own question; allow time for learners to think of responses. However, prolonged silence may indicate that they do not understand the question and that you need to rephrase it" (*Teaching, No Greater Call* [1999], 69).

Notes

1. In Conference Report, Apr. 1940, 96.

2. Francis M. Gibbons, *Joseph Fielding Smith: Gospel Scholar, Prophet of God* (1992), xiv–xv.

3. Personal correspondence, quoted in *Doctrines of Salvation,* ed. Bruce R. McConkie, 3 vols. (1954–56), 1:38; italics removed from original.

4. Personal correspondence, quoted in *Doctrines of Salvation,* 1:38.

5. "The Sin against the Holy Ghost," *Instructor,* Oct. 1935, 431; see also *Doctrines of Salvation,* 1:47–48.

6. "Out of the Darkness," *Ensign,* June 1971, 4.

7. "Address by Elder Joseph Fielding Smith before Seminary Teachers," *Deseret News,* Apr. 27, 1935, Church section, 7; see also *Doctrines of Salvation,* 1:42.

8. "Avoid Needless Speculations," *Improvement Era,* Dec. 1933, 866; see also *Doctrines of Salvation,* 1:38–39.

9. "Address by Elder Joseph Fielding Smith before Seminary Teachers," 7; see also *Doctrines of Salvation,* 1:41; *Teachings of Presidents of the Church: Joseph Smith* (2007), 95.

10. In Conference Report, Apr. 1915, 118.

11. *Answers to Gospel Questions,* comp. Joseph Fielding Smith Jr., 5 vols. (1957–66), 2:149–50.

12. "Seek Ye Earnestly the Best Gifts," *Ensign,* June 1972, 2.

13. Personal correspondence, quoted in *Doctrines of Salvation,* 1:42.

14. In Conference Report, Oct. 1959, 19.

15. *Answers to Gospel Questions,* 4:90.

16. "Seek Ye Earnestly the Best Gifts," 3.

17. In Conference Report, Oct. 1963, 22.

18. In Conference Report, Oct. 1952, 59–60; see also *Doctrines of Salvation,* 1:43.

19. In Conference Report, Apr. 1962, 45.

20. In Conference Report, Apr. 1931, 68.

21. In Conference Report, Apr. 1940, 96.

22. In Conference Report, Apr. 1916, 74; see also *Doctrines of Salvation,* 3:290.

23. "What a Prophet Means to Latter-day Saints," *Relief Society Magazine,* Jan. 1941, 7.

24. In Conference Report, Apr. 1955, 51.

Eternal Marriage

*"The fullness and blessings of the Priesthood
and Gospel grow out of Celestial marriage.
This is the crowning ordinance of the Gospel
and crowning ordinance of the temple."*

From the Life of Joseph Fielding Smith

Eighteen-year-old Joseph Fielding Smith had been told that a young woman named Louie Emily Shurtliff would be coming to live with the Smith family while she attended college. But he was still surprised—and pleased—when he came home from work one day and found Louie playing a hymn on his family's piano. Beginning that day, in the late summer of 1894, Joseph and Louie developed a friendship that gradually deepened until they fell in love. They were sealed in the Salt Lake Temple on April 26, 1898.[1]

Louie and Joseph enjoyed a loving relationship. When he was called to serve a two-year mission in England shortly after they were married, she worked for her father to support him financially. She also supported him emotionally and spiritually by sending him encouraging letters. After he returned, they established a happy home and welcomed two daughters into their family. But after 10 years of marriage, Louie became gravely ill during her third pregnancy and died at the age of 31.

Joseph found comfort in the assurance that Louie had departed "for a better world," and he recorded in his journal a prayer that he would "be worthy to meet her in eternal glory, to be united again with her."[2] But despite the consolation and hope he found in the gospel, he missed Louie terribly. He also worried about his daughters without a mother at home. Soon after Louie's death, Joseph met Ethel Georgina Reynolds. Although his love for Louie had not

191

*"Marriage as understood by Latter-day Saints
is a covenant ordained to be everlasting."*

diminished, he came to love Ethel, and so did his daughters. With the approval of his parents, Louie's parents, and Ethel's parents, Joseph asked Ethel to marry him. They were sealed on November 2, 1908. They had a joyful and eventful life together as they had nine more children. Their home was characterized by order, hard work, respect, cleanliness, tender discipline, love, and wholesome fun.[3]

After 29 years of marriage, Ethel died of a debilitating illness that had sapped her strength for 4 years. Once again, Joseph was lonely but comforted by the assurance of eternal marriage.[4] And once again, he met someone with whom he could share his life. He and Jessie Evans were sealed on April 12, 1938. "During their 33 years of life together she accompanied him most everywhere, near and far. He in turn helped her do the grocery shopping, dry the supper dishes, and bottle fruit in the fall. He had no qualms about being an apostle with an apron on."[5] Jessie often said of her husband: "He is the kindest man I have ever known. I have never heard him speak an unkind word." He would respond, with a smile, "I don't know any unkind words."[6]

Biographer John J. Stewart wrote of President Smith's gentleness and compassion toward Jessie: "From the pulpit he admonished husbands to be loving and devoted to their wives. But the sermon that touches me is his climbing nine blocks up Salt Lake City's steep north avenues to the Latter-day Saint Hospital on a hot July day in 1971 and spending his 95th birthday anniversary sitting at the bedside of his sick wife Jessie. As her condition worsened, he stayed right with her day and night for several weeks keeping an anxious vigil, giving her what comfort and encouragement he could to the end."[7]

Jessie died on August 3, 1971. Two months later, President Smith gave the opening address at general conference. His testimony showed that his sadness was calmed by trust in the Lord and hope for eternal life:

"I feel to say with Job of old, whose knowledge came from the same source from which mine has come: 'For I know that my redeemer liveth, and that he shall stand at the latter day upon the earth,' and that 'in my flesh shall I see God: Whom I shall see for myself, and mine eyes shall behold. . . .' (Job 19:25–27.)

"And as I join my testimony with that of Job, may I also unite with him in thanksgiving, for the cry, uttered out of the anguish and sorrow of his soul: '. . . the Lord gave, and the Lord hath taken away; blessed be the name of the Lord.' (Job 1:21.)

"I pray that we may all be guided by the power of the Holy Spirit, that we may walk uprightly before the Lord, and that we may inherit eternal life in the mansions and kingdoms that are prepared for the obedient."[8]

After President Smith's address, President Harold B. Lee, who was conducting the meeting, said: "I am sure that all members of the Church everywhere, realizing the circumstances under which he has delivered this powerful message, are greatly uplifted by the power and strength he has manifested before us here this morning. Thank you, President Smith, from the bottom of our hearts."[9]

Teachings of Joseph Fielding Smith

1

Celestial marriage is the crowning ordinance of the gospel of Jesus Christ.

There is no ordinance connected with the Gospel of Jesus Christ of greater importance, of more solemn and sacred nature, and more necessary to [our] eternal joy . . . than marriage.[10]

The fullness and blessings of the Priesthood and Gospel grow out of Celestial marriage. This is the crowning ordinance of the Gospel and crowning ordinance of the temple.[11]

I want to plead to my good brethren and sisters, good members of the Church, to go to the temple to be married for time and all eternity.[12]

2

In contrast to the practices of the world, marriage endures forever in the gospel plan.

Marriage is considered by a great many people as merely a civil contract or agreement between a man and a woman that they will live together in the marriage relation. It is, in fact, an eternal principle upon which the very existence of mankind depends. The Lord gave this law to man in the very beginning of the world as part of the Gospel law, and the first marriage was to endure forever. According to the law of the Lord every marriage should endure forever. If all mankind would live in strict obedience to the Gospel and in that love which is begotten by the Spirit of the Lord, all marriages would be eternal. . . .

. . . Marriage as understood by Latter-day Saints is a covenant ordained to be everlasting. It is the foundation for eternal exaltation, for without it there could be no eternal progress in the kingdom of God.[13]

It is very apparent to all of us who read the newspapers, who listen to the news accounts on the radio and who watch what comes over television that all too many do not hold marriage and the family unit in that respect which the Lord intends.[14]

Marriage is a sacred covenant, yet in many instances it is made the butt of coarse jokes, a jest, a passing fancy, by the vulgar and the unclean, and, too, by many who think themselves refined but who do not regard the sacredness of this great principle.[15]

The Lord has given us his everlasting gospel to be a light and a standard to us, and this gospel includes his holy order of matrimony, which is eternal in nature. We should not and must not follow the marriage practices of the world. We have greater light than the world has, and the Lord expects more of us than he does of them.

We know what the true order of marriage is. We know the place of the family unit in the plan of salvation. We know that we should be married in the temple, and that we must keep ourselves clean and pure so as to gain the approving seal of the Holy Spirit of Promise upon our marriage unions.

We are spirit children of our Eternal Father, who ordained a plan of salvation whereby we might come to earth and progress and advance and become like him; that is, he provided a gospel plan which would enable us to have eternal family units of our own and to enjoy eternal life.[16]

Marriage was never intended by the Lord to end at death of the mortal body; but to add honor, dominion, power to the covenanting

"The family relation, and the unity of the family, shall continue, where properly organized, in righteousness in the life to come."

parties, and the continued and eternal unity of the family in the kingdom of God. Such blessings are held in reserve for those who are willing to abide in this covenant as the Lord revealed it. It is not merely a partnership between a man and a woman, for as the Lord has said, in marriage they become one flesh and enter into a partnership with God.[17]

3

Faithfulness to the marriage covenant brings happiness and leads to blessings of eternal glory.

I am thankful to the Lord for the knowledge of the eternity of the marriage covenant, which gives the husband the right to claim his wife, and the wife the right to claim her husband in the world to come, providing they have gone to the House of the Lord and been united for time and all eternity by one holding this sealing power, for in no other way can this great blessing be obtained. I am also thankful for the knowledge that the family relation, and the unity of the family, shall continue, where properly organized, in righteousness in the life to come.[18]

I want to plead with those who have been to the temple and have been so married to be faithful and true to their covenants and their obligations, for in the House of the Lord they have made solemn covenants.[19]

Nothing will prepare mankind for glory in the kingdom of God as readily as faithfulness to the marriage covenant. . . .

If properly received this covenant becomes the means of the greatest happiness. The greatest honor in this life, and in the life to come, honor, dominion and power in perfect love, are the blessings which come out of it. These blessings of eternal glory are held in reserve for those who are willing to abide in this and all other covenants of the Gospel.[20]

What does marriage mean to members of the Church? It means that they are receiving in that ordinance the greatest, the crowning blessing, the blessing of eternal lives. Now that's the way the Lord puts it, "eternal lives," which means not only will the husband and the wife enter into eternal life, but their children who were born under the covenant likewise will be entitled through their faithfulness to eternal lives. And further, that the husband and the wife after the resurrection of the dead will not come to an end. By that the Lord means that they will have a continuation of the seeds forever, and the family organization does not come to an end. [See D&C 132:19–24.][21]

In order to fulfill the purposes of our Eternal Father, there must be a union, husbands and wives receiving the blessings that are promised to those who are faithful and true that will exalt them to Godhood. A man cannot receive the fulness of the blessings of the kingdom of God alone, nor can the woman, but the two together can receive all the blessings and privileges that pertain to the fulness of the Father's kingdom.[22]

4

Every soul whose heart is right will have the opportunity to receive the blessings of eternal marriage, whether in this life or the next.

In the great plan of salvation nothing has been overlooked. The gospel of Jesus Christ is the most beautiful thing in the world. It embraces every soul whose heart is right and who diligently seeks him and desires to obey his laws and covenants. Therefore, if a person is for any cause denied the privilege of complying with any of the covenants, the Lord will judge him or her by the intent of the heart. There are thousands of members of the Church [without access to temples] who have married and reared families in the Church, who were deprived of the privilege of being "sealed" for time and all eternity. Many of these have passed away, and their blessings are given them vicariously. The gospel is a vicarious work. Jesus vicariously performed a labor for us all because we could not do it for ourselves. Likewise, he has granted to the living members of the Church that they may act as proxies for the dead who died without the opportunity of acting in their own behalf.

Furthermore, there are thousands of young men as well as young women, who have passed to the world of spirits without the opportunity of these blessings. Many of them have laid down their lives in battle; many have died in their early youth; and many have died in their childhood. The Lord will not forget a single one of them. All the blessings belonging to exaltation will be given them, for this is the course of justice and mercy. So with those who live in the stakes of Zion and in the shadows of our temples; if they are deprived of blessings in this life these blessings will be given to them during the millennium.[23]

No one can be deprived of exaltation who remains faithful. . . . An undeserving husband cannot prevent a faithful wife from an exaltation and vice versa.[24]

_____ ⟨∞⟩ **5** ⟨∞⟩ _____

Children and youth prepare for eternal marriage as they learn about the marriage covenant, develop abiding faith, and keep themselves clean and pure.

May all Latter-day Saint fathers and mothers see to it that they teach their children the sacredness of the marriage covenant. Let them impress upon their children that in no other way than by honoring the covenants of God, among which the covenant of eternal marriage is one of the greatest and most mandatory, can they obtain the blessings of *eternal lives*.[25]

This life is short, and eternity is long. When we contemplate that the marriage covenant will endure forever, it is well that it should be given careful consideration. . . . The proper advice to our youth is to consider carefully with the view of choosing well a companion with an abiding faith in the Gospel. Such a person is more likely to prove true to every vow and covenant. When the young man and the young woman are thoroughly grounded in the divine mission of our Lord and believe the Gospel as revealed through Joseph Smith, the Prophet, the chances are all in favor of a happy union that will endure forever.[26]

I plead with you, the youth of Zion everywhere, to keep yourselves clean and pure so that you will be entitled to go to the house of the Lord and, together with the companions of your choice, enjoy all these great blessings the Lord offers to you.[27]

One thing . . . that I would like to call attention to—young people, when they marry, are not satisfied to begin with a little and humbly, but they want to receive just about as much as their parents have at the time they, the children, get married. . . . They want to start out with every convenience under the sun to make them comfortable. I think this is a mistake. I think they should begin humbly, putting their faith in the Lord, building here a little and there a little as they can, accumulating piecemeal, until they can reach a position of prosperity such as they wish to have.[28]

6

As a husband and wife faithfully observe all the ordinances and principles of the gospel, their joy in marriage grows sweeter.

Marriage was ordained of God. It is a righteous principle when in holiness it is received and practiced. If men and women today would enter into this covenant in the spirit of humility, love and faith, as they are commanded to do, walking righteously in the ways of eternal life, there would be no divorce, no broken homes; but a happiness, a joy, beyond expression.[29]

I want to impress upon all my good brethren and sisters who have been married in the temple that they should never forget the

*As a husband and wife faithfully observe the gospel together,
their joy and happiness in marriage "grow sweeter."*

great blessings which were bestowed upon them: That the Lord has
given unto them, through their faithfulness, the right to become his
sons and his daughters, joint heirs with Jesus Christ, possessing, as
stated here, all that the Father has [referring to Romans 8:13–19 and
Doctrine and Covenants 76:54–60].

And yet, there are members of the Church who fail to comprehend this and after they are married for time and all eternity, . . .
receiving the promise of the fulness of the Father's kingdom, they
permit things to come into their lives that bring friction and separate
them. And they forget that they have made a covenant for time and
all eternity with each other; and not only that, but they have made
a covenant with their Father in heaven.[30]

If a man and his wife were earnestly and faithfully observing all
the ordinances and principles of the gospel, there could not arise
any cause for divorce. The joy and happiness pertaining to the
marriage relationship would grow sweeter, and husband and wife
would become more and more attached to each other as the days
go by. Not only would the husband love the wife and the wife the
husband, but children born to them would live in an atmosphere of

love and harmony. The love of each for the others would not be impaired, and moreover the love of all towards our Eternal Father and his Son Jesus Christ would be more firmly rooted in their souls.[31]

Suggestions for Study and Teaching

Questions

- This chapter begins with examples of the joy and sadness that can be part of marriage and family life. How can the doctrine of eternal families sustain us through happy and sad times in our lives?

- What is it about celestial marriage that makes it "the crowning ordinance of the temple"? (See section 1.)

- President Smith contrasted the Lord's view of marriage to the world's view of marriage (see section 2.) What is significant to you about this contrast? How can we protect and fortify marriage and family in the world today?

- In section 3, President Smith lists at least five blessings that come to those who are "faithful and true" to the marriage covenant. What does it mean to you to be faithful and true to the marriage covenant?

- What are some things parents can do to "teach their children the sacredness of the marriage covenant"? (For some ideas, see section 5.)

- In section 6, President Smith explains how a marriage relationship can "grow sweeter." What examples have you seen of this principle? If you are married, think about what you can do to bring greater joy and love into your marriage.

Related Scriptures

1 Corinthians 11:11; D&C 42:22; 131:1–4; Moses 3:18–24

Teaching Help

"Questions written on the chalkboard before class will help learners begin to think about topics even before the lesson begins" (*Teaching, No Greater Call* [1999], 93).

Notes

1. See Joseph Fielding Smith Jr. and John J. Stewart, *The Life of Joseph Fielding Smith* (1972), 65–75; Francis M. Gibbons, *Joseph Fielding Smith: Gospel Scholar, Prophet of God* (1992), 51–55.

2. In *The Life of Joseph Fielding Smith,* 162.

3. See *The Life of Joseph Fielding Smith,* 214–41.

4. See *The Life of Joseph Fielding Smith,* 249.

5. *The Life of Joseph Fielding Smith,* 12–13.

6. In *The Life of Joseph Fielding Smith,* 268.

7. John J. Stewart, in *The Life of Joseph Fielding Smith,* 11; although this book was coauthored by John J. Stewart and Joseph Fielding Smith Jr., this comment is a personal observation by John J. Stewart.

8. "I Know That My Redeemer Liveth," *Ensign,* Dec. 1971, 27.

9. In Conference Report, Oct. 1971, 7.

10. "The Law of Chastity," *Improvement Era,* Sept. 1931, 643; see also *Doctrines of Salvation,* ed. Bruce R. McConkie, 3 vols. (1954–56), 2:58.

11. In "Lay Cornerstone at Provo Temple," *Deseret News,* May 22, 1971, B2.

12. In Conference Report, Oct. 1951, 120.

13. "The Perfect Marriage Covenant," *Improvement Era,* Oct. 1931, 704.

14. "President Joseph Fielding Smith Speaks to 14,000 Youth at Long Beach, California," *New Era,* July 1971, 7–8.

15. *The Restoration of All Things* (1945), 259.

16. "President Joseph Fielding Smith Speaks to 14,000 Youth at Long Beach, California," 8.

17. *The Restoration of All Things,* 259.

18. In Conference Report, Apr. 1915, 119.

19. In Conference Report, Oct. 1951, 120.

20. "The Law of Chastity," 643; see also *Doctrines of Salvation,* 2:58–59.

21. In Conference Report, Oct. 1951, 120–21.

22. "Obedience to the Truth," *Relief Society Magazine,* Jan. 1960, 6.

23. *Answers to Gospel Questions,* comp. Joseph Fielding Smith Jr., 5 vols. (1957–66), 2:37–38.

24. Personal correspondence, quoted in *Doctrines of Salvation,* 2:65.

25. In Conference Report, Oct. 1965, 30.

26. "Marriage Ordained of God," *Young Woman's Journal,* June 1920, 307–8; see also *Doctrines of Salvation,* 2:77–78.

27. "President Joseph Fielding Smith Speaks to 14,000 Youth at Long Beach, California," 10.

28. In Conference Report, Apr. 1958, 30.

29. *The Restoration of All Things,* 259.

30. In Conference Report, Apr. 1949, 135.

31. In Conference Report, Apr. 1965, 11.

Bringing Up Children in Light and Truth

"The first duty pertaining to the training of the children of the Church belongs in the home."

From the Life of Joseph Fielding Smith

President Joseph Fielding Smith described his father, President Joseph F. Smith, as "one in whom I have had more confidence than in anyone else I have known in this world."[1] He recalled that his father frequently gathered the family, "instructing his children in the principles of the gospel. They one and all rejoiced in his presence and were grateful for the words of counsel and instruction which he imparted. . . . They have never forgotten what they were taught, and the impressions have remained with them and will likely do so forever."[2] He also said: "My father was the most tender-hearted man I ever knew. . . . Among my fondest memories are the hours I have spent by his side discussing principles of the gospel and receiving instruction as only he could give it. In this way the foundation for my own knowledge was laid in truth, so that I too can say I know that my Redeemer lives, and that Joseph Smith is, was, and always will be a prophet of the living God."[3]

Joseph Fielding Smith also spoke lovingly of his mother, Julina L. Smith, and her teachings. He said: "I was trained at my mother's knee to love the Prophet Joseph Smith and to love my Redeemer. . . . I am grateful for the training that I received and I tried to follow the counsel that was given to me by my father. But I must not give him all the credit. I think a good part of it, a very great part of it, should go to my mother whose knee I used to sit by as a little child and listen to her stories about the pioneers. . . . She used to teach me and put in my hands, when I was old enough to read, things that I could understand. She taught me to pray [and] to be true and

*President Joseph Fielding Smith and his
great-granddaughter Shanna McConkie*

faithful to my covenants and obligations, to attend to my duties as a deacon and as a teacher . . . and later as a priest. . . . I had a mother who saw to it that I did read, and I loved to read."[4]

When Joseph Fielding Smith became a father, he followed his parents' example. His daughter Amelia said:

"Father was the perfect student and teacher, one who not only taught us from his great store of knowledge but encouraged us to learn on our own. . . .

"With his children he followed the counsel found in D&C 93:40: 'But I have commanded you to bring up your children in light and truth.'

"He taught us at the breakfast table as he told us stories from the scriptures, and had the ability to make each one sound new and exciting though we had heard it many times before. The suspense I felt wondering if Pharaoh's soldiers would find the gold cup in Benjamin's sack of grain is real even today. We learned about Joseph Smith finding the plates of gold, and the visit of the Father and the Son. If Father had time to walk to school with us, the stories continued. We walked past the [Salt Lake] Temple on the way to school and he told us about the Angel Moroni. We learned the temple was a very special place, that you had to be good to go there, and when you got married there it was forever. He taught us by the things he prayed for in our family prayers when we knelt by our chairs before breakfast and again at dinner time. . . .

"Today his teachings not only lift and sustain his descendants but countless numbers of faithful members of the Church as well. What a great privilege and blessing it has been to be his daughter."[5]

Teachings of Joseph Fielding Smith

—————————— ⟨⟨⟨ **1** ⟩⟩⟩ ——————————

To withstand the influence of the adversary, parents must bring up their children in light and truth.

The importance of family unity—love and consideration for one another in the family—cannot be overemphasized. Spiritual solidarity in family relationships is the sure foundation upon which the Church and society itself will flourish. This fact is well known and appreciated by the adversary, and as never before, he is using every clever device, influence, and power within his control to undermine and destroy this eternal institution. Only the gospel of Jesus Christ applied in family relationships will thwart this devilish destructiveness.[6]

There are many great and real dangers to be reckoned with, and those which concern us more than all others combined have to do with our children. The only real protection or adequate defense can be afforded by the home and its influences.[7]

Our children will have to be taught to discern between good and evil, otherwise in many respects they will not be able to understand why they are not permitted to indulge in practices that are common with their neighbors. Unless they are instructed in the doctrines of the Church, they will not, perhaps, understand why there is any harm in the Sunday concert, a Sunday theatre, picture show, ball game, or something of that kind, when their playmates, without restraint and with encouragement, indulge in these things forbidden of the Lord on his holy day. The parents are responsible for the proper teaching of their children, [and] the Lord will condemn the parents if their children grow up outside of the influence of the principles of the gospel of our Lord Jesus Christ.[8]

The Lord has commanded us, one and all, to bring our children up in light and truth. Where this spirit exists, disharmony, disobedience, and neglect of sacred duties will not, cannot, succeed.[9]

꧁ 2 ꧂

Parents are primarily responsible for the teaching of their children.

The Father has never relinquished his claim upon the children born into this world. They are still His children. He has placed them in the care of mortal parents with the admonition that they be brought up in light and truth. The primary responsibility, and fundamentally so, is upon the parents to teach their children in light and truth.[10]

The first duty pertaining to the training of the children of the Church belongs in the home. It is the responsibility of the parents to bring up their children in light and truth, and the Lord has declared that wherein they fail to do it, they will stand before the judgment seat to give answer.[11]

The Lord said in a revelation given to the Church in 1831:

"And again, inasmuch as parents have children in Zion, or in any of her stakes which are organized, that teach them not to understand the doctrine of repentance, faith in Christ the Son of the living God, and of baptism and the gift of the Holy Ghost by the laying on of the hands, when eight years old, the sin be upon the heads of the parents.

"For this shall be a law unto the inhabitants of Zion, or in any of her stakes which are organized." [D&C 68:25–26.]

. . . The Lord requires this at our hands.[12]

Parents will be responsible for the actions of their children, if they have failed to teach their children by example and by precept.

If parents have done all in their power to teach their children correctly by example and precept and the children then go astray, the parents will not be held responsible and the sin will be upon the children.[13]

3

The Church helps parents in their efforts to teach their children.

The chief responsibility to do [the] things which lead to salvation rests with each individual. All of us have been placed on earth to undergo the testing experiences of mortality. We are here to see if we will keep the commandments and overcome the world, and we must do all that we can for ourselves.

The next responsibility for our salvation rests with our families. Parents are set to be lights and guides to their children and are commanded to bring them up in light and truth, teaching them the gospel and setting proper examples. Children are expected to obey their parents, and to honor and respect them.

The Church and its agencies constitute in effect a service organization to help the family and the individual.[14]

"The Church and its agencies constitute in effect a service organization to help the family and the individual."

I appeal to you, my dear brethren and sisters, husbands and wives, fathers and mothers, to take advantage of every opportunity the Church affords to have your children trained in the various organizations provided for them by the revelations of the Lord: the Primary, the Sunday School, the Mutual Improvement organizations [Young Men and Young Women], and the quorums of the Lesser Priesthood under the direction of our bishoprics. . . .

. . . We have throughout the Church, wherever it is possible for us to have this opportunity, seminaries and institutes. . . . Brethren and sisters, send your children to these seminaries. Those who are going to college will be old enough, if they have the proper training in their youth, to attend the institutes of the Church.[15]

—————————— ⟨⟨⟨⟨⟩ **4** ⟨⟨⟨⟩ ——————————

Parents should do all they can to help their children understand and live the gospel of Jesus Christ.

Individual, personal testimony is and always will be the strength of The Church of Jesus Christ of Latter-day Saints. A testimony is best nurtured in the family setting. . . . The gaining and the keeping of testimonies should be a family project. Do not neglect anything that will help to strengthen the testimony of any member of your family.[16]

We must shelter [children] from the sins and evils of the world as much as we can so they will not be led away from paths of truth and righteousness.[17]

Help your children in every way you can to grow up with a knowledge of the gospel of Jesus Christ. Teach them to pray. Teach them to observe the Word of Wisdom, to walk faithfully and humbly before the Lord so that when they grow up to manhood and womanhood they can thank you for what you have done for them and look back over their lives with grateful hearts and with love for their parents for the manner in which those parents cared for them and trained them in the gospel of Jesus Christ.[18]

Set a righteous example

We ask parents to set an example of righteousness in their own lives and to gather their children around them and teach them the gospel, in their home evenings and at other times.[19]

Parents must try to be, or at least put forth their best efforts to be, what they wish the children to be. It is impossible for you to be an example of what you are not.[20]

You are to teach by example as well as precept. You are to kneel with your children in prayer. You are to teach them, in all humility, of the mission of our Savior, Jesus Christ. You have to show them the way, and the father who shows his son the way will not say to him: "Son, go to Sunday School, or go to Mutual, or go to the priesthood meeting," but he will say: "Come and go with me." He will teach by example.[21]

Begin teaching children when they are young

No person can begin too early to serve the Lord. . . . Young people follow the teaching of their parents. The child who is taught in righteousness from birth will most likely follow righteousness always. Good habits are easily formed and easily followed.[22]

There should be prayer and faith and love and obedience to God in the home. It is the duty of parents to teach their children these saving principles of the gospel of Jesus Christ, so that they will know why they are to be baptized and that they may be impressed in their hearts with a desire to continue to keep the commandments of God after they are baptized, that they may come back into his presence. Do you, my good brethren and sisters, want your families, your children; do you want to be sealed to your fathers and to your mothers before you, do you want to have this family unit perfect when you, if you are permitted, shall enter the celestial kingdom of God? If so, then you must begin by teaching at the cradle-side.[23]

Teach children to pray

What is a home without the spirit of prayer? It is not a Latter-day Saint home. We should pray; we ought not to let a morning pass without thanking the Lord on our knees in the family circle, thanking Him for His blessings and asking for His guidance. We should not let the night pass away, should not retire until we have assembled the members of that family again and thanked the Lord for His protection, and asked for His guidance every day of our lives.[24]

I hope that you are teaching your children in your homes to pray. I hope that you are having family prayers, morning and evening, that your children are taught by example and by precept to observe the commandments that are so precious and so sacred and mean so much to our salvation in the kingdom of God.[25]

Introduce children to the scriptures

There is not a home in any part of the world where the Bible should not be found. There is not a home in which the Book of Mormon should not be found. I am speaking of Latter-day Saint homes. There is no home where the Doctrine and Covenants and the Pearl of Great Price should not be. Don't keep them on the shelves or in the cupboard, but opened where they can easily be reached, that the members of the family might find access to them and sit down and read and study the principles of the gospel for themselves.[26]

Hold family home evening

Children who grow up in homes where they have participated in family home evenings, where love and unity abound, build solid foundations for sound citizenship and for active Church participation. There is no greater legacy that parents can leave to their children than the memory and blessings of a happy, unified, and loving home.

Well-planned family home evenings can be a source of long-lasting joy and influence. These evenings are times for group activity, for organizing, for the expressions of love, for the hearing of testimony, for learning gospel principles, for family fun and recreation, and of all things, for family unity and solidarity.

Fathers and mothers who faithfully hold family home evenings and who build family unity in every way possible, fulfill with honor the greatest of all responsibilities—that of parenthood.[27]

Fathers can provide no greater leadership in the kingdom of God than to lead their families in holding family home evenings. When such experiences are a part of home life there builds up a unity and family respect which influence each person toward increased righteousness and happiness.[28]

Parents who ignore the great help of this program [family home evening] are gambling with the future of their children.[29]

Teach virtue, chastity, and morality

You should teach your children virtue, chastity, and they should be taught from their early childhood. And they should be made aware of the pitfalls and the dangers that are so prevalent throughout the world.[30]

We have great concern for the spiritual and moral welfare of all youth everywhere. Morality, chastity, virtue, freedom from sin—these are and must be basic to our way of life, if we are to realize its full purpose.

We plead with fathers and mothers to teach personal purity by precept and example and to counsel with their children in all such things. . . .

We have confidence in the young and rising generation in the Church and plead with them not to follow the fashions and customs of the world, not to partake of a spirit of rebellion, not to forsake the paths of truth and virtue. We believe in their fundamental goodness and expect them to become pillars of righteousness and to carry on the work of the Church with increasing faith and effectiveness.[31]

Prepare children to be witnesses of the truth and to serve missions

Our young people are among the most blessed and favored of our Father's children. They are the nobility of heaven, a choice and chosen generation who have a divine destiny. Their spirits have been reserved to come forth in this day when the gospel is on earth, and when the Lord needs valiant servants to carry on his great latter-day work.[32]

We must prepare [children] to be living witnesses of the truth and divinity of this great latter-day work, and particularly in the case of our sons, see that they are worthy and qualified to go on missions to preach the gospel to our Father's other children.[33]

Help children prepare to have eternal families of their own

Are you training [your children] so that when they are married they will want to go to the house of the Lord? Are you teaching them so that they will want to receive the great endowment which the Lord has in store for them? Have you impressed upon them the fact that they can be sealed as husbands and wives and have bestowed upon them every gift and every blessing that pertains to the celestial kingdom?[34]

We must . . . so guide and lead [children] that they will choose proper companions and marry in the house of the Lord and thus become inheritors of all the great blessings of which we have been talking.[35]

Let us try humbly to keep our families intact, to keep them under the influence of the Spirit of the Lord, trained in the principles of the gospel that they may grow up in righteousness and truth. . . . [Children] are given unto us that we might train them in the ways of life, eternal life, that they might come back again into the presence of God, their Father.[36]

Suggestions for Study and Teaching

Questions
- In "From the Life of Joseph Fielding Smith," note the examples of parents showing love for their children. Think of ways you can follow these examples, regardless of your family responsibilities. How can parents organize themselves to be able to spend more time with their children?

- President Smith mentioned spiritual dangers that existed during his lifetime (see section 1). What are some additional dangers that exist today? How can parents and grandparents help children withstand these influences?

- Consider the trust Heavenly Father places in parents when He allows them to care for His children (see section 2). What guidance and help does He offer?

- In what ways is the Church "a service organization to help the family and the individual"? (See section 3.) How have Church organizations helped you and your family? What can we do to help children and youth participate fully?

- Section 4 lists several ways to help children and youth live the gospel. As you review the counsel, consider the following questions: What are some things you and your family are doing well? In what ways might you improve? What can you do to help the youth of the Church strengthen their testimonies?

Related Scriptures
   Deuteronomy 6:1–7; Psalm 132:12; Mosiah 1:4; 4:14–15; D&C 68:25–28; 93:36–40; see also "The Family: A Proclamation to the World"

Teaching Help

"Be careful not to end good discussions too soon in an attempt to present all the material you have prepared. Although it is important to cover the material, it is more important to help learners feel the influence of the Spirit, resolve their questions, increase their understanding of the gospel, and deepen their commitment to keep the commandments." However, it is also "important to end discussions at the right time. Much of the spirit of an uplifting discussion is lost when it lasts too long. . . . Manage the time. Know when the lesson should end. Give yourself enough time to summarize what has been said and to bear your testimony" (*Teaching, No Greater Call* [1999], 64, 65).

Notes

1. In Joseph Fielding Smith Jr. and John J. Stewart, *The Life of Joseph Fielding Smith* (1972), 40.

2. In *The Life of Joseph Fielding Smith*, 40.

3. In Bryant S. Hinckley, "Joseph Fielding Smith," *Improvement Era*, June 1932, 459.

4. In *The Life of Joseph Fielding Smith*, 56.

5. Amelia Smith McConkie, "Joseph Fielding Smith," *Church News*, Oct. 30, 1993, 8, 10.

6. Message from the First Presidency, in *Family Home Evenings 1970–71* (family home evening lesson manual, 1970), v.

7. "Our Children—'The Loveliest Flowers From God's Own Garden,'" *Relief Society Magazine*, Jan. 1969, 5.

8. In Conference Report, Oct. 1916, 71–72.

9. In Conference Report, Apr. 1965, 11.

10. "The Sunday School's Responsibility," *Instructor*, May 1949, 206; see also *Doctrines of Salvation*, ed. Bruce R. McConkie, 3 vols. (1954–56), 1:316.

11. *Take Heed to Yourselves!* (1966), 221.

12. In Conference Report, Apr. 1958, 29–30.

13. Personal correspondence, quoted in *Doctrines of Salvation*, 1:316; italics removed.

14. "Use the Programs of the Church," *Improvement Era*, Oct. 1970, 3.

15. In Conference Report, Apr. 1958, 29–30.

16. "The Old and the New Magazines," *Improvement Era*, Nov. 1970, 11.

17. "Mothers in Israel," *Relief Society Magazine*, Dec. 1970, 886.

18. In Conference Report, Apr. 1958, 30.

19. In Conference Report, Apr. 1970, 6.

20. "Our Children—'The Loveliest Flowers From God's Own Garden,'" 6.

21. In Conference Report, Oct. 1948, 153.

22. *Take Heed to Yourselves!* 414.

23. In Conference Report, Oct. 1948, 153.

24. "How to Teach the Gospel at Home," *Relief Society Magazine*, Dec. 1931, 685.

25. In Conference Report, Apr. 1958, 29.

26. "Keeping the Commandments of Our Eternal Father," *Relief Society Magazine*, Dec. 1966, 884.

27. Message from the First Presidency, in *Family Home Evenings 1970–71*, v.

28. Message from the First Presidency, in *Family Home Evenings* (family home evening lesson manual, 1971), 4.

29. In "Message from the First Presidency," *Ensign*, Jan. 1971, 1.

30. "Teach Virtue and Modesty," *Relief Society Magazine*, Jan. 1963, 5.

31. In Conference Report, Apr. 1970, 5–6.

32. In Conference Report, Apr. 1970, 6.

33. "Mothers in Israel," 886.

34. In Conference Report, Oct. 1948, 154.

35. "Mothers in Israel," 886.

36. In Conference Report, Apr. 1958, 30.

Sealing Power and Temple Blessings

"Elijah came to restore to the earth . . . the fulness
of the power of priesthood. This priesthood holds
the keys of binding and sealing on earth and
in heaven of all the ordinances and principles
pertaining to the salvation of man."

From the Life of Joseph Fielding Smith

In 1902 Joseph Fielding Smith traveled to the state of Massachusetts, where he was able to find information about his Smith ancestors. While he was there, he met a genealogist named Sidney Perley. Mr. Perley told him, "It is my ambition, if I can do it, to search out the records of every individual who came to Essex County before the year 1700."

President Smith later recounted: "I said to him, 'Mr. Perley, you have cut out for yourself a big work, haven't you?' He replied, 'Yes, and I am afraid I'll never finish it.' Then I said to him, 'Why are you doing this work?' He thought a moment and looked rather puzzled and then replied, 'I do not know why, but I got started, and I cannot stop.' I said, 'I can tell you why you are doing this and why you cannot stop, but if I did, you would not believe me and would laugh at me.'

"'Oh,' he said, 'I don't know. If you can tell me, I am sure I will be interested.' Then I told him of the prophecy concerning Elijah and the fulfilment of this promise to the Prophet Joseph Smith and Oliver Cowdery, April 3, 1836, in the Kirtland Temple, and how this spirit of research had taken hold of many people, and they had turned their hearts to the seeking after the dead in fulfilment of this great promise which was to come before the second coming, so that

All members of the family can participate in family history work.

the earth would not be smitten with a curse. Now the children were turning their hearts toward their fathers, and we were doing the ordinance work for the dead that they might find redemption and have the privilege of coming into the kingdom of God, although dead.

"When I got through, he laughed and said, 'It is a very pretty story, but I do not believe it.' Yet he admitted that there was something compelling him to carry on this research, and he could not stop. I have met a great many others who also started and could not stop, men and women who are not members of the Church. So we find today thousands of men and women searching out the records of the dead. They do not know why, but it is so that we can obtain these compiled records and go into our temples and do the work for our dead."[1]

President Smith taught that family history is about more than finding names, dates, and places and gathering stories. It is about providing temple ordinances that unite families for eternity, sealing faithful people of all generations as members of the family of God. "Parents must be sealed to each other, and children to parents in order to receive the blessings of the celestial kingdom," he said. "Therefore our salvation and progression depends upon the salvation of our worthy dead with whom we must be joined in family ties. This can only be accomplished in our Temples."[2] Before offering the dedicatory prayer in the Ogden Utah Temple, he said, "May I remind you that when we dedicate a house to the Lord, what we really do is dedicate ourselves to the Lord's service, with a covenant that we shall use the house in the way he intends that it shall be used."[3]

Teachings of Joseph Fielding Smith

───────────────── 1 ─────────────────

Elijah restored the power to seal,
or bind, on earth and in heaven.

Malachi, the last of the prophets of the Old Testament, closed his predictions with these words:

"Behold, I will send you Elijah the prophet, before the coming of the great and dreadful day of the Lord:

"And he shall turn the heart of the fathers to the children, and the heart of the children to their fathers, lest I come and smite the earth with a curse." (Mal. 4:5–6.)

It seems to be most fitting that the last of the old prophets should close his words with a promise to future generations, and in that promise predict a time to come when there would be a linking of the dispensations past with those of later times. . . .

We have a much clearer interpretation of the words of Malachi given by the Nephite prophet Moroni, who appeared to Joseph Smith September 21, 1823. This is the way the angel quoted them:

"Behold, I will reveal unto you the Priesthood, by the hand of Elijah the prophet, before the coming of the great and dreadful day of the Lord.

"And he shall plant in the hearts of the children the promises made to the fathers, and the hearts of the children shall turn to their fathers.

"If it were not so, the whole earth would be utterly wasted at his coming." (D&C 2:1–3.)

Moroni informed Joseph Smith that this prediction was about to be fulfilled. The fulfillment came some twelve years later, on April 3, 1836. On this day Elijah appeared to Joseph Smith and Oliver Cowdery in the Kirtland Temple and there conferred upon them . . . the power to bind, or seal, on earth and in heaven. The keys of this priesthood were held by Elijah, to whom the Lord gave power over the elements as well as over men, with the authority to seal for time and eternity on the righteous all the ordinances pertaining to the fullness of salvation.[4]

Some members of the Church have been confused in thinking that Elijah came with the keys of baptism for the dead or of salvation for the dead. Elijah's keys were greater than that. They were the keys of sealing, and those keys of sealing pertain to the living and embrace the dead who are willing to repent.[5]

Elijah came to restore to the earth, by conferring on mortal prophets duly commissioned of the Lord, the fulness of the power of Priesthood. This Priesthood holds the keys of binding and sealing on earth and in heaven of all the ordinances and principles pertaining to the salvation of man, that they may thus become valid in the celestial kingdom of God. . . .

It is by virtue of this authority that ordinances are performed in the temples for both the living and the dead. It is the power which unites for eternity husbands and wives when they enter into marriage according to the eternal plan. It is the authority by which parents obtain the claim of parenthood concerning their children through all eternity and not only for time, which makes eternal the family in the Kingdom of God.[6]

⟨⟨⟨ 2 ⟩⟩⟩

The restoration of the sealing authority saves the earth from being utterly wasted at the coming of Jesus Christ.

If Elijah had not come we are led to believe that all the work of past ages would have been of little avail, for the Lord said the whole earth, under such conditions, would be utterly wasted at his coming. Therefore his mission was of vast importance to the world. It is not the question of baptism for the dead alone, but also the sealing of parents and children to parents, so that there should be a "whole and complete and perfect union, and welding together of dispensations, and keys and powers and glories," from the beginning down to the end of time [see D&C 128:18]. If this sealing power were not on the earth, then confusion would reign and disorder would take place of order in that day when the Lord shall come, and, of course, this could not be, for all things are governed and controlled by perfect law in the kingdom of God.[7]

Why would the earth be wasted? Simply because if there is not a welding link between the fathers and the children—which is the work for the dead—then we will all stand rejected; the whole work of God will fail and be utterly wasted. Such a condition, of course, shall not be.[8]

The restoration of this [sealing] authority is the leaven that saves the earth from being utterly wasted at the coming of Jesus Christ. When we get this truth firmly and clearly fixed in our minds, it is easy to see that there would be only confusion and disaster should Christ come and the power of sealing not be here.[9]

The sealing power of the priesthood "unites for eternity husbands and wives when they enter into marriage according to the eternal plan."

———————— ⬿⬿⬿ 3 ⬿⬿⬿ ————————

To prepare for salvation in its fullest, we must receive temple ordinances through the sealing power.

The Lord [has] given unto us privileges and blessings, and the opportunity of entering into covenants, accepting ordinances that pertain to our salvation beyond what is preached in the world, beyond the principles of faith in the Lord Jesus Christ, repentance from sin and baptism for the remission of sins and the laying on of hands for the gift of the Holy Ghost; and these principles and covenants are received nowhere else but in the temple of God.[10]

Temple work is so interwoven with the plan of salvation, that one cannot exist without the other. In other words, there can be no salvation where there [are] no temple ordinances peculiarly belonging to the temple.[11]

There are thousands of Latter-day Saints who . . . are willing to go to meeting, willing to pay their tithing and attend to the regular duties of the Church, but they do not seem to feel or understand the importance of receiving the blessings in the temple of the Lord which will bring them into exaltation. It is a strange thing. People seem to be content just to slide along without taking advantage of the opportunities presented to them and without receiving these necessary covenants that will bring them back into the presence of God as sons and daughters.[12]

If you want salvation in the fullest, that is exaltation in the kingdom of God, . . . you have got to go into the temple of the Lord and receive these holy ordinances which belong to that house, which cannot be had elsewhere. No man shall receive the fulness of eternity, of exaltation alone; no woman shall receive that blessing alone; but man and wife, when they receive the sealing power in the temple of the Lord, shall pass on to exaltation, and shall continue and become like the Lord. And that is the destiny of men, that is what the Lord desires for His children.[13]

Note: To read some of President Smith's words of hope and promise for faithful people who are unable to receive all the ordinances of the temple in their lifetimes, see chapter 15 in this book.

───────── 4 ─────────

Because of the sealing power, we can perform saving ordinances for those who have died without receiving them.

Who are the fathers spoken of by Malachi, and who are the children? The fathers are our dead ancestors who died without the privilege of receiving the Gospel, but who received the promise that the time would come when that privilege would be granted them. The children are those now living who are preparing genealogical data and who are performing the vicarious ordinances in the Temples.[14]

Elijah came, having the keys of sealing, and the power has been given unto us by which we may reach out after the dead. This sealing power embraces those who are dead who are willing to repent and to receive the Gospel who died without that knowledge, just the same as it reaches out for those who repent who are living.[15]

The Lord has decreed that all of his spirit children, every soul who has lived or shall live on earth, shall have a fair and just opportunity to believe and obey the laws of his everlasting gospel. Those who accept the gospel and live in harmony with its laws, including baptism and celestial marriage, shall have eternal life.

It is obvious that only a small portion of mankind has so far heard the word of revealed truth from the voice of one of the Lord's true servants. In the wisdom and justice of the Lord, all must do so. As Peter said:

"For this cause was the gospel preached also to them that are dead, that they might be judged according to men in the flesh, but live according to God in the spirit." (1 Peter 4:6.)

Those who did not have the opportunity to hear the message of salvation in this life but who would have accepted it with all their hearts if such an opportunity had come to them—they are the ones who will accept it in the spirit world; they are the ones for whom we shall perform the ordinances in the temples; and they are the ones who shall, in this way, become heirs with us of salvation and eternal life.[16]

The turning of the hearts of fathers to children and of children to fathers, is the power of salvation for the dead, by means of the vicarious work which the children may perform for their fathers, and is in every sense reasonable and consistent. I have heard it said many times by those who oppose this work that it is impossible for one person to stand vicariously for another. Those who express themselves in this way overlook the fact that the entire work of salvation is a vicarious work, Jesus Christ standing as the propitiator, redeeming us from death, for which we were not responsible, and also redeeming us from the responsibility of our own sins, on condition of our repentance and acceptance of the gospel. He has done this on a grand infinite scale and by the same principle he has delegated authority to the members of his Church to act for the dead who are helpless to perform the saving ordinances for themselves.[17]

I think sometimes we look at this work for the salvation of the dead rather narrowly. It is a wrong conception to think of the people for whom we are doing work in the temple of the Lord as being dead. We should think of them as living; and the living proxy but represents them in receiving the blessings which they should have received and would have received in this life had they been living in a gospel dispensation. Therefore every dead person for whom work is done in the temple is considered to be living at the time the ordinance is given.[18]

This doctrine of salvation for the dead is one of the most glorious principles ever revealed to man. It is the way in which the gospel shall be offered to all men. It establishes the fact that God is no respecter of persons [see Acts 10:34]; that every soul is precious in His sight; and that all men will, in fact and in reality, be judged according to their works.

Now, I thank the Lord that He has restored His everlasting gospel to us in this day. I thank Him for the sealing power returned to earth by the Prophet Elijah. I thank Him for the eternal family unit, for the privilege we have of being sealed ourselves in his holy temples, and for then making available these sealing blessings to be given to our ancestors who died without a knowledge of the gospel.[19]

5

Family history work and temple work for the dead are labors of love.

There are many good, humble souls who have deprived themselves of the comforts, and at times the necessities, of life, in order that they might prepare the records and perform the labor for their dead that the gift of salvation might be taken unto them. These labors of love shall not go for naught, for all those who have worked in this goodly cause shall find their treasure and riches in the celestial kingdom of God. Great shall be their reward, yea, even beyond the power of mortals to understand.[20]

There is no work connected with the gospel that is of a more unselfish nature than the work in the House of the Lord, for our dead. Those who work for the dead do not expect to receive any earthly remuneration or reward. It is, above all, a work of love, which is begotten in the heart of man through faithful and constant labor in these saving ordinances. There are no financial returns, but there shall be great joy in heaven with those souls whom we have helped

223

to their salvation. It is a work that enlarges the soul of man, broadens his views regarding the welfare of his fellowman, and plants in his heart a love for all the children of our Heavenly Father. There is no work equal to that in the temple for the dead in teaching a man to love his neighbor as himself. Jesus so loved the world that he was willing to offer himself as a sacrifice for sin that the world might be saved. We also have the privilege, in a small degree, of showing our great love for Him and our fellow beings by helping them to the blessings of the gospel which now they cannot receive without our assistance.[21]

6

Through family history work and temple work, we complete the family organization from generation to generation.

The doctrine of salvation for the dead and temple work holds out to us the glorious prospect of the continuance of the family relation. Through it we learn that family ties are not to be broken, that husbands and wives will eternally have a claim upon each other and upon their children to the latest generation. However, in order to receive these privileges the sealing ordinances in the temple of our God must be obtained. All contracts, bonds, obligations and agreements made by men shall come to an end, but the obligations and agreements entered into in the house of the Lord, if faithfully kept, will last forever [see D&C 132:7]. This doctrine gives us a clearer concept of the purposes of the Lord toward his children. It shows his abundant and unlimited mercy and love to all who obey him, aye, even to those who are rebellious, for in his goodness he will grant great blessings even unto them.[22]

We are taught in the gospel of Jesus Christ that the family organization will be, so far as celestial exaltation is concerned, one that is complete, an organization linked from father and mother and children of one generation to the father and mother and children of the next generation, and thus expanding and spreading out down to the end of time.[23]

There must be a welding, a joining together of the generations from the days of Adam to the end of time. Families will be joined

As we turn our hearts to ancestors who have died, we can also turn our hearts to living family members

and linked together, parents to children, children to parents, one generation to another, until we shall be joined together in one great grand family with our father Adam at the head, where the Lord placed him. So we cannot be saved and exalted in the kingdom of God unless we have within our hearts the desire to do this work and perform it so far as it is within our power on behalf of our dead. This is a glorious doctrine, one of the grand principles of truth revealed through the Prophet Joseph Smith. We should take advantage of our opportunities and prove ourselves worthy and acceptable in the sight of the Lord, that we might receive this exaltation for ourselves, and there rejoice in the kingdom of God with our relatives and friends in this grand reunion and assemblage of the Saints of the Church of the First Born, who have kept themselves free and unspotted from the sins of the world.

The Lord bless us and grant that we may have the desire in our hearts to magnify our calling and to serve Him in faithfulness in all these things, is my prayer.[24]

Suggestions for Study and Teaching

Questions

- In "From the Life of Joseph Fielding Smith," read President Smith's counsel about "what we really do" at a temple dedication. What can we do to follow this counsel?

- How do the teachings in section 1 relate to our efforts to help our ancestors who have died? How can these teachings relate to our relationships with living family members?

- As you read section 2, look for President Smith's explanation of why the sealing power "saves the earth from being utterly wasted at the coming of Jesus Christ." What does this teach about the place of families in the plan of salvation?

- In what ways is temple work "interwoven with the plan of salvation"? (See section 3.) How can this principle influence our feelings about temple work?

- President Smith counseled that when we do temple work for the dead, we should think of the people as living (see section 4). What does this mean to you? How might this idea influence the way you serve in the temple?

- As you review section 5, look for blessings that President Smith said would come to those who do family history work. How have you found these things to be true?

- Study section 6, and imagine the experience of rejoicing with your ancestors in a "grand reunion." Think about what you can do to prepare yourself and your family for that privilege.

Related Scriptures

1 Corinthians 15:29; D&C 95:8; 97:15–16; 128:16–19

Teaching Help

"When an individual asks a question, consider inviting others to answer it instead of answering it yourself. For example, you could say, 'That's an interesting question. What do the rest of you think?'

or 'Can anyone help with this question?'" (*Teaching, No Greater Call* [1999], 64).

Notes

1. In Conference Report, Apr. 1948, 134.

2. "Salvation for the Dead," *Improvement Era,* Feb. 1917, 361; see also *Doctrines of Salvation,* ed. Bruce R. McConkie, 3 vols. (1954–56), 2:147.

3. "Ogden Temple Dedicatory Prayer," *Ensign,* Mar. 1972, 6.

4. "The Coming of Elijah," *Ensign,* Jan. 1972, 2, 5.

5. "The Keys of the Priesthood Restored," *Utah Genealogical and Historical Magazine,* July 1936, 100.

6. "A Peculiar People: The Authority Elijah Restored," *Deseret News,* Jan. 16, 1932, Church section, 8; see also *Doctrines of Salvation,* 2:117.

7. "Salvation for the Living and the Dead," *Relief Society Magazine,* Dec. 1918, 677–78; see also *Doctrines of Salvation,* 2:121.

8. *Doctrines of Salvation,* 2:122.

9. "The Coming of Elijah," 5.

10. In "Relief Society Conference Minutes," *Relief Society Magazine,* Aug. 1919, 466; see also *Doctrines of Salvation,* 2.40.

11. "One Hundred Years of Progress," *Liahona: The Elders' Journal,* Apr. 15, 1930, 520.

12. "The Duties of the Priesthood in Temple Work," *Utah Genealogical and Historical Magazine,* Jan. 1939, 4.

13. "Elijah the Prophet and His Mission— IV," *Instructor,* Mar. 1952, 67.

14. "Salvation for the Dead," *Millennial Star,* Dec. 8, 1927, 775; see also *Doctrines of Salvation,* 2:127.

15. "The Keys of the Priesthood Restored," 101.

16. *Sealing Power and Salvation,* Brigham Young University Speeches of the Year (Jan. 12, 1971), 2–3; italics removed.

17. *The Restoration of All Things* (1945), 174–75.

18. "The Keys of the Priesthood Restored," 100–101.

19. *Sealing Power and Salvation,* 3.

20. "A Greeting," *Utah Genealogical and Historical Magazine,* Jan. 1935, 5; see also *Doctrines of Salvation,* 2:180.

21. "Salvation for the Dead," *Improvement Era,* Feb. 1917, 362; see also *Doctrines of Salvation,* 2:144.

22. "Salvation for the Dead," *Improvement Era,* Feb. 1917, 362–63; see also *Doctrines of Salvation,* 2:173.

23. In Conference Report, Apr. 1942, 26; see also *Doctrines of Salvation,* 2:175.

24. In Conference Report, Oct. 1911, 122.

"If ye love me, keep my commandments" (John 14:15).

Living by Every Word That Proceeds from the Mouth of God

"The supreme act of worship is to keep the commandments, to follow in the footsteps of the Son of God, to do ever those things that please him."

From the Life of Joseph Fielding Smith

"I am seeking after my salvation," President Joseph Fielding Smith declared, "and I know that I can find it only in obedience to the laws of the Lord in keeping the commandments, in performing works of righteousness, following in the footsteps of our file leader, Jesus, the exemplar and the head of all."[1]

In addition to seeking his own salvation, President Smith worked diligently to help others do the same. Elder Francis M. Gibbons, who served as a secretary to the First Presidency, observed that President Smith "saw it as his duty to raise a warning voice when the people began to drift away from the path marked by the scriptures. And he had no intention to abandon that duty, regardless of what anyone said. That speaking out made him unpopular in some circles seems not to have had any deterring effect upon him; his purpose was not to become popular or famous in the eyes of the people. Instead, he saw his role as that of a watchman on the tower whose duty it was to sound the warning call to those below who could not see the approaching danger."[2]

President Smith once shared an experience that illustrated the change of heart that can come to a person who heeds this warning call:

"I attended a stake conference a number of years ago and spoke on the Word of Wisdom. . . . When I went to the rear of the building [at the close of the conference,] nearly everybody had left, but a man held out his hand and said:

"'Brother Smith, that is the first discourse on the Word of Wisdom that I ever liked.'

"I said: 'Haven't you heard other discourses on the Word of Wisdom?'

"He said: 'Yes, but this is the first one that I ever enjoyed.'

"I said: 'How is that?'

"He said: 'Well, you see, I am keeping the Word of Wisdom now.'"[3]

Teachings of Joseph Fielding Smith

1

God governs the universe by law, and we are subject to that law.

It should be conceded by all people that since the Almighty governs the entire universe by immutable law, man, who is the greatest of all his creations, must himself be subject to such law. The Lord has stated this truth tersely and convincingly in a revelation to the Church:

"All kingdoms have a law given;

"And there are many kingdoms; for there is no space in the which there is no kingdom; and there is no kingdom in which there is no space, either a greater or a lesser kingdom.

"And unto every kingdom is given a law; and unto every law there are certain bounds also and conditions.

"All beings who abide not in those conditions are not justified." (D&C 88:36–39.)

This truth is self-evident. Thus, it is only reasonable that we should expect the kingdom of God to be governed by law and all who desire to enter there to be subject to the law. "Behold, mine house is a house of order, saith the Lord God, and not a house of confusion." (D&C 132:8.)

The Lord has given to man a code of laws that we call the gospel of Jesus Christ. Due to lack of inspiration and spiritual guidance, men may differ in relation to these laws and their application, but there can hardly be a dispute in regard to the fact that such laws do exist, and that all who seek entrance into that kingdom are subject to them.[4]

We have every truth, every doctrine, every law and requirement, every performance and ordinance needed to save and exalt us in the highest heaven of the celestial world.[5]

------------------ 2 ------------------

Keeping the commandments is an expression of our love for the Lord.

Our responsibility in the Church is to worship the Lord in spirit and in truth, and this we are seeking to do with all our heart, might, and mind. Jesus said: "Thou shalt worship the Lord thy God, and him only shalt thou serve." (Matt. 4:10.)

We believe that worship is far more than prayer and preaching and gospel performance. The supreme act of worship is to keep the commandments, to follow in the footsteps of the Son of God, to do ever those things that please him. It is one thing to give lip service to the Lord; it is quite another to respect and honor his will by following the example he has set for us. . . . I rejoice in the privilege of following in his footsteps. I am grateful for the words of eternal life which I have received, I am very glad to say, in this world, and for the hope of eternal life which is mine in the world to come if I will remain faithful and true to the end.[6]

This is the law to members of the Church, in the words of the Savior: "He that hath my commandments, and keepeth them, he it is that loveth me. . . ." (John 14:21.) Again, the Savior said: "If ye love me, keep my commandments." (John 14:15.) . . .

The Savior never committed any sin nor carried any troubled conscience. He was not under the necessity of repenting as you and I are; but in some way that I cannot understand, he carried the weight of my transgressions and yours. . . . He came and offered himself as a sacrifice to pay the debt for each of us who is willing to repent of his sins and return to him and keep his commandments. Think of it, if you can. The Savior carried that burden in some way beyond our comprehension. I know that, because I accept his word. He tells us of the torment he went through; the torment was so great that he pled with his Father that if it were possible he might not drink the bitter cup and shrink: ". . . nevertheless not my will, but thine, be done." (Luke 22:42.) The answer he got from his Father was, "You have to drink it."

Can I help loving him? No, I cannot. Do you love him? Then keep his commandments.[7]

3

If we turn from the Lord's commandments, we cannot expect to receive His blessings.

When we turn from the commandments the Lord has given unto us for our guidance then we do not have a claim upon his blessings.[8]

What good does it do for us to petition the Lord, if we have no intention of keeping His commandments? Such praying is hollow mockery and an insult before the throne of grace. How dare we presume to expect a favorable answer if such is the case? "Seek ye the Lord while he may be found, call ye upon him while he is near: Let the wicked forsake his way, and the unrighteous man his thoughts: and let him return unto the Lord, and he will have mercy upon him; and to our God, for he will abundantly pardon." So said Isaiah (Isaiah 55:6–7). But is not the Lord always near when we petition Him? Verily no! He has said, "They were slow to hearken unto the voice of the Lord their God; therefore, the Lord their God is slow to hearken unto their prayers, to answer them in the day of their trouble. In the day of their peace they esteemed lightly my counsel; but, in the day of their trouble, of necessity they feel after me" [D&C 101:7–8]. If we draw near unto Him, He will draw near unto us, and we will not be forsaken; but if we do not draw near to Him, we have no promise that He will answer us in our rebellion.[9]

Parents can help their children "walk in the full light of the truth."

We cannot pray to the Lord and say: "Listen to our cause, bring victory to us, do what we want you to do, but don't ask us to do what you want us to do." [10]

It is necessary for us to walk in the full light of the truth, not in part of the truth only. I haven't the privilege of discarding some of the principles of the gospel and believing others, and then feel that I am entitled to the full blessings of salvation and exaltation in the kingdom of God. If we want exaltation, if we want the place which the Lord has prepared for those who are just and true, then we must be willing to walk in the full light of the gospel of Jesus Christ, and keep all the commandments. We cannot say that some of them are small and insignificant and therefore the Lord will not care if we violate them. We are commanded to live by every word that proceeds from the mouth of God [see Deuteronomy 8:3; D&C 98:11]. "Why call ye me Lord, Lord," he says, "and do not the things that I say?" [See Luke 6:46.] [11]

_____ ⟨∽∾⟩ 4 ⟨∾∽⟩ _____

When we are keeping the commandments of the Lord, we are on the road to perfection.

The Lord expects us to believe in him, to accept his everlasting gospel, and to live in harmony with his terms and conditions. It is not our province to select and obey those gospel principles which appeal to us and forget the rest. It is not our prerogative to decide that some principles no longer apply to our social and cultural circumstances.

The Lord's laws are eternal, and we have the fullness of his everlasting gospel and are obligated to believe all of his laws and truths and then to walk in conformity with them. There is nothing more important to any individual than keeping the Lord's commandments. He expects us to cleave unto every true principle, to put first in our lives the things of his kingdom, to press forward with a steadfastness in Christ, and to serve him with all our might, mind, and strength. In the language of the scriptures, let us hear the conclusion of the whole matter: "Fear God, and keep his commandments: for this is the whole duty of man." (Eccles. 12:13.)[12]

I often think, and I suppose you do, too, of that great and wonderful discourse—the greatest that was ever preached, so far as we know—which we call the Sermon on the Mount. . . . If we will only hearken to those teachings, we may come back again into the presence of God, the Father, and His Son Jesus Christ.

I often think of that which is really a summation:

"Be ye therefore perfect, even as your Father which is in heaven is perfect." [Matthew 5:48.]

. . . I believe the Lord meant just what He said, that we should be perfect, as our Father in heaven is perfect. That will not come all at once, but line upon line and precept upon precept, example upon example, and even then not as long as we live in this mortal life, for we will have to go even beyond the grave before we reach that perfection and shall be like God.

But here we lay the foundation. Here is where we are taught these simple truths of the Gospel of Jesus Christ, in this probationary state, to prepare us for that perfection. It is my duty, it is yours, to be better today than I was yesterday, and for you to be better today than you were yesterday, and better tomorrow than you were today. Why? Because we are on that road, if we are keeping the commandments of the Lord, we are on that road to perfection, and that can only come through obedience and the desire in our hearts to overcome the world. . . .

. . . If we have a failing, if we have a weakness, there is where we should concentrate, with a desire to overcome, until we master and conquer. If a man feels that it is hard for him to pay his tithing, then that is the thing he should do, until he learns to pay his tithing. If it is the Word of Wisdom, that is what he should do, until he learns to love that commandment.[13]

5

As we keep the commandments, the Lord comforts and blesses us and strengthens us to become men and women worthy of exaltation.

To please [the Lord], we must not only worship him with thanksgiving and praise, but render willing obedience to his commandments. By so doing, he is bound to bestow his blessings; for it is upon this principle (obedience to law) that all things are predicated [see D&C 130:20–21].[14]

God has given unto us [commandments] that we might grow nearer unto Him and be built up in the faith and strengthened. No commandment, at any time, has He given us, that was not for our comfort and blessing. They are not given merely to please the Lord, but to make us better men and women, and worthy of salvation and exaltation in His kingdom.[15]

If we go into the temple we raise our hands and covenant that we will serve the Lord and observe his commandments and keep ourselves unspotted from the world. If we realize what we are doing then the endowment will be a protection to us all our lives—a protection which a man who does not go to the temple does not have.

I have heard my father say that in the hour of trial, in the hour of temptation, he would think of the promises, the covenants that he made in the House of the Lord, and they were a protection to him. . . . This protection is what these ceremonies are for, in part. They

In the temple, we covenant to "serve the Lord and observe his commandments and keep ourselves unspotted from the world."

save us now and they exalt us hereafter, if we will honor them. I know that this protection is given for I, too, have realized it, as have thousands of others who have remembered their obligations.[16]

The Lord will give us gifts. He will quicken our minds. He will give us knowledge that will clear up all difficulties and put us in harmony with the commandments that he has given us; he will give us a knowledge that will be so deeply rooted in our souls that it can never be rooted out, if we will just seek for the light and the truth and the understanding that are promised to us and that we can receive if we will only be true and faithful to every covenant and obligation pertaining to the gospel of Jesus Christ.[17]

The great promise that is made to the members of this Church who are willing to abide by the law and keep the commandments of the Lord is that they shall not only receive a place in the kingdom of God, but that they shall also have the presence of the Father and the Son; and that is not all, for the Lord has promised that all that he hath shall be given unto them [see D&C 84:33–39].[18]

Through obedience to those commandments which are set forth in the Gospel of Jesus Christ, and by continuance therein, we shall receive immortality, glory, eternal life, and dwell in the presence of God the Father and his Son Jesus Christ, where we shall truly know them.[19]

If we will walk in paths of virtue and holiness, the Lord will pour out his blessings upon us to a degree we have never supposed possible. We shall be in very deed, as Peter expressed it, "a chosen generation, a royal priesthood, an holy nation, a peculiar people." (1 Pet. 2:9.) And we will be peculiar because we will not be like other people who do not live up to these standards. . . .

As servants of the Lord, our purpose is to walk in the path he has charted for us. We not only desire to do and say what will please him, but we seek so to live that our lives will be like his.

He himself set the perfect example for us in all things and said to us: "Follow thou me." Of his Nephite disciples he asked: ". . . what manner of men ought ye to be?" and then answered: "Verily I say unto you, even as I am." (3 Ne. 27:27.)

Now we are engaged in the greatest work in the world. This priesthood which we possess is the power and authority of the Lord himself; and he has promised us that if we magnify our callings and walk in the light, as he is in the light, we shall have glory and honor with him forever in his Father's kingdom.

With such a glorious hope before us, can we do less than forsake the evil ways of the world? Shall we not put first in our lives the things of God's kingdom? Shall we not seek to live by every word that proceedeth forth from his mouth?[20]

I testify that the Lord has spoken in our day; that his message is one of hope and joy and salvation; and I promise you that if you will walk in the light of heaven, be true to your trust, and keep the commandments, you shall have peace and joy in this life and eternal life in the world to come.[21]

Keep the commandments. Walk in the light. Endure to the end. Be true to every covenant and obligation, and the Lord will bless you beyond your fondest dreams.[22]

Suggestions for Study and Teaching

Questions

- Review the account at the end of "From the Life of Joseph Fielding Smith." Why do our feelings about the gospel change when we are striving to keep the commandments?

- What do you learn from the scripture passages that are quoted in section 1?

- How is our obedience to the commandments an expression of love for Jesus Christ? How is it an expression of gratitude for His atoning sacrifice? How is it an expression of worship? (See section 2.)

- Ponder the teachings in section 3. Why is it wrong to expect the Lord to bless us if we are not striving to be obedient?

- How is it helpful for you to know that you should not expect to become perfect all at once or even in this life? (See section 4.) Think about what you can do each day, with the Lord's help, to stay "on that road to perfection."

- In section 5, President Smith lists at least 10 ways the Lord will bless us as we keep the commandments. What experiences can you share in which you have received some of these blessings?

Related Scriptures

Matthew 4:4; 2 Nephi 31:19–20; Omni 1:26; D&C 11:20; 82:8–10; 93:1; 130:20–21; 138:1–4

Teaching Help

"Ask participants to share what they have learned from their personal study of the chapter. It may be helpful to contact a few participants during the week and ask them to come prepared to share what they have learned" (from page vii in this book).

Notes

1. In Conference Report, Oct. 1969, 110.

2. Francis M. Gibbons, *Joseph Fielding Smith: Gospel Scholar, Prophet of God* (1992), 313.

3. In Conference Report, Oct. 1935, 12.

4. "Justice for the Dead," *Ensign,* Mar. 1972, 2.

5. In "President Smith's Last Two Addresses," *Ensign,* Aug. 1972, 46.

6. "I Know That My Redeemer Liveth," *Ensign,* Dec. 1971, 27.

7. In Conference Report, Apr. 1967, 121–22.

8. In Conference Report, Oct. 1935, 15.

9. In Conference Report, Apr. 1943, 14.

10. In Conference Report, Oct. 1944, 144–45.

11. In Conference Report, Apr. 1927, 111–12.

12. "President Joseph Fielding Smith Speaks on the New MIA Theme, *New Era,* Sept. 1971, 40.

13. In Conference Report, Oct. 1941, 95.

14. "The Virtue of Obedience," *Relief Society Magazine,* Jan. 1968, 5.

15. In Conference Report, Apr. 1911, 86.

16. "The Pearl of Great Price," *Utah Genealogical and Historical Magazine,* July 1930, 103.

17. "Seek Ye Earnestly the Best Gifts," *Ensign,* June 1972, 3.

18. "Keep the Commandments," *Improvement Era,* Aug. 1970, 3.

19. In Conference Report, Oct. 1925, 116.

20. "Our Responsibilities as Priesthood Holders," *Ensign,* June 1971, 50.

21. In Conference Report, British Area General Conference 1971, 7.

22. "Counsel to the Saints and to the World," *Ensign,* July 1972, 27.

Even in times of war, we can live in the world but not be of the world.

In the World but Not of the World

"While we are in the world, we are not of the world. We are expected to overcome the world and to live as becometh saints."

From the Life of Joseph Fielding Smith

On December 29, 1944, President Joseph Fielding Smith's son Lewis died while serving in the United States Army. Despite the grief President Smith experienced, he was comforted by the memory of Lewis's good life. "If Lewis ever did or said a mean thing I never heard of it," President Smith wrote in his journal. "His thoughts were pure as were his actions. . . . As severe as the blow is we have the peace and happiness of knowing that he was clean and free from the vices so prevalent in the world and found in the army. He was true to his faith and is worthy of a glorious resurrection, when we shall be reunited again."[1]

About 11 years later, President Joseph Fielding Smith and his wife Jessie saw similar characteristics in other military personnel. They toured the Church's missions in east Asia and also visited Latter-day Saints from the United States who were serving in the military. President and Sister Smith were impressed with these young men, who, in spite of the temptations of the world, lived good, clean lives. In the October 1955 general conference, President Smith reported:

"You fathers and mothers who have sons serving in the forces, be proud of them. They are fine young men. Some of our servicemen are converts, who have been brought into the Church by the teachings, by precept and by example—principally by example by the members of the Church who are also serving with them in the forces.

"I met a number of young men who said, 'We came in the Church because of the lives of these young men and because they taught us the principles of the gospel.'

"They are doing a good work. There might be one or two that may be careless, but those young men with whom I had the privilege of meeting, talking to, would bear their testimony of the truth and were walking humbly.

"And as I met with the officers and chaplains . . . , universally they said, 'We like your young men. They are clean. They are dependable.'"[2]

President Smith admonished members of the Church to be—like these young servicemen—"different from the rest of the world."[3] In such sermons, he often spoke about keeping the Sabbath day holy, obeying the Word of Wisdom, respecting the names of Heavenly Father and Jesus Christ, dressing modestly, and keeping the law of chastity. He assured the Latter-day Saints that the blessings they would receive if they would forsake the evils of the world and keep the commandments would "exceed anything we can now comprehend."[4]

Teachings of Joseph Fielding Smith

1

The Lord expects us to forsake the evils of the world and live as becometh Saints.

We are living in an evil and wicked world. But while we are in the world, we are not of the world. We are expected to overcome the world and to live as becometh saints. . . . We have greater light than the world has, and the Lord expects more of us than he does of them.[5]

In the seventeenth chapter of John—I can hardly read this chapter without tears coming to my eyes— . . . our Lord, in praying to his Father in the tenderness of all his soul because he knew the hour had come for him to offer himself as a sacrifice, prayed for his disciples. In that prayer he said,

"I pray not that thou shouldest take them out of the world, but that thou shouldest keep them from the evil.

"They are not of the world, even as I am not of the world.

"Sanctify them through thy truth: thy word is truth." (John 17:15–17.)

If we are living the religion which the Lord has revealed and which we have received, we do not belong to the world. We should have no part in all its foolishness. We should not partake of its sins and its errors—errors of philosophy and errors of doctrine, errors in regard to government, or whatever those errors may be—we have no part in it.

The only part we have is the keeping of the commandments of God. That is all, being true to every covenant and every obligation that we have entered into and taken upon ourselves.[6]

Do not get the impression from what I have said that I feel that we should keep aloof from everybody outside of the Church and not associate with them. I have not said that, but I do want us to be consistent Latter-day Saints, and if the people of the world walk in darkness and sin and contrary to the will of the Lord, there is the place for us to draw the line.[7]

When we join the Church . . . , we are expected to forsake many of the ways of the world and live as becometh saints. We are no longer to dress or speak or act or even think as others too often do. Many in the world use tea, coffee, tobacco, and liquor, and are involved in the use of drugs. Many profane and are vulgar and indecent, immoral and unclean in their lives, but all these things should be foreign to us. We are the Saints of the Most High. . . .

I call upon the Church and all its members to forsake the evils of the world. We must shun unchastity and every form of immorality as we would a plague . . .

As servants of the Lord, our purpose is to walk in the path he has charted for us. We not only desire to do and say what will please him, but we seek so to live that our lives will be like his.[8]

Keeping the Sabbath day holy

I want to say a few words in regard to the observance of the Sabbath day and keeping it holy. This commandment was given in the beginning, and God commanded the Saints and all peoples of the earth that they should observe the Sabbath day and keep it holy—one day in seven. Upon that day we should rest from our labors, we should go unto the house of the Lord and offer up our sacraments upon His holy day. For this is a day appointed unto us on which we should rest from our labors and pay our devotions unto the Most High. [See D&C 59:9–10.] On this day we should offer unto Him our thanks and honor Him in prayer, in fasting, in singing, and in edifying and instructing each other.[9]

The Sabbath day has become a day of pleasure, of revelry, anything but a day of worship, . . . and I regret to say that too many—one would be too many—members of the Church of Jesus Christ of Latter-day Saints have joined that procession, and the Sabbath day to some members of the Church is looked upon as a day of revelry, of pleasure, rather than one in which we can serve the Lord our God with all our hearts, with all our mights, mind, and strength. . . .

Now, this is the law to the Church today just as it was the law to ancient Israel, and some of our people get rather disturbed because they feel that observing the Sabbath day curtails their activities.[10]

We have no business violating the Sabbath day. . . . I regret very much that, even in communities of Latter-day Saints, this doctrine is not looked upon as it ought to be by some; that we have those among us who seem to feel that it is perfectly right to follow the custom of the world in this regard. They are partakers of the ideas and notions of the world in violation of the commandments of the Lord. But if we do this the Lord will hold us accountable, and we cannot violate his word and receive the blessings of the faithful.[11]

Obeying the Word of Wisdom

The Word of Wisdom is a basic law. It points the way and gives us ample instruction in regard to both food and drink, good for the body and also detrimental. If we sincerely follow what is written with the aid of the Spirit of the Lord, we need no further counsel. This wonderful instruction contains the following promise:

"And all saints who remember to keep and do these sayings, walking in obedience to the commandments, shall receive health in their navel and marrow to their bones;

*The Lord revealed the Word of Wisdom to the Prophet Joseph Smith
to help the Saints receive physical and spiritual strength.*

"And shall find wisdom and great treasures of knowledge, even hidden treasures;

"And shall run and not be weary, and shall walk and not faint." [D&C 89:18–20.][12]

Billions of dollars are spent annually for intoxicating liquors and tobacco. Drunkenness and the filthiness which these evils bring to the human family are undermining, not only the health, but the moral and spiritual bulwarks of humanity.[13]

Families are torn apart by increasing use of illegal drugs and the abuse of legal drugs.[14]

We must not listen to [the] enticings and to the wicked advertising of things that are detrimental to the body and condemned by our Father in heaven and his Son Jesus Christ, contrary to the gospel they have given to us. . . .

Our bodies must be clean. Our thinking must be clean. We must have in our hearts the desire to serve the Lord and keep his commandments; to remember our prayers, and in humility seek the counsels that come through the guidance of the Spirit of the Lord.[15]

Respecting the name of Deity

We should hold the name of Deity in the most sacred and solemn respect. Nothing is so distressing or shocks the feelings of a refined person more than to hear some uncouth, ignorant, or filthy creature bandy around the name of Deity. Some individuals have become so profane that it appears almost impossible for them to speak two or three sentences without the emphasis—as they think—of a vulgar or blasphemous oath. There are some individuals also who seem to think . . . that it is a manly accomplishment and elevates them from the common run of mankind, if they can use blasphemous language. . . . Filthiness in any form is degrading and soul-destroying, and should be avoided as a deadly poison by all members of the Church.

Good stories have been frequently ruined simply because the authors have not understood the propriety of the use of sacred names. When blasphemous expressions are placed in the mouths of otherwise respectable characters, instead of enhancing the story they detract from its value and interest. . . . How strange it is that some people, and good people at that, think that to use some expression involving the name of the Lord, adds interest, wit, or power, to their stories! . . .

Above all other peoples on the earth, the Latter-day Saints should hold in the utmost sacredness and reverence all things that are holy. The people of the world have not been trained as we have been in such matters, notwithstanding there are many honest, devout, and refined people in the world. But we have the guidance of the Holy Spirit and the revelations of the Lord, and He has solemnly taught us in our own day our duty in relation to all such things.[16]

Dressing modestly and keeping the law of chastity

The Latter-day Saints should not follow the fashions and the immodesty of the world. We are the people of the Lord. He expects us to live clean, virtuous lives, to keep our thoughts clean and minds pure and faithful in the observance of all his other commandments. Why should we follow the world, why can we not be modest, why can't we do the things the Lord would have us do?[17]

As I walk along the streets on my way to or from the Church Office Building, I see both young and older women, many of them "daughters of Zion," who are immodestly dressed [see Isaiah 3:16–24]. I realize that times and fashions do change. . . . [But] the principle of modesty and propriety is still the same. . . . The standards expressed by the General Authorities of the Church are that women, as well as men, should dress modestly. They are taught proper deportment and modesty at all times.

It is, in my judgment, a sad reflection on the "daughters of Zion" when they dress immodestly. Moreover, this remark pertains to the men as well as to the women. The Lord gave commandments to ancient Israel that both men and women should cover their bodies and observe the law of chastity at all times.

I am making a plea for modesty and chastity and for all the members of the Church, male and female alike, to be chaste, clean in their lives, and obedient to the covenants and commandments the Lord has given us. . . .

. . . The wearing of immodest clothing, which may seem like a small matter, take[s] something away from our young women or young men in the Church. It simply makes it more difficult to keep those eternal principles by which we all have to live if we are to return to the presence of our Father in heaven.[18]

   2

The blessings promised to the faithful are far greater than the temporary pleasures of the world.

[A member of the Church once said that he] could not quite understand when he paid his tithing and kept the Word of Wisdom, was prayerful, and tried to be obedient to all the commandments the Lord had given him, and yet he had to struggle to make a living; while his neighbor violated the Sabbath day, I suppose he smoked and drank; he had what the world would call a good time, he paid no attention to the teachings of our Lord and Savior Jesus Christ, and yet he prospered.

You know, we have a great many members of the Church that ponder that over in their hearts and wonder why. Why this man seems to be blessed with all the good things of the earth—incidentally, many of the bad things that he thinks are good—and yet so many members of the Church are struggling, laboring diligently to try to make their way through the world.

The answer is a simple thing. If I sometimes, and once in a while I do, go to a football game or a baseball game or some other place of amusement, invariably I will be surrounded by men and women who are puffing on cigarets or cigars or dirty pipes. It gets very annoying, and I get a little disturbed. I will turn to Sister Smith, and I will say something to her, and she will say, "Well, now, you know what you have taught me. You are in *their* world. This is their world." And that sort of brings me back to my senses. Yes, we are in their world, but we do not have to be of it.

So, as this is their world we are living in, they prosper, but, my good brethren and sisters, their world is coming to its end. . . .

The day will come when we will not have *this* world. It will be changed. We will get a better world. We will get one that is righteous, because when Christ comes, he will cleanse the earth.[19]

If we shall search diligently, pray always, be believing, and walk uprightly, we have the Lord's promise that all things shall work together for our good [see D&C 90:24]. This is not a promise that we shall be free from the trials and problems of life, for this probationary state is designed to give us experience and difficult and conflicting situations.

Life never was intended to be easy, but the Lord has promised that he will cause all trials and difficulties to result in our good. He will give us strength and ability to overcome the world and to stand firm in the faith despite all opposition. It is a promise that we shall have peace in our hearts despite the tumults and troubles of the world. And above all, it is a promise that when this life is over, we shall qualify for eternal peace in the presence of Him whose face we have sought, whose laws we have kept, and whom we have chosen to serve.[20]

⟨⟨⟨3⟩⟩⟩

As we put God's kingdom first in our lives, we act as lights to the world and set an example for others to follow.

The Latter-day Saints are as a city set on a hill that cannot be hid, and like the candle that gives light to all who are in the house. It is our duty to let our light shine as an example in righteousness, not only to the people among whom we live, but to the peoples of the whole earth. [See Matthew 5:14–16.][21]

We desire to see the Saints in every nation receive the full blessings of the gospel and stand as spiritual leaders in their nations.[22]

Brethren and sisters, let us keep the commandments of God as they have been revealed. Let us set the example before the people of the earth, that they, seeing our good works, may feel to repent and receive the truth and accept the plan of salvation, that they may receive salvation in the celestial kingdom of God.[23]

I pray that the Saints shall stand firm against the pressures and enticements of the world; that they shall put first in their lives the things of God's kingdom; that they shall be true to every trust and keep every covenant.

I pray for the young and rising generation that they shall keep their minds and bodies clean—free from immorality, from drug abuse, and from the spirit of rebellion and defiance of decency that is sweeping the land.

Our Father, pour out thy Spirit upon these thy children that they may be preserved from the perils of the world and kept clean and pure, fit candidates to return to thy presence and dwell with thee.

And let thy preserving care be with all those who seek thy face and who walk before thee in the integrity of their souls, that they may be lights to the world, instruments in thy hands to bring to pass thy purposes on earth.[24]

Suggestions for Study and Teaching

Questions

- As you read "From the Life of Joseph Fielding Smith," think about challenges young people face today when their parents or adult leaders are not with them. What can we do to help youth remain faithful in such situations?

- What are some blessings that come to us as we keep the commandments mentioned in section 1?

- How might you use the teachings in section 2 to help someone who is distracted by the things of the world? How can we find "peace in our hearts despite the tumults and troubles of the world"?

- How can our examples help others forsake the ways of the world? (See section 3.) When have you seen the power of righteous example? Think about what you can do to set a righteous example for your family and others.

Related Scriptures

Matthew 6:24; Mark 8:34–36; John 14:27; Philippians 2:14–15; Moroni 10:30, 32

Teaching Help

"You can express love for those you teach by listening attentively to them and being sincerely interested in their lives. Christlike love has the power to soften hearts and help people be receptive to the whisperings of the Spirit" (*Teaching, No Greater Call* [1999], 46).

Notes

1. Joseph Fielding Smith Jr. and John J. Stewart, *The Life of Joseph Fielding Smith* (1972), 287–88.
2. In Conference Report, Oct. 1955, 43–44.
3. In Conference Report, Apr. 1947, 60–61.
4. "Our Responsibilities as Priesthood Holders," *Ensign,* June 1971, 50.
5. "President Joseph Fielding Smith Speaks to 14,000 Youth at Long Beach, California," *New Era,* July 1971, 8.
6. In Conference Report, Apr. 1952, 27–28.
7. "The Pearl of Great Price," *Utah Genealogical and Historical Magazine,* July 1930, 104.
8. "Our Responsibilities as Priesthood Holders," 49–50.
9. In Conference Report, Apr. 1911, 86.
10. In Conference Report, Apr. 1957, 60–61.
11. In Conference Report, Apr. 1927, 111.
12. *Answers to Gospel Questions,* comp. Joseph Fielding Smith Jr., 5 vols. (1957–66), 1:199.
13. "Be Ye Clean!" *Church News,* Oct. 2, 1943, 4; see also *Doctrines of Salvation,* ed. Bruce R. McConkie, 3 vols. (1954–56), 3:276.
14. In "Message from the First Presidency," *Ensign,* Jan. 1971, 1.

15. In Conference Report, Oct. 1960, 51.

16. "The Spirit of Reverence and Worship," *Improvement Era,* Sept. 1941, 525, 572; see also *Doctrines of Salvation,* 1:12–14.

17. "Teach Virtue and Modesty," *Relief Society Magazine,* Jan. 1963, 6.

18. "My Dear Young Fellow Workers," *New Era,* Jan. 1971, 5.

19. In Conference Report, Apr. 1952, 28.

20. "President Joseph Fielding Smith Speaks on the New MIA Theme," *New Era,* Sept. 1971, 40.

21. In Conference Report, Oct. 1930, 23.

22. In Conference Report, British Area General Conference 1971, 6.

23. In Conference Report, Apr. 1954, 28.

24. "A Witness and a Blessing," *Ensign,* June 1971, 110.

"Then Peter said, Silver and gold have I none; but such as I have give I thee: In the name of Jesus Christ of Nazareth rise up and walk" (Acts 3:6).

Love and Concern for All Our Father's Children

"I think if all men knew and understood who they are, and were aware of the divine source from whence they came, . . . they would have feelings of kindness and kinship for each other that would change their whole way of living and bring peace on earth."

From the Life of Joseph Fielding Smith

Joseph Fielding Smith Jr. and John J. Stewart observed, "It is in the thoughtful little things of life that the real Joseph Fielding Smith could be seen most clearly." Then they shared three examples of "thoughtful little things" he had done:

"One day at a church conference in the Mormon Tabernacle on Temple Square a 12-year-old boy, excited to be there for the first time, had come early to be sure to get a seat close to the front. . . . Just before the meeting began, and when all the seats were taken, an usher asked the boy to give up his seat so that a late arriving United States Senator could have it. Meekly the boy complied, and stood in the aisle, disappointed, embarrassed, in tears." President Joseph Fielding Smith "noticed the youngster and motioned him to come up [on the stand]. When the boy told him what had happened he said, 'That usher had no right to do that to you. But here, you sit by me,' and shared his seat with him, in the midst of the apostles of the Church.

"One day as he was interviewing a group of young men leaving on two-year missions for the Church, [he] noticed a farm boy who had been assigned to eastern Canada. 'Son, it's cold up there. Do you have a good warm coat?' 'No sir, I haven't.' He took the boy across the street to [a] department store and bought him the warmest coat in stock.

"The day he was sustained in conference as president of the Church a little girl worked her way through the throng after the meeting and reached for his hand. So touched was he by the gesture that he stooped down and took the child into his arms. He learned that her name was Venus Hobbs, . . . soon to be four years old. On her birthday Venus received a surprise telephone call: Joseph Fielding Smith and his wife calling long distance to sing 'Happy Birthday' to her."[1]

These acts of kindness were not isolated occurrences but part of a lifelong pattern. President Smith was "a man of great tenderness and compassion. His life has been one repeated instance after another of giving aid to the needy, comfort to the brokenhearted, counsel to the confused and in exemplifying that charity which is 'the pure love of Christ.' [Moroni 7:47.]"[2]

Teachings of Joseph Fielding Smith

1

With the knowledge that God is the Father of all people, we desire to love and bless others.

I think if all men knew and understood who they are, and were aware of the divine source from whence they came, and of the infinite potential that is part of their inheritance, they would have feelings of kindness and kinship for each other that would change their whole way of living and bring peace on earth.

We believe in the dignity and divine origin of man. Our faith is founded on the fact that God is our Father, and that we are his children, and that all men are brothers and sisters in the same eternal family.

As members of his family, we dwelt with him before the foundations of this earth were laid, and he ordained and established the plan of salvation whereby we gained the privilege of advancing and progressing as we are endeavoring to do.

The God we worship is a glorified Being in whom all power and perfection dwell, and he has created man in his own image and likeness, with those characteristics and attributes which he himself possesses.

And so our belief in the dignity and destiny of man is an essential part both of our theology and of our way of life. It is the very basis of our Lord's teaching that "the first and great commandment" is: "Thou shalt love the Lord thy God with all thy heart, and with all thy soul, and with all thy mind"; and that the second great commandment is: "Thou shalt love thy neighbour as thyself." (See Matt. 22:37–39.)

Because God is our Father, we have a natural desire to love and serve him and to be worthy members of his family. We feel an obligation to do what he would have us do, to keep his commandments and live in harmony with the standards of his gospel— all of which are essential parts of true worship.

And because all men are our brothers, we have a desire to love and bless and fellowship them—and this too we accept as an essential part of true worship.

Thus, everything we do in the Church centers around the divine law that we are to love and worship God and serve our fellowmen.

It is no wonder, then, that as a church and as a people we have deep and abiding concern for the welfare of all our Father's children. We seek their temporal and spiritual well-being along with our own. We pray for them as we do for ourselves, and we try to live so that they, seeing our good works, may be led to glorify our Father who is in heaven. [See Matthew 5:16.][3]

2

As we love and support one another in the Church, we become a power in the world for good.

"If ye love me, keep my commandments." [John 14:15.]

These words were addressed by the Master to his disciples but a few hours before his death, as he had assembled with them to eat the passover, and give them the final instruction before he should suffer for the sins of the world. On that same occasion, and shortly before these remarks were made, he referred to the same subject, when he said:

"Little children, yet a little while I am with you. Ye shall seek me; and as I said unto the Jews, Whither I go ye can not come; so now

I say to you. A new commandment I give unto you, That ye love one another; as I have loved you, that ye also love one another." [John 13:33–34.] . . .

. . . We are not merely friends; we are brothers and sisters, the children of God, who have come out, as I have said, from the world to enter into covenants, to observe his laws and to abide by all things which are given us by inspiration. We are commanded to love one another. "A new commandment," the Lord has said, and yet like many other commandments it is as old as eternity. There never was a time when that commandment did not exist and was not essential to salvation, and yet it is always new. It never grows old, because it is true.[4]

I believe it is our solemn duty to love one another, to believe in each other, to have faith in each other, that it is our duty to overlook the faults and the failings of each other, and not to magnify them in our own eyes nor before the eyes of the world. There should be no faultfinding, no back-biting, no evil speaking, one against another, in the Church of Jesus Christ of Latter-day Saints. We should be true to each other and to every principle of our religion and not be envious one of another. We should not be jealous one of another, nor angry with each other, and there should not arise in our hearts a feeling that we will not forgive one another our trespasses. There should be no feeling in the hearts of the children of God of unforgiveness against any man, no matter who he may be. . . .

. . . We ought not to harbor feelings one against another, but have a feeling of forgiveness and of brotherly love and sisterly love, one for another. Let each one of us remember his or her own individual failings and weaknesses and endeavor to correct them. We have not reached a condition of perfection yet, it is hardly to be expected that we will in this life, and yet, through the aid of the Holy Ghost, it is possible for us to stand united together seeing eye to eye and overcoming our sins and imperfections. If we will do this, respecting all the commandments of the Lord, we shall be a power in the world for good; we shall overwhelm and overcome all evil, all opposition to the truth, and bring to pass righteousness upon the face of the earth. For the Gospel will be spread and the people in the world will feel the influence which will be shed forth from the

When we extend a helping hand to others, we show our love for them.

people of Zion, and they will be inclined more to repent of their sins and to receive the truth.[5]

_____ 3 _____

We express love for our fellowmen by serving them.

Our Savior came into the world to teach us love for each other, and as that great lesson was made manifest through his great suffering and death that we might live, should we not express our love for our fellowmen by service rendered in their behalf? . . .

Service must be given in behalf of others. We must extend the helping hand to the unfortunate, to those who have not heard the truth and are in spiritual darkness, to the needy, the oppressed. Are you failing? Let us think of the words of the poet, Will L. Thompson. . . . The poem starts this way:

> "Have I done any good in the world today?
> Have I helped anyone in need?
> Have I cheered up the sad,
> And made someone feel glad?
> If not I have failed indeed." [*Hymns,* no. 223.][6]

Our mission is to all the world—for the peace, and hope, and happiness, and temporal and eternal salvation of all of our Father's children. . . . With all my powers of persuasion I urge this people to continue to reach out and bless the lives of all our Father's children everywhere.[7]

───────────────── 4 ─────────────────

We need to appreciate and love people for themselves.

When I was a boy, we had a horse named Junie. She was one of the most intelligent animals I ever saw. She seemed almost human in her ability. I couldn't keep her locked in the barn because she would continually undo the strap on the door of her stall. I used to put the strap connected to the half-door of the stall over the top of the post, but she would simply lift it off with her nose and teeth. Then she would go out in the yard.

There was a water tap in the yard used for filling the water trough for our animals. Junie would turn this on with her teeth and then leave the water running. My father would get after me because I couldn't keep that horse in the barn. She never ran away; she just turned on the water and then walked around the yard or over the lawn or through the garden. In the middle of the night, I would hear the water running and then I would have to get up and shut it off and lock Junie up again.

My father suggested that the horse seemed smarter than I was. One day he decided that he would lock her in so that she couldn't get out. He took the strap that usually looped over the top of the post and buckled it around the post and under a crossbar, and then he said, "Young lady, let's see you get out of there now!" My father and I left the barn and started to walk back to the house; and before we reached it, Junie was at our side. She then went over and turned the water on again.

I suggested that now, perhaps, she was about as smart as either one of us. We just couldn't keep Junie from getting out of her stall. But that doesn't mean she was bad, because she wasn't. Father wasn't about to sell or trade her, because she had so many other good qualities that made up for this one little fault.

The horse was as reliable and dependable at pulling our buggy as she was adept at getting out of the stall. And this was important, because Mother was a licensed midwife. When she would get called to a confinement somewhere in the valley, usually in the middle of the night, I would have to get up, take a lantern out to the barn, and hitch Junie up to the buggy.

I was only about ten or eleven years old at the time; and that horse had to be gentle and yet strong enough to take me and Mother all over the valley, in all kinds of weather. One thing I never could understand, however, was why most of the babies had to be born at night and so many of them in winter.

Often I would wait in the buggy for Mother, and then it was nice to have the company of gentle old Junie. This experience with this horse was very good for me, because early in life I had to learn to love and appreciate her for herself. She was a wonderful horse with only a couple of bad habits. People are a lot the same way. None of us is perfect; yet each of us is trying to become perfect, even as our Father in heaven. We need to appreciate and love people for themselves.

Maybe you need to remember this when you evaluate your parents or teachers or ward and stake leaders or friends or brothers and sisters. This lesson has always stayed with me—to see the good in people even though we are trying to help them overcome one or two bad habits. . . .

I learned early in life to love and not to judge others, trying always to overcome my own faults.[8]

⟨ 5 ⟩

**When we love the Lord with all our hearts
and our neighbors as ourselves, we are
in harmony with all sacred law.**

"Thou shalt love the Lord thy God with all thy heart, and with all thy soul, and with all thy mind.

"This is the first and great commandment.

"And the second is like unto it, Thou shalt love thy neighbour as thyself.

"On these two commandments hang all the law and the prophets." (Matthew 22:37–40.)

In other words, all that has been revealed for the salvation of man from the beginning to our own time is circumscribed, included in, and a part of these two great laws. If we love the Lord with all the heart, with all the soul, and with all the mind, and our neighbors as ourselves, then there is nothing more to be desired. Then we will be in harmony with the total of sacred law. If we were willing to live in harmony with these two great commandments—and we must do so eventually if we are worthy to live in the presence of God—then wickedness, jealousy, ambition, covetousness, bloodshed, and all sin of every nature would be banished from the earth. Then would come a day of eternal peace and happiness. What a glorious day that would be! We have been endowed with sufficient reason to know that such a state is most desirable and would establish among men the Fatherhood of God and the perfect brotherhood of man.

. . . Can we say that we love the Lord with all the soul? Can we say we are as solicitous for the welfare of our neighbor as we are for our own?[9]

Let us love the Lord for this is the foundation of all things. It is the first commandment, and the second commandment, to love our neighbors as ourselves, is like unto it, and when we have done that we have fulfilled the law, because there is nothing that will be left undone.[10]

Suggestions for Study and Teaching

Questions

- Consider the "thoughtful little things" President Joseph Fielding Smith did for others (see "From the Life of Joseph Fielding Smith"). What can we do to establish similar patterns of kindness in our lives?

- How can the doctrines in section 1 help us be kind and loving to those around us?

- What impresses you about President Smith's counsel in section 2? Why do you think we will be "a power in the world for good" as we follow this counsel?

- What has Jesus Christ done to "teach us love for each other"? (See section 3.) In what ways can we follow His example?

- Review the story about Junie the horse (see section 4). Why do you think it is important to "appreciate and love people for themselves"? What can we do to see the good in others even if we are trying to help them overcome bad habits?

- What does it mean to you to keep the commandments in Matthew 22:37–40? (For some examples, see section 5.) Why are we "in harmony with the total of sacred law" when we keep these commandments?

Related Scriptures

Acts 17:28–29; Romans 8:16–17; 1 John 4:18–21; Mosiah 2:17; 18:8–10; Moroni 7:45–48

Teaching Help

Consider inviting participants to read the subheadings in the chapter and select a section that is meaningful to them or their family. Invite them to study President Smith's teachings in that section, including corresponding questions at the end of the chapter. Then ask class members to share what they have learned.

Notes

1. In Joseph Fielding Smith Jr. and John J. Stewart, *The Life of Joseph Fielding Smith* (1972), 10–11.
2. S. Perry Lee, "Church Expresses Devotions to President Smith," *Church News*, July 14, 1956, 2.
3. In Conference Report, Apr. 1970, 4–5.
4. In Conference Report, Oct. 1920, 53–55.
5. In Conference Report, Apr. 1915, 119–20.
6. In Conference Report, Apr. 1968, 12.
7. In Conference Report, Apr. 1970, 4.
8. "My Dear Young Fellow Workers," *New Era*, Jan. 1971, 4–5.
9. In Conference Report, Apr. 1943, 12.
10. In Conference Report, Oct. 1920, 59.

Elder Joseph Fielding Smith in 1910, soon after he was ordained an Apostle

Proclaiming the Gospel to the World

"We have tasted the fruits of the gospel and know they are good, and we desire that all men shall receive the same blessings and the same spirit that have been poured out so abundantly upon us."

From the Life of Joseph Fielding Smith

Joseph Fielding Smith and his wife, Louie, were not surprised when they received a letter, signed by President Lorenzo Snow, calling Joseph to serve a full-time mission. In those early days of the Church, married men often served away from home. So when that letter arrived on March 17, 1899, about a month before their first wedding anniversary, Joseph and Louie accepted the opportunity with faith and courage, mixed with sadness at the thought of being separated for two years.

Elder Smith served in England, about 4,700 miles (about 7,600 kilometers) from home. He and Louie sent letters to each other often—letters filled with expressions of love and testimony. In one of Elder Smith's first letters to Louie, he wrote: "I know that the work I have been called to do is the work of God or I would not stay here one minute, no, I would not have left home. But I know that our happiness is dependent upon my faithfulness while I am here. I should be willing to do this much for the love of mankind when our Savior could suffer as He did for us. . . . I am in the hands of our Heavenly Father and he will watch over me and protect me if I do his will. And he will be with you while I am away and watch over you and protect you in all things."[1]

Elder Smith and his missionary companions were dedicated servants of the Lord. In one letter to Louie, he reported that each month, he and the other missionaries distributed about 10,000 tracts, or pamphlets, and visited about 4,000 homes. However, he followed this report with a sobering observation: "I don't believe one, or more than one, tract in every hundred is read."[2] During the time Elder Smith was in England, very few of the people there accepted the message of the restored gospel. In his two years of service, "he did not make one convert, did not have opportunity to perform one baptism, although he did confirm one convert."[3] Unable to see many results of his labors, he found comfort in knowing that he was doing the Lord's will and that he was helping prepare people who might receive the gospel later in their lives.

For about two weeks of his mission, Elder Smith was confined in a hospital with four other missionaries. The five elders had been exposed to smallpox, so they were quarantined to prevent the illness from spreading. Although Elder Smith referred to their stay as an "imprisonment," he and his companions made the best of it. They even shared the gospel with the hospital staff. At the end of the confinement, Elder Smith wrote the following report in his journal: "We have made friends with the nurses and others who visited us during our imprisonment. Many times we have had talks with them about the gospel; also left with them books to read. When we left the hospital we sang a hymn or two, which among other things impressed those who listened, for we left them with tears in their eyes. I think we have made an impression at the hospital for good, especially with the nurses, who confess that we are not the people they thought we were and [that] they will now defend us at all times."[4]

Elder Smith concluded his mission in June 1901. Seventy years later, he returned to England as President of the Church to preside over an area conference. By that time, the seeds he and others had planted had sprouted and flourished. He rejoiced to see so many British Saints come to the meetings.[5] He said, "Several stakes of Zion, a temple dedicated to the Lord, a considerable number of ward and stake buildings, and some highly successful missionary work—all testify to the fact that the Church is coming of age in Great Britain." And he said that this progress in Great Britain was representative of what would happen throughout the world. He declared that the gospel is for all people and that "the Church shall be established everywhere, in all nations, even to the ends of the earth, before the second coming of the Son of Man."[6]

Teachings of Joseph Fielding Smith

1

We alone have the fulness of the restored gospel, and we desire that all people receive the same blessing.

In his infinite wisdom, and to fulfill the covenants and promises made to the prophets of old, the Lord has restored in these last days the fullness of his everlasting gospel. This gospel is the plan of salvation. It was ordained and established in the councils of eternity before the foundations of this earth were laid, and it has been revealed anew in our day for the salvation and blessing of all our Father's children everywhere. . . .

Nearly six hundred years before Christ—that is, his coming—the great prophet Nephi said to his people: ". . . there is one God and one Shepherd over all the earth.

"And the time cometh that he shall manifest himself unto all nations. . . ." (1 Ne. 13:41–42.)

That promised day is now dawning. This is the appointed time for the preaching of the gospel in all the world and for the building up of the Lord's kingdom in every nation. There are good and upright people in all nations who will respond to the truth; who will come into the Church; and who will become lights to guide their own people. . . .

. . . The gospel is for all people, and the Lord expects those who receive it to live its truths and to offer them to those of their own nation and tongue.

And so now, in the spirit of love and brotherhood, we invite all men everywhere to give heed to the words of eternal life revealed in this day through the Prophet Joseph Smith and his associates.

We invite our Father's other children to "come unto Christ, and be perfected in him," and to deny themselves of "all ungodliness." (Moro. 10:32.)

We invite them to believe in Christ and his gospel, to come into his church, and to be one with his saints.

We have tasted the fruits of the gospel and know they are good, and we desire that all men shall receive the same blessings and the same spirit that have been poured out so abundantly upon us.[7]

I am not unmindful that there are good and devout people among all sects, parties, and denominations, and they will be blessed and rewarded for all the good they do. But the fact remains that we alone have the fullness of those laws and ordinances which prepare men for the fullness of reward in the mansions above. And so we say to the good and noble, the upright and devout people everywhere: Keep all the good you have; cleave unto every true principle which is now yours; but come and partake of the further light and knowledge which that God who is the same yesterday, today, and forever is again pouring out upon his people.[8]

I pray that the Lord's purposes on earth, both in and out of the Church, may speedily be brought to pass; that he will bless his faithful Saints; and that the hearts of hosts of men who seek truth and whose hearts are right before the Lord may become inheritors with us of the fullness of the blessings of the restored gospel.[9]

2

All Church members have a responsibility to use their strength, energy, means, and influence to proclaim the gospel.

We have heard that we are all missionaries. . . . We are all set apart, not by the laying on of hands; we have not had a special calling; we have not been singled out to do missionary labor, but as members of the Church, having pledged ourselves to the advancement of the gospel of Jesus Christ we become missionaries. That is part of the responsibility of every member of the Church.[10]

With a heart full of love for all men, I ask the members of the Church to learn and live the gospel and to use their strength, energy, and means in proclaiming it to the world. We have received a commission from the Lord. He has given a divine mandate. He has commanded us to go forth with unwearying diligence and offer

*"Every person who receives the light of the gospel becomes a
light and a guide to all those whom he is able to teach."*

to his other children those saving truths revealed to the Prophet
Joseph Smith.[11]

Our mission, I say, is, so far as it is within our power, to regen-
erate, to bring to repentance, just as many of the children of our
Father in heaven as it is possible for us to do. . . . That is an obligation the Lord has placed upon the Church, and more particularly
upon the quorums of the priesthood of the Church, and yet this
obligation belongs to every soul.[12]

There are among us a great many honest souls who have never
accepted the opportunity, or have never taken the trouble to search,
that they might find these glorious truths which have been made
known in the revelations of the Lord. They do not think of these
things, they live among us, we associate with them and we come
in contact with them daily. They think we are a pretty nice sort of
people, but peculiar in our religious views, and therefore they pay

no attention to our faith, and therefore this great missionary work that is being carried on now in the stakes of Zion is gathering in a harvest of honest, faithful souls right here from among those who before had never taken the opportunity, I say, which has been theirs, to hear the gospel.[13]

We who have received the truth of the everlasting gospel ought not to be satisfied with anything short of the best, and the best is the fulness of the Father's kingdom; and for that I hope and pray we shall live and set examples in righteousness to all men that none may stumble, that none may falter, that none may turn from the path of righteousness, due to anything that we may do or say.[14]

There is an influence that radiates not only from the individual but from the Church. I believe that our success in the world depends largely upon the attitude of the Saints. If we were united wholly, in thought, in deed, in our actions; if we loved the word of truth, if we walked in it as the Lord would have us do, then there would radiate from this community, from [congregations] of the Latter-day Saints in all of these communities, out into all the world, an influence that would be irresistible. More honest men and women would be converted, for the Spirit of the Lord would go before us to prepare the way. . . . If they, this people, would keep the commandments of the Lord it would be a force and a power and influence that would break down opposition and would prepare people to receive the light of the everlasting Gospel; and when we fail to do it we take upon ourselves a responsibility that is dreadful in its consequences.

How will I feel, or you, when called before the judgment seat if someone shall point his finger at me or you and say that "if it had not been for the actions of this man or this group I would have received the truth, but I was blinded because they, professing to have the light, did not live it."[15]

The Lord says if we labor all our days and save but one soul, how great will be our joy with him [see D&C 18:15]; on the other hand how great will be our sorrow and our condemnation if through our acts we have led one soul away from this truth.[16]

The Latter-day Saints, wherever they may be, are and should be a light to the world. The gospel is a light breaking forth in darkness, and every person who receives the light of the gospel becomes a light and a guide to all those whom he is able to teach.

Your responsibility . . . is to be living witnesses of the truth and divinity of the work. We hope you will live the gospel and work out your own salvation, and that others seeing your good works may be led to glorify our Father in heaven [see Matthew 5:16].[17]

3

The Church needs more missionaries to go forth on the Lord's errand.

We need missionaries. . . . The field is wide; the harvest is great; but the laborers are few [see Luke 10:2]. Likewise the field is white and ready for the harvest [see D&C 4:4]. . . .

. . . Our missionaries go forth. No power has been able to stay their hands. It has been tried. Great efforts were made in the very beginning when there was only a handful of missionaries, but the progress of this work could not be stopped. It cannot be stopped now. It must and will go forth that the inhabitants of the earth may have the opportunity of repenting of their sins and receive the remission of their sins and come into the Church and kingdom of God, before these final destructions come upon the wicked, for they have been promised. . . .

And these missionaries, mostly young men, untrained in the ways of the world, go forth with this message of salvation and confound the great and the mighty, because they have the truth. They are proclaiming this gospel; the honest and sincere are hearing it and are repenting of their sins and coming into the Church.[18]

We hope to see the day when every worthy and qualified young Latter-day Saint man will have the privilege of going forth on the Lord's errand to stand as a witness of the truth in the nations of the earth.

We now have many and can use many more stable and mature couples in this great missionary cause, and we hope that those who are worthy and qualified will set their affairs in order and respond

*"We commend those who are serving so valiantly
in the great missionary cause."*

to calls to preach the gospel and will perform their obligations acceptably.

We also have and can use many young sisters in this work, although the same responsibility does not rest upon them that rests upon the brethren, and our greater concern with reference to young sisters is that they enter proper marital unions in the temples of the Lord.

We invite members of the Church to assist financially in sustaining the missionary cause and to contribute liberally of their means for the spread of the gospel.

We commend those who are serving so valiantly in the great missionary cause. Joseph Smith said: "After all that has been said, the greatest and most important duty is to preach the gospel." [19]

_____ ⌒⌒⌒ **4** ⌒⌒⌒ _____

We are to preach the doctrines of salvation as they are recorded in the scriptures, in plainness and simplicity and as guided by the Spirit.

In the early days of this dispensation, the Lord said to those called in his ministry, "that every man might speak in the name of God the Lord, even the Savior of the world; . . . That the fulness of my gospel might be proclaimed by the weak and the simple unto the ends of the world, and before kings and rulers." (D&C 1:20, 23.)

To those called "to go forth to preach" his gospel and to all "the elders, priests and teachers" of his church, he said: They "shall teach the principles of my gospel, which are in the Bible and the Book of Mormon," and the other scriptures, "as they shall be directed by the Spirit." (See D&C 42:11–13.)

As agents of the Lord we are not called or authorized to teach the philosophies of the world or the speculative theories of our scientific age. Our mission is to preach the doctrines of salvation in *plainness* and simplicity as they are revealed and recorded in the scriptures.

After directing us to teach the principles of the gospel found in the standard works, as guided by the Spirit, the Lord then made that great pronouncement which governs all the teaching of his gospel by anyone in the Church: "And the Spirit shall be given unto you by the prayer of faith; and if ye receive not the Spirit ye shall not teach." (D&C 42:14.)[20]

_____ ⌒⌒⌒ **5** ⌒⌒⌒ _____

The gospel is the sole hope of the world, the one way that will bring peace on earth.

Do you know what is the greatest power, the most potent factor in all the world, for the permanent establishment of peace in the earth? Having asked the question I will answer it, at least I will express my view in regard to it—not saying anything about other movements. The greatest factor in all the world is the power of the Holy Priesthood, and that is in the possession of the Latter-day Saints. Right from the beginning the Lord sent out the elders into the world, commanding them to call upon the people, saying, Repent, come unto Zion. Believe in my gospel and you shall have peace.

Peace will come, of course, through righteousness, through justice, through the mercy of God, through the power which he will grant unto us by which our hearts will be touched and we will have love one for another. Now our duty is to declare these things among all people, call upon them to come unto Zion where the standard is set up—the standard of peace—and to receive of the blessings of the house of the Lord and the influence of his Holy Spirit which is here manifest. And I want to tell you that we ourselves, if we will serve the Lord, have wonderful power in regard to the establishment of peace in the world.

Now we are willing that other movements in this direction should go on. We are in favor of all that will bring peace unto the world; but let us not lose sight of the fact that we, Latter-day Saints, if we will band together, and stand as one serving the Lord and will send forth the word of eternal life among the nations, will have greater power, in my judgment, for the establishment of peace in the world than any other force. I am in full accord with the idea that has been expressed that the Lord is using many agencies; his work is not confined to the Latter-day Saints, for he has called many to his service outside of the Church and has endowed them with power, has inspired them to do his work. . . . However, my brethren and sisters, do not let us lose sight of the fact that we are a power in the earth for good and for the spread of the truth and the establishment of peace among all nations, kindreds, tongues and peoples. . . . Our mission has been and is, "Repent ye, for the kingdom of God is at hand." [See D&C 33:10.]

We must continue until all the righteous are gathered out, until all men are warned, until those who will hear shall hear, and those who will not hear also shall hear, for the Lord has declared that there shall not be a soul that shall not hear, not a heart that shall not be penetrated [see D&C 1:2], for his word will go forth, whether it be the word of his elders or by some other means, it mattereth not, but in his due time he shall cut short his work in righteousness; he shall establish his truth and he shall come and reign upon the earth.[21]

We respect our Father's other children of all sects, parties, and denominations, and have no desire except to see them receive the added light and knowledge that has come to us by revelation, and to become with us inheritors of the great blessings of the restoration of the gospel.

But we have the plan of salvation; we administer the gospel; and the gospel is the sole hope of the world, the one way that will bring peace on earth and right the wrongs that exist in all nations.[22]

We know that if men will have faith in Christ, repent of their sins, covenant in the waters of baptism to keep his commandments, and then receive the Holy Ghost by the laying on of hands by those who are called and ordained unto this power—and if they will then keep the commandments—they shall have peace in this life and eternal life in the world to come [see D&C 59:23].[23]

There is no cure for the ills of the world except the gospel of the Lord Jesus Christ. Our hope for peace, for temporal and spiritual prosperity, and for an eventual inheritance in the kingdom of God is found only in and through the restored gospel. There is no work that any of us can engage in that is as important as preaching the gospel and building up the Church and kingdom of God on earth.[24]

Suggestions for Study and Teaching

Questions

- Think about the way Joseph Fielding Smith responded to challenges as a full-time missionary (see "From the Life of Joseph Fielding Smith"). How might his example influence your service in the Church?

- Ponder the blessing of tasting "the fruits of the gospel" (section 1). Think about people with whom you can share these "fruits."

- How can President Smith's words in section 2 help us share the gospel with others?

- President Smith said that the Church needs more full-time missionaries, including "mature couples" (section 3). What can we do to help youth prepare to serve? What can you do to prepare yourself to serve?

- In what ways can our words and actions communicate the plainness and simplicity of the gospel? (See section 4.) When have you felt the Holy Ghost guide you in these efforts?

- What teachings in section 5 are particularly inspiring to you? What are your feelings as you think about sharing "the sole hope of the world, the one way that will bring peace on earth"?

Related Scriptures

Matthew 24:14; Mark 16:15; 1 Nephi 13:37; 2 Nephi 2:6–8; 3 Nephi 12:13–16; D&C 1:17–24; 4; 50:13–14; 88:81; 133:57–58

Teaching Help

When a participant reads aloud from President Smith's teachings, invite the other participants to "listen and look for specific principles or ideas. If a passage contains unusual or difficult words or phrases, explain these before the passage is read. If anyone in the group might have difficulty reading, ask for volunteers instead of having them take turns" (*Teaching, No Greater Call* [1999], 56).

Notes

1. Joseph Fielding Smith to Louie Shurtliff Smith, in Joseph Fielding Smith Jr. and John J. Stewart, *The Life of Joseph Fielding Smith* (1972), 114–15.

2. Joseph Fielding Smith to Louie Shurtliff Smith, in *The Life of Joseph Fielding Smith,* 102.

3. See *The Life of Joseph Fielding Smith,* 91.

4. Journal of Joseph Fielding Smith, Apr. 30, 1901, Church History Library; punctuation and capitalization standardized.

5. See Conference Report, British Area General Conference 1971, 85.

6. In Conference Report, British Area General Conference 1971, 176.

7. "I Know That My Redeemer Liveth," *Ensign,* Dec. 1971, 26–27.

8. "A Witness and a Blessing," *Ensign,* June 1971, 109–10.

9. "Out of the Darkness," *Ensign,* June 1971, 4.

10. *Take Heed to Yourselves,* comp. Joseph Fielding Smith Jr. (1966), 27–28.

11. In Conference Report, Oct. 1970, 5–6.

12. In Conference Report, Apr. 1944, 50; see also *Doctrines of Salvation,* ed. Bruce R. McConkie, 3 vols. (1954–56), 1:308.

13. In Conference Report, Apr. 1921, 42.

14. In Conference Report, Apr. 1923, 139.

15. In Conference Report, Oct. 1933, 62–63.

16. In Conference Report, Apr. 1951, 153.

17. In Conference Report, British Area General Conference 1971, 176.

18. In Conference Report, Apr. 1953, 19–20.

19. In Conference Report, Oct. 1970, 7; see also *Teachings of Presidents of the Church: Joseph Smith* (2007), 330.

20. In Conference Report, Oct. 1970, 5.

21. In Conference Report, Oct. 1919, 89–90.

22. "To the Saints in Great Britain," *Ensign,* Sept. 1971, 3–4.

23. In Conference Report, Oct. 1970, 7.

24. "Counsel to the Saints and to the World," *Ensign,* July 1972, 27.

Prayer—a Commandment and a Blessing

"Few things in life are as important as communing with Deity in prayer."

From the Life of Joseph Fielding Smith

President Joseph Fielding Smith taught that we should make the spirit of prayer "part of our very being."[1] He set an example of this principle by the way he lived and by the way he prayed—alone, with family members, and in public.

After the death of his first wife, Louie, he penned this tender supplication in his journal, providing a glimpse into his personal prayers: "O my Father in heaven, help me, I pray Thee, to so live that I shall be worthy to meet her in eternal glory, to be united again with her, never again to be separated, throughout the countless ages of eternity. Help me to be humble, to trust in Thee. Give me wisdom and knowledge of heavenly things that I may have power to resist all evil and remain steadfast to Thy *truth*. O Lord, help me, grant unto me eternal life in thy Kingdom. Guide my footsteps in righteousness, give unto me Thy Whole Spirit. Help me to rear my precious babies that they shall remain pure and spotless throughout their lives, and when we have finished our course, take us unto thy Celestial Kingdom, we pray thee. In the name of our Redeemer, let it be, Amen."[2]

President Smith's son Joseph Jr. told of a memorable prayer President Smith offered when the two of them were on their way home to Salt Lake City after a trip in eastern Utah. They "became engulfed in a heavy rain storm and took a wrong turn," ending up in a place called Indian Canyon. "The storm became heavier and the road very muddy and slippery, so much so that it was not only dangerous but impossible to travel farther. The heavy mist shrouded the

*"It is the duty of parents to teach their children to pray
as soon as they commence to understand."*

deep chasm off the one-lane dirt road, and young Joseph Jr. and
Dr. David E. Smith who were passengers attempted to push and
steady the car for fear of its sliding into the deep canyon below.
The wheels began to spin in the mud, and eventually the car came
to a standstill. . . . Joseph recall[ed] that his father said, 'We have
done all we can. We will call upon the Lord.' He bowed his head
in prayer, calling upon the Lord to prepare the way that he might
right his mistake and get out of the dangerous canyon and proceed
on the journey home. He told the Lord that he had important com-
mitments that needed his attention the next day, and that it was
imperative that he be back in Salt Lake City. Miraculously, the storm
abated, a wind came up, drying off the road sufficiently that they
were able to . . . eventually get back onto a highway. No sooner had
they reached low ground than the storm settled in again, stalling
traffic in the immediate area for several hours. As they proceeded
down Provo Canyon headed for Salt Lake City, after many hours
of extra travel, they were stopped by a highway patrolman who
asked where they had come from. When informed that they had
come through Indian Canyon the officer said, 'That's impossible! It's
reported that all the bridges in that area have been washed out.' To
their surprise, the headlines of the next day's paper reported 200
cars stranded in the area from which they had escaped."[3]

During President Smith's 62-year apostolic ministry, many of his
sermons included public prayers in which he sought the blessings
of heaven for members of the Church and people throughout the
world. For example, in his first general conference as President of
the Church, he petitioned, "I pray that God our Heavenly Father will
open the windows of heaven and pour out upon his children in all
the earth those great and eternal blessings which will better their
lot temporally and spiritually."[4]

President Smith's prayers revealed the depth of his testimony and
his love for his Father in Heaven and his Savior. President Boyd K.
Packer, who was called to serve in the Quorum of the Twelve Apostles when Joseph Fielding Smith was President of the Church, said:
"It was an experience to hear President Joseph Fielding Smith pray.
Even when he was past ninety he would pray that he would 'keep
his covenants and obligations and endure to the end.'"[5]

Teachings of Joseph Fielding Smith

─────────── ⟨⟨⟨⟩⟩ 1 ⟨⟨⟩⟩⟩ ───────────

We are commanded to draw near
to Heavenly Father in prayer.

It is a commandment from the Lord that we seek him constantly in humble prayer. When the Savior was with his disciples he taught them to pray and he set the example before them in frequent prayers to his Father. We may be sure, since it is a commandment from the Lord, that there is virtue in prayer, and when we seek the Lord it should be in the spirit of humility and reverence. . . .

. . . It is the duty of parents to teach their children to pray as soon as they commence to understand. Let them form the habit of approaching their Father in heaven, and with the understanding of the reason for prayer. If this habit is formed in childhood, it may remain through mature years, and the man or woman who has earnestly sought the Lord and thanked him for blessings, may expect that the Lord will not forsake them in the hour of need.[6]

I wonder if we ever stop to think why the Lord has asked us to pray. Did he ask us to pray because he wants us to bow down and worship him? Is that the main reason? I don't think it is. He is our Heavenly Father, and we have been commanded to worship him and pray to him in the name of his Beloved Son, Jesus Christ. But the Lord can get along without our prayers. His work will go on just the same, whether we pray or whether we do not. . . . Prayer is something that *we* need, not that the Lord needs. He knows just how to conduct his affairs and how to take care of them without any help from us. Our prayers are not for the purpose of telling him how to run his business. If we have any such idea as that, then of course we have the wrong idea. Our prayers are uttered more for our sakes, to build us up and give us strength and courage, and to increase our faith in him.

Prayer is something that humbles the soul. It broadens our comprehension; it quickens the mind. It draws us nearer to our Father in heaven. We need his help; there is no question about that. We need the guidance of his Holy Spirit. We need to know what principles have been given to us by which we may come back into his presence. We need to have our minds quickened by the inspiration that comes from him; and for these reasons we pray to him, that he may help us to live so that we will know his truth and be able to walk in its light, that we may, through our faithfulness and our obedience, come back again into his presence.[7]

Few things in life are as important as communing with Deity in prayer. The Lord has drawn over our minds a curtain of forgetfulness so that we do not remember him and our association with him as members of his family in the premortal life. Prayer is the avenue of communication which he has provided for us to commune with him again. Thus, one of the chief purposes of our mortal probation is to see if we can learn with the spirit of prayer always in our hearts so that when the Lord chooses to speak, we shall hear his voice in our souls.[8]

2

The season for prayer is always.

"And a commandment I give unto them (that is, unto the parents in Zion), that he that observeth not his prayers before the Lord in the season thereof, let him be had in remembrance before the judge of my people." [D&C 68:33.]

I do not suppose that we have read that verse in this section any too much, and I wonder sometimes if we realize how important this command really is. No man can retain the Spirit of the Lord, unless he prays. No man can have the inspiration of the Holy Spirit, unless in his heart is found this spirit of prayer. . . .

Now I want to dwell upon this passage for a moment or two. . . . What is the season of prayer?

Some of us may have the idea that the season of prayer is when we arise in the morning, and when we are about to retire at night when our work is done, and that there is no other season for prayer. But I say unto you, and I have good backing for it, that the season for prayer is always. Let me read it to you. You know I like to prove what I say; I like to bring witnesses to bear on that which I express, and I do not ask the people to accept that which I say unless it is in harmony, absolutely, with what the Lord has said either directly or

Amulek, pictured here with Alma, encouraged the people to "cry unto [the Lord] for mercy, for he is mighty to save" (Alma 34:18).

through his prophets. We read in the Book of Mormon the word of [Amulek] to the poor Zoramites who had departed from the truth, and having been cast out of their synagogues, because they were poor, and feeling that they could only pray one at a time as they ascended in the rameumptom, as it is called [see Alma 31:12–23], they knew not what to do. [Amulek] taught them as follows:

"Yea, cry unto him for mercy, for he is mighty to save; yea, humble yourselves and continue in prayer unto him; cry unto him when ye are in your fields, yea, over all your flocks; cry unto him in your houses, yea, over all your household, both morning, mid-day, and evening; yea, cry unto him against the power of your enemies; yea, cry unto him against the devil, who is an enemy to all righteousness. Cry unto him over the crops of your fields, that ye may prosper in them; cry over the flocks of your fields, that they may increase. But this is not all; ye must pour out your souls in your closets and your secret places and in your wilderness; yea, and when you do not cry unto the Lord, let your hearts be full, drawn out in prayer unto him continually for your welfare, and also for the welfare of those who are around you. And now, behold, my beloved brethren, I say unto you, do not suppose this is all, for after ye have done all these things, if ye turn away the needy and the naked, and visit not the sick and afflicted, and impart of your substance, if ye have, to those who stand in need; I say unto you, if ye do not anything of these things, behold, your prayer is vain and availeth you nothing, and ye are as hypocrites who deny the faith." [Alma 34:18–28.]

I think that is very excellent doctrine, and I read it to impress upon your minds the season of prayer. The season of prayer is in the morning before the family separates. A good time for prayer is when you assemble at the table before you partake of the morning meal, and let the members of the family take turn in the praying. That is the season of prayer. The season of prayer for the merchant is in the morning when he goes to his place of business and before he begins his day's work, over his merchandise. The time of prayer for the shepherd, is when he is out with his flocks watching over them. The time for the farmer to pray is when he goes with his plow into the field, when he goes to sow his grain, and when he goes to gather his harvest. And if a man will pray as he is commanded to do in this passage of scripture which I have read, then he more than likely will be found in all things righteously keeping the commandments of the Lord.[9]

3

All we do should be in harmony with the expressions of our prayers.

We should not pray merely with our lips; but in every act, in our conversation, in all that we undertake to do, we should try to carry out the expressions of our prayers, and be in harmony with the thoughts that we declare to the Lord in our daily supplications.[10]

Are we in possession of the spirit of prayer? Have we made it a part of our very being? Are we in touch with our heavenly Father through the Holy Spirit, or are we not?[11]

⟨⟨ 4 ⟩⟩

In our prayers we should pour out our souls in thanksgiving.

How careful we should be to cultivate, through the medium of a prayerful life, a thankful attitude. I believe that one of the greatest sins of which the inhabitants of the earth are guilty today is the sin of ingratitude, the want [or lack] of acknowledgment, on their part, of the Lord and his right to govern and control.[12]

In our prayers we should pour out our souls in thanksgiving for life and being, for the redeeming sacrifice of the Son of God, for the gospel of salvation, for Joseph Smith and the mighty work of restoration brought to pass through him. We should acknowledge the hand of the Lord in all things and thank him for all things both temporal and spiritual.[13]

⟨⟨ 5 ⟩⟩

We should plead with Heavenly Father for all our righteous desires.

We should plead with [Heavenly Father] for faith and integrity and for every godly attribute, for the triumph and success of his work, for the guidance of his Holy Spirit, and for salvation in his kingdom. We should pray for our families, for our wives and children, for food and shelter and clothing, for our business concerns, and for all our righteous desires.[14]

I pray that the blessings of heaven may be and abide with us and all men.

O that the heavens might pour down righteousness and truth upon all the world!

O that all men everywhere might have a listening ear, and that they might heed the words of truth and light which come from the Lord's servants!

O that the Lord's purposes among all people in every nation might speedily be fulfilled!

I pray for the members of the Church, who are the saints of the Most High, that they may be strengthened in their faith, and that desires for righteousness may increase in their hearts, and that they may work out their salvation with fear and trembling before the Lord [see Philippians 2:12; Mormon 9:27].

I pray for the good and the upright among all people, that they may be led to seek truth, to sustain every true principle, and to further the cause of freedom and justice.

In these troublesome and difficult times, I pray that all men may be guided by that light which lighteth every man who cometh into the world [see John 1:9; D&C 93:2], and that they may gain thereby the wisdom to solve the problems which beset mankind.

I beseech a gracious Father to pour out his blessings upon all men, upon the young and old, upon those who have cause to mourn, upon the hungry and needy, upon those who are entrapped in unfortunate circumstances and unwholesome environments, and upon all who need aid, and help, and succor, and wisdom, and all those good and great things that only he can give.

Along with all of you, I have love and concern and compassion for our Father's children in all the earth, and pray that their conditions may be bettered both temporally and spiritually; I pray that they may come unto Christ, and learn of him, and take his yoke upon them, that they may find rest to their souls, for his yoke is easy and his burden is light [see Matthew 11:29–30].

I pray that the Latter-day Saints and all who will join with them in keeping the commandments of the Father of us all may so live as to gain peace in this life and eternal life in the world to come [see D&C 59:23]—all of which I ask in humility and in thanksgiving, and in the name of the Lord Jesus Christ. Amen.[15]

Suggestions for Study and Teaching

Questions

- "From the Life of Joseph Fielding Smith" contains four examples of prayers offered by President Smith. What can we learn from each of these examples?

- Reflect upon your personal approach to prayer. What can we do so that our prayers will help us draw "nearer to our Father in heaven"? (See section 1.)

- President Smith taught, "The season for prayer is always" (section 2). In what ways can we follow the counsel to pray always?

- What does it mean to you to "carry out the expressions of our prayers"? (See section 3.) Think about what you can do to improve in this area.

- How does our attitude change when we "pour out our souls in thanksgiving" to our Heavenly Father? (See section 4.)

- As you study President Smith's prayer in section 5, consider your own prayers. Silently ponder this question: What people and matters should you include more often in your prayers?

Related Scriptures

Matthew 7:7–8; Philippians 4:6; 1 Thessalonians 5:17–18; James 1:5–6; 2 Nephi 32:8–9; Alma 34:38–39; 3 Nephi 18:18–21; D&C 10:5

Teaching Help

"To encourage discussion, use the questions at the end of each chapter. You may also develop your own questions especially for those you are teaching" (from page vi in this book).

Notes

1. In Conference Report, Apr. 1918, 156.

2. In Joseph Fielding Smith Jr. and John J. Stewart, *The Life of Joseph Fielding Smith* (1972), 162–63; italics in original.

3. Joseph Fielding Smith Jr. and John J. Stewart, *The Life of Joseph Fielding Smith,* 232–33.

4. In Conference Report, Apr. 1970, 6.

5. Boyd K. Packer, "Covenants," *Ensign,* Nov. 1990, 84; italics removed from original.

6. *Answers to Gospel Questions,* comp. Joseph Fielding Smith Jr., 5 vols. (1957–66), 3:83–85.

7. In Conference Report, Apr. 1968, 10; italics in original.

8. "President Joseph Fielding Smith Speaks on the New MIA Theme," *New Era,* Sept. 1971, 40.

9. In Conference Report, Oct. 1919, 142–43.

10. In Conference Report, Oct. 1913, 73.

11. In Conference Report, Apr. 1918, 156.

12. In Conference Report, Oct. 1969, 110.

13. "President Joseph Fielding Smith Speaks on the New MIA Theme," 40.

14. "President Joseph Fielding Smith Speaks on the New MIA Theme," 40.

15. In Conference Report, Apr. 1970, 149.

"The Lord . . . expects us to have knowledge of temporal things."

Individual Responsibility

"We expect our members everywhere to learn correct principles and to govern themselves."

From the Life of Joseph Fielding Smith

Brother D. Arthur Haycock was walking toward the Church Administration Building one day when he saw that President Joseph Fielding Smith was unlocking the side door. Needing to enter the building, where he worked as the secretary to the Quorum of the Twelve Apostles, Brother Haycock "hurried up the stairs, two or three at a time, to get his foot in the door before it closed. He barely made it. As he got inside the building he hurried again to catch up with President Smith to walk to the elevator with him. He commented to him, 'I hope I can be that lucky to squeeze into heaven through the door you open.'" At first President Smith did not reply, and Brother Haycock worried that in his attempt to be humorous, he had said something wrong. But "as they reached the elevator President Smith said, with a twinkle in his eye, 'Now, brother, don't ever count on that!'"[1]

Through sermons and actions, President Smith repeatedly taught the principle he shared with Brother Haycock: He emphasized that although Latter-day Saints should diligently help others receive the blessings of the gospel, salvation is an individual responsibility. He also encouraged the Saints to be self-reliant and to work industriously in temporal pursuits. "That is what life is all about," he said, "to develop our potential, and especially to gain self-mastery."[2]

Joseph Fielding Smith learned to work when he was a young boy. His father was often away from home, so "he spent much of his childhood doing the work of an adult." In fact, he was such a diligent worker that he "unwittingly inherited one job earlier than he need have, when in boyish pride he secretly milked one of the family cows to prove he was capable of doing it, and thus was assigned the job permanently."[3]

His willingness to work continued when he served a full-time mission in England. His wife Louie wrote the following to him while he was there: "I know that you love duty far more than you do pleasure and so I have so much love and trust that I feel as though you are about as near being a perfect young man as could be."[4] In addition to fulfilling his duty to teach the gospel to others, he worked hard to learn the gospel himself. In one letter he sent home, he told of his efforts to memorize a scripture passage: "I have tried all day to learn a passage of scripture and have not got it yet. But I am determined to learn it before I am through."[5]

President Smith passed his work ethic on to his children. He told them: "People die in bed. And so does ambition." With this principle in mind, he and his wife made sure the children arose early every morning and did their part to keep the home clean and organized. "Somehow it seemed immoral to Dad for us to lie in bed after six o'clock," recalled one of his sons. "Of course I only tried it once. Father saw to that."[6] President Smith helped around the house as well. When he and Louie were newly married, he did as much work as he could on the construction of their first home. Over the years, he did most home repairs himself, helped in the kitchen, and helped pick fruit in season and preserve it in bottles.[7]

Brother Haycock, the same man who once rushed to follow President Smith into the Church Administration Building, later became the personal secretary to five Presidents of the Church, including President Smith. In this close association, he saw President Smith's continual efforts to improve himself spiritually. He said that he often walked into President Smith's office and found the prophet studying the scriptures or reading another book.[8]

Teachings of Joseph Fielding Smith

―――――――――――――― 1 ――――――――――――――

The Lord expects us to be industrious in seeking temporal and spiritual blessings.

The Lord said to [Adam]: "In the sweat of thy face shalt thou eat bread," [Genesis 3:19; see also Moses 4:25] and all down through the ages the Lord has called upon his people to be diligent, to serve him in faithfulness, to work. . . .

In the early days of the Church in these valleys [in Utah], great stress was placed upon industry by President Brigham Young and the other brethren, and it was necessary because our forefathers came here with nothing. They had to work. They had to be industrious. It was essential that they produce the things they needed, and therefore counsel to that extent and in that direction was given to them constantly that they should be industrious. They were taught not to be proud in their hearts. They came out here where they could worship the Lord their God and keep his commandments. They were told to be humble as well as to be diligent. . . . Oh, I wish we could remember that. I am sorry that we have forgotten. . . .

. . . The Lord said, "Thou shalt not be idle for he that is idle shall not eat the bread, nor wear the garments of the laborer." [D&C 42:42.] That is good sound sense, isn't it? Why should a man in idleness partake of the industry of the industrious—provided that this man who is idle, is in a physical condition that he can work? I am not at all in sympathy with any kind of movement that tends to destroy manhood by encouraging men to be idle, and I don't care what age that is. It doesn't matter how old he gets, if a man is physically strong and is able to perform services, he should take care of himself; that the Lord expects him to do.

The Lord said in another revelation:

"And again, verily I say unto you, that every man who is obliged to provide for his own family, let him provide, and he shall in nowise lose his crown; and let him labor in the Church. Let every man be diligent in all things. And the idler shall not have place in the Church, except he repent and mend his ways." [D&C 75:28–29.]

So that is the counsel the Lord has given the Church today. And this is not merely to be applied to plowing fields, or to reaping and harvesting and engaging in industry, but it means likewise that a man should be industrious in spiritual things as well as in the temporalities by which he makes his living.[9]

We are here for a great purpose. That purpose is not to live 100 years, or less, and plant our fields, reap our crops, gather fruit, live in houses, and surround ourselves with the necessities of mortal life. That is not the purpose of life. These things are necessary to our existence here, and that is the reason why we should be industrious. But how many men spend their time thinking that all there is in life is to accumulate the things of this world, to live in comfort, and surround themselves with all the luxuries, and privileges, and pleasures it is possible for mortal life to bestow, and never give a thought to anything beyond?

Why, all these things are but temporary blessings. We eat to live. We clothe ourselves to keep warm and covered. We have houses to live in for our comfort and convenience, but we ought to look upon all these blessings as temporary blessings needful while we journey through this life. And that is all the good they are to us. We cannot take any of them with us when we depart. Gold, silver and precious stones, which are called wealth, are of no use to man only as they enable him to take care of himself and to meet his necessities here.[10]

The Lord . . . expects us to have knowledge of temporal things so we can care for ourselves temporally; so we can be of service to our fellowmen; and so we can take the gospel message to his other children throughout the world.[11]

The object of our being here is to do the will of the Father as it is done in heaven, to work righteousness in the earth, to subdue wickedness and put it under our feet, to conquer sin and the adversary of our souls, to rise above the imperfections and weaknesses of poor fallen humanity, by the inspiration of the Lord and his power made manifest, and thus become the saints and servants of the Lord in the earth.[12]

_____ ⌒⌒ 2 ⌒⌒ _____

We are ultimately accountable to the Lord for our observance of duty.

We are dealing with our faith and conscience; you are dealing not with me, not with the Presidency of the Church, but with the Lord. I am not dealing with men respecting my tithing—my dealings are with the Lord; that is, with reference to my own conduct in the Church and with reference to my observance of the other laws and rules of the Church. If I fail to observe the laws of the Church, I am responsible to the Lord and will have to answer to him, by and by, for my neglect of duty, and I may have to answer to the Church for my fellowship. If I do my duty, according to my understanding of the requirements that the Lord has made of me, then I ought to have a conscience void of offense. I ought to have satisfaction in my soul that I have simply done my duty as I understand it, and I will accept the consequences. With me, it is a matter between me and the Lord; so it is with every one of us.

He who sent his Only Begotten Son into the world, to accomplish the mission that he did, also sent every soul within the sound of my voice, and indeed every man and woman in the world, to accomplish a mission, and that mission cannot be accomplished by neglect, nor by indifference, nor can it be accomplished by ignorance.

We should learn the obligation that we are under to the Lord and to each other; these things are essential, and we cannot prosper in spiritual things, we cannot grow in knowledge of the Lord or in wisdom, without devoting our thoughts and our efforts toward our own betterment, toward the increase of our own wisdom and knowledge in the things of the Lord.[13]

It is so easy for humankind to blame somebody else for their own mistakes, and so easy for us, because of our human nature, to take credit when the thing that is accomplished is something that pleases and benefits. But we never want to shoulder a responsibility for our mistakes that do not please, and so we endeavor to place that kind of responsibility somewhere else and on others. . . . Let us shoulder our own responsibilities, and not endeavor to place them somewhere else.[14]

"No person, by any decree of the Father, has ever been compelled to do good. . . . Each may act for himself."

⟨⟨⟨ 3 ⟩⟩⟩

God has given us agency and expects us to do all we can for ourselves.

Agency [is] the great gift the Lord has bestowed upon every soul to act for himself, to make his own choice, to be an agent with a power to believe and accept the truth and receive eternal life or to reject the truth and receive remorse of conscience. This is one of the greatest gifts of God. What would we be without it, if we were compelled as some people would like to have their fellows compelled to do their will? There could be no salvation; there could be no rewards of righteousness; no one could be punished for unfaithfulness because men would not be accountable before their Maker.[15]

Joseph Smith was asked how he governed so great and diverse a people as the Latter-day Saints. He replied: "I teach them correct principles and they govern themselves."

This is the principle upon which we operate in the Church. We expect our members everywhere to learn correct principles and to govern themselves.[16]

This great gift of agency, that is the privilege given to man to make his own choice, has never been revoked, and it never will be. It is an eternal principle giving freedom of thought and action to every soul. No person, by any decree of the Father, has ever been compelled to do good; no person has ever been forced to do evil. Each may act for himself. It was Satan's plan to destroy this agency and force men to do his will. There could be no satisfactory existence without this great gift. Men must have the privilege to choose even to the extent that they may rebel against the divine decrees. Of course salvation and exaltation must come through the free will without coercion and by individual merit in order that righteous rewards may be given and proper punishment be meted out to the transgressor.[17]

We believe it is by grace that we are saved after all that we can do, and that building upon the foundation of the atonement of Christ, all men must work out their salvation with fear and trembling before the Lord [see 2 Nephi 25:23; Mormon 9:27].[18]

It is an important fact, shown by direct acts and by implication in all the scriptures, that God has done for men all that men cannot do for themselves to secure salvation, but he expects men to do all for themselves that is in their power.

By this principle it is contrary to the order of heaven instituted before the foundation of the earth, for holy messengers who have passed through the resurrection, or messengers who belong to the heavenly sphere, to come to earth and perform work for men which they can do for themselves. . . .

It is a most serious error to believe that Jesus did everything for men if they would but confess him with their lips, and there is nothing else for them to do. Men have work to do if they would obtain salvation. It was in harmony with this eternal law that the angel directed Cornelius to Peter [see Acts 10], and that Ananias was sent to Paul [see Acts 9:1–22]. It was likewise in obedience to this law that Moroni, who understood the writings upon the Nephite plates, did not do the translating, but under the direction of the Lord, gave to Joseph Smith the Urim and Thummim by which he was able to accomplish that important work by the gift and power of God.[19]

─────────────── ⤖ 4 ⤖ ───────────────

Our two great responsibilities are to seek our own salvation and to work diligently for the salvation of others.

We have these two great responsibilities. . . . First, to seek our own salvation; and, second, our duty to our fellow men. Now I take it that my first duty is, so far as I am individually concerned, to seek my own salvation. That is your individual duty first, and so with every member of this Church.[20]

Our first concern should be our own salvation. We should seek every gospel blessing for ourselves. We should be baptized and enter into the order of celestial marriage so that we can become inheritors in the fulness of our Father's kingdom. Then we should be concerned about our families, our children, and our ancestors.[21]

It is . . . our duty to save the world, the dead as well as the living. We are saving the living who will repent by preaching the gospel among the nations and gathering out the children of Israel, the honest in heart. We are saving the dead by going into the house of the Lord and performing these ceremonies—baptism, the laying on of hands, confirmation, and such other things as the Lord requires at our hands—in their behalf.[22]

It is my duty, as it is your duty, my brethren and my sisters like-wise—for responsibility is placed also upon you—to do the very best that is within our power, and not to shirk, but endeavor with all our soul to magnify the callings the Lord has given us, to labor diligently for the salvation of our own house, each one of us, and for the salvation of our neighbors, the salvation of those who are abroad.[23]

Suggestions for Study and Teaching

Questions

- What impresses you about President Smith's efforts to teach his children to work? (See "From the Life of Joseph Fielding Smith.") What can we do to help children be more responsible?

- How do the teachings in section 1 increase your understanding of self-reliance? Think about what you can do to be more self-reliant.

- Review the counsel in section 2. What does it mean to you to be "responsible to the Lord"?

- President Smith taught, "We expect our members everywhere to learn correct principles and to govern themselves" (section 3). How can this teaching benefit families? How can it guide priesthood quorums and Relief Societies?

- In our efforts to serve others, why do you think "our first concern should be our own salvation"? (See section 4.)

Related Scriptures

Philippians 2:12; 2 Nephi 2:14–16, 25–30; D&C 58:26–28

Teaching Help

"As you teach from this book, invite others to share their thoughts, ask questions, and teach one another. When they actively participate, they will be more prepared to learn and to receive personal revelation" (from pages v–vi in this book).

Notes

1. Joseph Fielding Smith Jr. and John J. Stewart, *The Life of Joseph Fielding Smith* (1972), 358–59.
2. Joseph Fielding Smith, in *The Life of Joseph Fielding Smith*, 10.
3. Joseph Fielding Smith Jr. and John J. Stewart, *The Life of Joseph Fielding Smith*, 51–52.
4. Louie Shurtliff Smith, in *The Life of Joseph Fielding Smith*, 113.
5. Joseph Fielding Smith, in *The Life of Joseph Fielding Smith*, 116.
6. In Joseph Fielding McConkie, "Joseph Fielding Smith," in Leonard J. Arrington, ed. *The Presidents of the Church* (1986),

336–37; see also *The Life of Joseph Fielding Smith,* 217–21.
7. See *The Life of Joseph Fielding Smith,* 12–13, 155–57; Francis M. Gibbons, *Joseph Fielding Smith: Gospel Scholar, Prophet of God* (1992), 202.
8. See Jay M. Todd, "A Day in the Life of President Joseph Fielding Smith," *Ensign,* July 1972, 5.
9. In Conference Report, Apr. 1945, 48–49.
10. "Salvation for the Dead," *Utah Genealogical and Historical Magazine,* Apr. 1926, 154–55; see also *Doctrines of Salvation,* ed. Bruce R. McConkie, 3 vols. (1954–56), 1:68–69.

11. Address at the Logan Utah Institute of Religion, Jan. 10, 1971, 2, Church History Library; unpublished manuscript.

12. In Conference Report, Oct. 1969, 108.

13. In Conference Report, Oct. 1969, 108.

14. In Conference Report, Oct. 1932, 88.

15. In Conference Report, Oct. 1949, 88.

16. In Conference Report, British Area General Conference 1971, 6; see also *Teachings of Presidents of the Church: Joseph Smith* (2007), 284.

17. *Answers to Gospel Questions,* comp. Joseph Fielding Smith Jr., 5 vols. (1957–66), 2:20.

18. "Out of the Darkness," *Ensign,* June 1971, 4.

19. "Priesthood—Restoration of Divine Authority," *Deseret News,* Sept. 2, 1933, Church section, 4; see also *Doctrines of Salvation,* 3:90–91.

20. "The Duties of the Priesthood in Temple Work," *Utah Genealogical and Historical Magazine,* Jan. 1939, 3; see also *Doctrines of Salvation,* 2:145.

21. *Sealing Power and Salvation,* BYU Speeches of the Year (Jan. 12, 1971), 2.

22. In Conference Report, Oct. 1911, 120; see also *Doctrines of Salvation,* 2:192–93.

23. In Conference Report, Apr. 1921, 41.

The Work of Latter-day Saint Women: "Unselfish Devotion to This Glorious Cause"

"There is no limit to the good that our sisters can do."

From the Life of Joseph Fielding Smith

At a general Relief Society meeting on October 2, 1963, President Joseph Fielding Smith said, "We, the Brethren of the Church, honor and respect our good sisters for their unselfish devotion to this glorious cause."[1]

In making this declaration, President Smith spoke from years of experience. He had spent a lifetime serving alongside faithful Latter-day Saint women. This service began in the late 1880s, when he was about 10 years old. At that time, Latter-day Saint women were encouraged to gain an education in medicine and health care. His mother, Julina L. Smith, followed this counsel and received training to serve as a midwife. She often awoke him in the middle of the night so he could drive their horse-drawn carriage to a home where a baby was about to be born. Serving with his mother in this way, young Joseph Fielding Smith saw an example of the strength and compassion of the women of the Church.[2] Sister Smith later served as a counselor in the Relief Society general presidency.

President Smith had great respect for the Relief Society, which he said "is a vital part of the kingdom of God on earth."[3] His second wife, Ethel, served as a member of the general Relief Society board for 21 years. Sister Amy Brown Lyman, who served with Ethel on the board and later served as general Relief Society president, said: "Sister Smith was one of the most brilliant women I ever knew. I considered her the finest writer and speaker [on the] board."[4] In this capacity, Ethel attended stake conferences to provide instruction for

*Throughout the history of the Church, women have played
essential roles in the Lord's latter-day work.*

local Relief Society sisters. She and President Smith went on some Church assignments together, and the two of them often shared the pulpit to teach the members.[5]

After Ethel died, President Smith married Jessie Evans. Jessie went with him almost every time he traveled to teach the Saints. She had a beautiful singing voice, and President Smith always wanted her to sing at the meetings they attended. Elder Francis M. Gibbons, who served as a secretary to the First Presidency, recounted: "Whenever Joseph Fielding presided, he wanted her to perform if for no other reason than that he never tired of hearing her sing. Beyond that, however, her well-trained contralto voice, singing sacred hymns, added a special touch of spirituality to the meetings, inspiring the listeners and elevating his own capabilities in delivering the spoken word. Later, through the persistent and playful urging of his wife, Joseph would occasionally join Jessie in a duet, blending his own fine baritone voice with hers. On these occasions, they would usually sit together on the piano bench while Jessie played the accompaniment, moderating her usual, full-throated voice so as not to drown out the singing of her husband."[6]

As President of the Church, Joseph Fielding Smith regularly worked with Sister Belle S. Spafford, the Relief Society general president. Sister Spafford later spoke of her experience working with him: "President Joseph Fielding Smith, a man of tenderness and great love for the people, evidenced at all times a depth of understanding of the work of the women of the Church, and he passed this on to the Relief Society presidency countless times and in many ways, opening our vision and directing our ways."[7]

Teachings of Joseph Fielding Smith

1

The scriptures tell of faithful women who have had responsibilities in the Lord's Church.

We may read in the Pearl of Great Price that after the consequences brought upon Adam and Eve by the fall, Eve preached the discourse. It is brief but wonderfully full of meaning and is as follows:

". . . Were it not for our transgression we never should have had seed, and never should have known good and evil, and the joy of our redemption, and the eternal life which God giveth unto all the obedient." [Moses 5:11.]

"And Adam and Eve blessed the name of God, and *they* made all things known unto their sons and their daughters." [Moses 5:12; italics added.]

We learn from this that Eve as well as Adam received revelation and commandment to teach their children in the ways of eternal life.[8]

We read that in [early] days of Israel women were active and had duties to perform [see Exodus 15:20; Judges 4–5].[9]

In the New Testament we read of a great number of faithful women who sought and gave counsel. Many of these followed the Lord and ministered to him [see Luke 8:1–3; 10:38–42].[10]

2

In the latter days, Relief Society sisters play vital roles in the restored Church of Jesus Christ.

On the 17th day of March, 1842, the Prophet Joseph Smith met with a number of the sisters of the Church in Nauvoo and organized them into a society which was given the name of "The Female Relief Society of Nauvoo." . . . That this organization was by revelation, there can be no doubt. This truth has been abundantly demonstrated throughout the years and today its value and necessity are abundantly attested.[11]

Surely the Church of Jesus Christ would not have been completely organized had not this wonderful organization come into existence. . . . This restoration would not have been complete without the Relief Society in which the sisters are able to accomplish a divinely appointed service so essential to the welfare of the Church.[12]

The "Female Relief Society of Nauvoo" was organized by the Prophet Joseph Smith assisted by Elder John Taylor. The Lord had revealed that the women of the Church should be organized into a society, for there was important work for them to do in aiding to "bring forth and establish the cause of Zion." [D&C 6:6.] This labor of the sisters was primarily to be for the benefit, encouragement, and advancement of the women of the Church that they might be prepared in all things for a place in the celestial kingdom. The responsibility was also given them to aid in the work of mercy and relief from distress and suffering of the poor, the sick, and afflicted throughout the Church. All through the years since that organization, the sisters of this society have been true to their calling and have magnified themselves in their faithfulness in that work. No task assigned has been too hard; no responsibility neglected, and through their ministrations thousands have been blessed.[13]

The Relief Society . . . has grown to be a power in the Church. Absolutely necessary—we speak of it as an auxiliary, which means a help, but the Relief Society is more than that. It is needed.[14]

I wish to commend the sisters of this great organization for their integrity and faithfulness which have been manifest constantly since the days of Nauvoo.[15]

The Lord is pleased with your labors. You, through your service, have helped to build up and strengthen the kingdom of God. Just as necessary is the labor of the Relief Society in the Church as it is—shall I say?—with the quorums of the Priesthood. Now some may feel that I am expressing this a little too strongly, but my own judgment is that the work that you, our good sisters, are doing, finds its place and is just as important in the building up of this kingdom, strengthening it, causing it to expand, laying a foundation upon which we all may build, just as much as it is for the brethren who hold the Priesthood of God. We can't get along without you.[16]

[Relief Society sisters] are members of the greatest women's organization in the world, an organization which is a vital part of the kingdom of God on earth and which is so designed and operated that it helps its faithful members to gain eternal life in our Father's kingdom. . . .

The Relief Society was established by the spirit of inspiration, has been guided by that spirit [ever since], and has instilled into the hearts of countless of our good sisters those desires for righteousness which have been pleasing to the Lord.[17]

Relief Society is "the greatest women's organization in the world, an organization which is a vital part of the kingdom of God on earth."

---◇◇◇ 3 ◇◇◇---

Relief Society sisters help look after the temporal and spiritual welfare of God's children.

The Lord through his wisdom has called upon our sisters to be aids to the Priesthood. Because of their sympathy, tenderness of heart, and kindness, the Lord looks upon them and gives unto them the duties and responsibilities of being ministers to the needy and to the afflicted. He has pointed out the path which they should follow, and he has given to them this great organization where they have authority to serve under the directions of the bishops of the wards and in harmony with the bishops of the wards, looking after the interest of our people both spiritually and temporally.

And the Lord can call upon our sisters to go into the homes to comfort the needy, to aid and assist the afflicted, to kneel with them and pray with them, and the Lord will hearken to the sisters' prayers when they are offered sincerely in behalf of the sick, just as he will listen to the prayers of the elders of the Church.[18]

The purpose and duties of the Relief Society are many. . . . My father, President Joseph F. Smith [said:] "This is an organization that was established by the Prophet Joseph Smith. It is, therefore, the oldest auxiliary organization of the Church, and it is of the first importance. It has not only to deal with the necessities of the poor, the sick and the needy, but a part of its duty—and the larger part, too—is to look after the spiritual welfare and salvation of the mothers and daughters of Zion; to see that none is neglected, but that all are guarded against misfortune, calamity, the powers of darkness, and the evils that threaten them in the world. It is the duty of the Relief Societies to look after the spiritual welfare of themselves and of all the female members of the Church."[19]

It is the duty of the Relief Society, not only to look after those who are members of the Relief Society, but their labor should extend beyond those borders. Wherever anybody is in trouble, needs help, in difficulties, sick or afflicted, we call upon the Relief Society. . . . They can perform a great and wonderful work by encouraging the wayward, helping them, bringing them back into activity, helping them to overcome their weaknesses or sins and imperfections, and bringing them to an understanding of the truth. I say there is no limit to the good that our sisters can do.

. . . I don't know what in the world our stake presidents and bishops in the wards would do if they didn't have these good sisters of the Relief Society upon whom to depend; whom they can call to their service, many times, to handle situations that would be very delicate, that is for our brethren, but which our sisters may perform to the very greatest advantage. It would be a wonderful thing if all the members of the Church were perfect. If that were the case we would all have less responsibility, both the men and the women, but that time has not come. We have members among our sisters who need encouragement, a little help spiritually as well as temporally, and nobody can do it better than our sisters who belong to this great and wonderful organization.

In this work the sisters may lend their aid in encouraging and helping the wayward, indifferent, the careless, just as the brethren of the Priesthood are called upon to do in behalf of the wayward, careless, and indifferent among the brethren. We should all work to bring to pass righteousness and endeavor to bring back into activity those who have drifted and neglected the duties of the Church.[20]

From [its] humble start under the most difficult conditions, when the membership of the Church was small, we have seen this Society grow. . . . The good that has been accomplished in the care of the poor, care of the sick and the afflicted, and those who are in physical, mental, or spiritual need, will never correctly be known. . . . All of this has been accomplished through the spirit of love in accordance with the true spirit of the gospel of Jesus Christ.[21]

4

The Lord expects women to seek for light and truth that they may be entitled to celestial glory.

The gospel means just as much to our sisters as it does to the brethren. They are just as much concerned in it as are the brethren. And when the Lord said to the Prophet Joseph Smith, "Search these commandments, for they are true and faithful, and the prophecies and promises which are in them shall all be fulfilled," [D&C 1:37] he did not limit that commandment to the male members of the Church. . . . It is just as important that our sisters understand the Plan of Salvation as it is for the men. It is just as essential that they keep the commandments. No woman is going to be saved in the kingdom of God without baptism for the remission of sins and the laying on of hands for the gift of the Holy Ghost. . . .

. . .When the Lord said that no person could be saved in ignorance [see D&C 131:6], I think he meant women as well as he did men, and I think the women of the church are under the obligation of studying the scriptures.[22]

The Lord requires of the women, as well as of the men in the Church, that they know his divine will and have an abiding testimony in their hearts of the revealed truth pertaining to salvation in the kingdom of God. The Lord did not reveal The Book of Mormon for the benefit of those who hold the Priesthood only, but for every soul who seeks the truth, male and female alike.[23]

The Lord expects the sisters to be qualified with a testimony of the truth to understand the doctrines of the Church just as he does those who hold the Priesthood. If we gain exaltation, which we hope to obtain, it is necessary that we prepare ourselves by knowledge, by faith, by prayer. And when the Lord said, "Seek ye first the kingdom of God and his righteousness," [Matthew 6:33; 3 Nephi 13:33] he was not talking just to a body of men, it was a mixed congregation.[24]

Every woman baptized into the Church has the hands of the elders laid on her head for the gift of the Holy Ghost that she may have the guidance of that Spirit in all truth. It is the will of the Lord that none may be without divine guidance which will reveal to them the truth and enable them to discern the light from the darkness and, thus, be fortified and given power to resist all false doctrines, theories, and notions, which are so prevalent in the world today.[25]

Our sisters are entitled just as much to the inspiration for their needs of the Holy Spirit as are the men, every bit. They are entitled to the gift of prophecy concerning matters that would be essential for them to know. . . . When they pray they should pray earnestly, expecting to have an answer to their prayers. The Lord will hear them, if they are earnest, true, just as well as he will the brethren.[26]

The Lord has promised to all, males and females alike, the gift of the Holy Ghost on conditions of faithfulness, humility, and true repentance. They are required to study and to know the truths of the gospel and to prepare themselves by study, faith, and obedience to all commandments to seek for light and truth that they may be entitled to celestial glory.[27]

5

Through the priesthood, God offers to His daughters every spiritual gift and blessing that can be obtained by His sons.

I think we all know that the blessings of the priesthood are not confined to men alone. These blessings are also poured out . . . upon all the faithful women of the Church. These good sisters can

"The Lord requires of the women . . . in the Church, that they know his divine will and have an abiding testimony in their hearts."

prepare themselves, by keeping the commandments and by serving in the Church, for the blessings of the house of the Lord. The Lord offers to his daughters every spiritual gift and blessing that can be obtained by his sons, for neither is the man without the woman, nor the woman without the man in the Lord [see 1 Corinthians 11:11].[28]

We are all aware that the Lord told Abraham he would be a father of many nations and that his seed would be like the stars of the heaven and as the sand which is upon the seashore in number, but what we must not overlook is that the same promises were made to Sarah.

"And God said unto Abraham, As for Sarai thy wife, thou shalt not call her name Sarai, but Sarah shall her name be. And I will bless her, and give thee a son also of her: yea, I will bless her, and she shall be a mother of nations; kings of people shall be of her." [Genesis 17:15–16.][29]

The Lord, speaking of the priesthood and the power of the priesthood, and the ordinances of the Church which we receive through the priesthood, had this to say: "And this greater priesthood administereth the gospel and holdeth the key of the mysteries of the kingdom, even the key of the knowledge of God."

. . . Let me read that again: "And this greater priesthood administereth the gospel and holdeth the key of the mysteries of the kingdom, even the key of the knowledge of God. Therefore, in the ordinances thereof, the power of Godliness is manifest. And without the ordinances thereof and the authority of the priesthood, the power of Godliness is not manifest unto men in the flesh; for without this, no man can see the face of God, even the Father and live." [D&C 84:19–22.]

When we read things of this nature, it ought to make every man among us who holds the priesthood rejoice to think that we have that great authority by which we may know God. Not only the men holding the priesthood know that great truth, but because of that priesthood and the ordinances thereof, every member of the Church, men and women alike, may know God.[30]

Suggestions for Study and Teaching

Questions

- What can we learn from the experiences described in "From the Life of Joseph Fielding Smith"? What similar experiences have you had?

- President Smith spoke of women in different eras who have fulfilled important responsibilities in the kingdom of God (see section 1). In what ways have you seen women contribute to the strength of their families and the Church?

- How have you seen that Relief Society service is "essential to the welfare of the Church"? (See section 2.) In what ways do Relief Society sisters and priesthood bearers work together to build up the kingdom of God?

- In what ways does the Relief Society look after the spiritual welfare of Latter-day Saint women? In what ways do Relief Society sisters extend their influence beyond their organization? (For some examples, see section 3.)

- President Smith emphasized that all women and men need to understand gospel doctrines, strengthen their testimonies, and receive revelation (see section 4). Why do you think it is important for all of us to seek these gifts?

- President Smith taught that the blessings of the priesthood are "poured out . . . upon all the faithful women of the Church" (section 5). Why do women need the blessings of the priesthood to carry out their responsibilities in the home and in the Church? What examples have you seen of women receiving spiritual gifts?

Related Scriptures

Acts 5:12–14; Alma 32:22–23; D&C 46:8–9

Teaching Help

"It is often helpful to begin thinking about an upcoming lesson soon after you have taught the preceding lesson. You will probably be most aware of those you teach and their needs and interests immediately after you have been with them" (*Teaching, No Greater Call* [1999], 97).

Notes

1. "Purpose of the Relief Society," *Relief Society Magazine,* Jan. 1964, 5.

2. For more about Joseph Fielding Smith helping his mother with her duties as a midwife, see chapter 20 in this book.

3. "Mothers in Israel," *Relief Society Magazine,* Dec. 1970, 883.

4. Amy Brown Lyman, in Joseph Fielding Smith and John J. Stewart, *The Life of Joseph Fielding Smith* (1972), 243.

5. See Francis M. Gibbons, *Joseph Fielding Smith: Gospel Scholar, Prophet of God* (1992), 261.

6. Francis M. Gibbons, *Joseph Fielding Smith: Gospel Scholar, Prophet of God,* 281.

7. Belle S. Spafford, *Latter-day Prophet-Presidents I Have Known* (speech given at Brigham Young University, May 29, 1973), 4.

8. *Answers to Gospel Questions,* comp. Joseph Fielding Smith Jr., 5 vols. (1957–66), 3:66.

9. "The Relief Society Organized by Revelation," *Relief Society Magazine,* Jan. 1965, 5.

10. *Answers to Gospel Questions,* 3:67.

11. "Purpose of the Relief Society," 4.

12. "The Relief Society Organized by Revelation," 6.

13. "Relief Society Responsibilities," *Relief Society Magazine,* Oct. 1954, 644.

14. "Relief Society—An Aid to the Priesthood," *Relief Society Magazine,* Jan. 1959, 4.

15. "Relief Society Responsibilities," *Relief Society Magazine,* Oct. 1954, 646.

16. "Relief Society—An Aid to the Priesthood," 6; punctuation standardized.

17. "Mothers in Israel," 883.

18. "Relief Society—An Aid to the Priesthood," 5.

19. "Teaching the Gospel," *Relief Society Magazine,* Jan. 1966, 5; see also Joseph F. Smith, in Conference Report, Apr. 1906, 3.

20. "Relief Society Responsibilities," *Relief Society Magazine,* Mar. 1954, 151–52.

21. "Purpose of the Relief Society," 5.

22. "Obedience to the Truth," *Relief Society Magazine,* Jan. 1960, 6–7.

23. "Relief Society Responsibilities," *Relief Society Magazine,* Oct. 1954, 644.

24. "Relief Society Responsibilities," *Relief Society Magazine,* Mar. 1954, 152.

25. "Relief Society Responsibilities," *Relief Society Magazine,* Oct. 1954, 644.

26. "Obedience to the Truth," 7.

27. *Answers to Gospel Questions,* 3:68–69.

28. In Conference Report, Apr. 1970, 59.

29. "Mothers in Israel," 885.

30. "And the Truth Shall Make You Free," *Deseret News,* Mar. 30, 1940, Church section, 4; see also *Doctrines of Salvation,* comp. Bruce R. McConkie, 3 vols. (1954–56), 3:142–43.

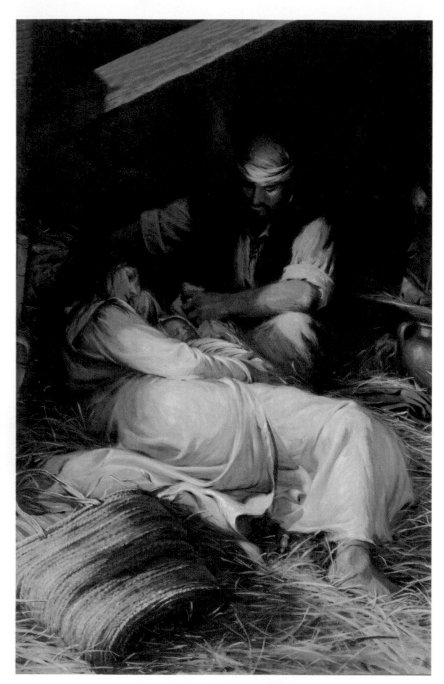

The story of the Savior's birth "never grows old no matter how often told."

The Birth of Jesus Christ: "Good Tidings of Great Joy"

"What of this wonderful story? Have we permitted it to permeate and influence our lives? Have we accepted it in its full meaning without reservations?"

From the Life of Joseph Fielding Smith

During the Christmas season of 1971, a newspaper reporter had the opportunity to spend time with President Joseph Fielding Smith and members of his family. The reporter shared a glimpse into the prophet's life:

"Christmas is a special time for President Joseph Fielding Smith. It is a day for family and a day for remembering. But, most of all for President Smith, Christmas is a day for children.

"'I think the thing I like most about Christmas is the children,' President Smith said, as he squeezed his great-granddaughter closer to him.

"With a large picture Bible nestled on his lap, President Smith and two of his great-granddaughters, Shanna McConkie, 4, and Sherri, 2, turned the pages that told of the Christ child's birth. They lingered for a long time on the page with the picture of the manger scene. There was a closeness between President Smith and the girls. . . .

"President Smith has enjoyed many family visitors during the Christmas season. 'Christmas is a time for families to be together,' he said."[1]

For President Smith, Christmas traditions centered on the Savior's birth, ministry, and Atonement. In response to Christmas greetings he received from Church members, he said: "I appreciate the

311

thoughtfulness of those who send Christmas cards. I regard them as an expression of love and a reminder of the birth of the Savior whom we honor and worship as the head of the church. His message was of peace and good will. This is my wish to my fellowmen everywhere."[2]

In December 1970, President Smith published a Christmas message for Church members throughout the world. In part, he said:

"I greet you at this Christmas Season, in love and fellowship, and with a prayer that our Eternal Father will look down upon you in mercy and pour out His bounteous blessings upon you.

"In these times when iniquity abounds, when there are great tribulations on the earth, when there are wars and rumors of wars, we are all in need, as never before, of the guiding and preserving care of the Lord.

"We need to know that in spite of all the troubles and ills which befall us, still the Lord is governing in the affairs of the earth and that if we keep His commandments and are true and faithful to His laws, He will bless us here and now and reward us with eternal life in His kingdom in due course. . . .

". . . I now pray that at this Christmas Season, and at all times, we may center our faith in the Son of God and gain for ourselves that peace which passeth understanding."[3]

Teachings of Joseph Fielding Smith

<hr>

1

The story of the birth of our Redeemer is eloquent in its humble simplicity.

There is no story quite as beautiful, or which can stir the soul of the humble quite to the depths, as this glorious story can of the birth of our Redeemer. No words that man may utter can embellish or improve or add to the eloquence of its humble simplicity. It never grows old no matter how often told, and the telling of it is by far too infrequent in the homes of men. Let us try to imagine ourselves out with the shepherds who were watching over their flock that memorable night. These were humble men who had not lost the faith of their fathers, whose hearts had not become hardened as were the hearts of the rulers of the Jews in the days of our Lord's ministry, for had they been, the angels would not have appeared to them with their glorious message. Let us repeat this wondrous story.

"And there were in the same country shepherds abiding in the field, keeping watch over their flock by night.

"And, lo, the angel of the Lord came upon them, and the glory of the Lord shone round about them: and they were sore afraid.

"And the angel said unto them, Fear not: for, behold, I bring you good tidings of great joy, which shall be to all people.

"For unto you is born this day in the city of David a Savior, which is Christ the Lord.

"And this shall be a sign unto you; ye shall find the babe wrapped in swaddling clothes, lying in a manger.

"And suddenly there was with the angel a multitude of the heavenly host praising God, and saying,

"Glory to God in the highest, and on earth peace, good will towards men.

"And it came to pass, as the angels were gone away from them into heaven, the shepherds said one to another, Let us now go even unto Bethlehem, and see this thing which is come to pass, which the Lord hath made known unto us.

"And they came with haste, and found Mary, and Joseph, and the babe lying in a manger." [Luke 2:8–16.]

Can any soul read this and not be touched with the spirit of humility and be impressed with the simple truth of the story?[4]

2

Although Jesus Christ was the Son of God, He came into this world as a baby and progressed from grace to grace until He received a fulness.

I suppose that we all understand the fact that Jesus Christ was Jehovah, who led Israel in the days of Abraham and Moses, and in fact from the days of Adam. Also that Jehovah, or Jesus Christ, as a personage of Spirit appeared to the Brother of Jared, and that he was born a babe in this world and grew to manhood in this world.[5]

In His youth, Jesus gained knowledge
"line upon line and precept upon precept."

Our Savior was a God before he was born into this world, and he brought with him that same status when he came here. He was as much a God when he was born into the world as he was before. But as far as this life is concerned it appears that he had to start just as all other children do and gain his knowledge line upon line. Luke says he "increased in wisdom and stature, and in favour with God and man." [Luke 2:52.] John records that "he received not of the fulness at the first," but had to progress "from grace to grace, until he received a fulness." [D&C 93:13.] . . .

Evidently, before he was 12 years old—for then he astonished the doctors and wise men in the temple—he had learned a great deal about his Father's business [see Luke 2:46–49]. This knowledge could come to him by revelation, by the visitation of angels, or in some other way. But his knowledge, so far as this life was concerned, had to come line upon line and precept upon precept. Without question he was in communication, from time to time, with his Heavenly Father.

. . . "Jesus grew up with his brethren, and waxed strong, and waited upon the Lord for the time of his ministry to come. And he served under his father, and he spake not as other men, neither could he be taught; for he needed not that any man should teach him. And after many years, the hour of his ministry drew nigh." [Joseph Smith Translation, Matthew 3:24–26.]

The statement of our Lord that he could do nothing but what he had seen the Father do, means simply that it had been revealed to him what his Father had done [see John 5:19–20]. Without doubt, Jesus came into the world subject to the same condition as was required of each of us—he forgot everything, and he had to grow from grace to grace. His forgetting, or having his former knowledge taken away, would be requisite just as it is in the case of each of us, to complete the present temporal existence.

The Savior did not have a fulness at first, but after he received his body and the resurrection all power was given unto him both in heaven and in earth. Although he was a God, even the Son of God, with power and authority to create this earth and other earths, yet there were some things lacking which he did not receive until after his resurrection. In other words he had not received the fulness until he got a resurrected body.[6]

<hr>

3

Jesus Christ came into this world to redeem us from physical and spiritual death.

Jesus came here to fulfill a definite mission which was assigned to him before the foundation of this earth was laid. He is spoken of in the scriptures as "the Lamb slain from the foundation of the world." [Revelation 13:8.] He volunteered to come, in the Meridian of Time, to redeem men from the fall which would come upon them through the transgression of Adam.

. . . Jesus is the only person born into this world who did not have an earthly father. The Father of his body is also the Father of his Spirit, and the Father of the spirits of all men. From his Father he obtained eternal life; from his mother he obtained the power to die, for his mother was a mortal woman. From her he got his blood, and from his Father he got his immortality. Thus having the power to lay down his life and take it again, he was able to pay the price of Adam's transgression, and redeem all creatures from the grave.[7]

The true reason for the coming of Jesus Christ into the world . . . was, first, to redeem *all* men from the physical or mortal death, which Adam brought into the world, and second, to redeem all men from spiritual death or banishment from the presence of the Lord on conditions of their repentance and remission of sins and endurance to the end of the mortal probation.[8]

We rejoice in the birth of the Son of God among men.

We are grateful for the atoning sacrifice He worked out by the shedding of His own blood.

We are thankful that He has redeemed us from death and opened the door so that we may gain eternal life.

We pray for peace on earth, for the spread of the gospel, and for the final triumph of truth.

We plead with our Father's children everywhere to join with us in doing those things which will give us all peace in this world and eternal glory in the world to come [see D&C 59:23].[9]

―――――――――――― 4 ――――――――――――

We should permit the story of the Savior's birth to permeate and influence our lives.

When [Christmas morning] comes some will bow their heads in humble supplication to the Father of Lights for the blessings they have received through the sufferings of his beloved Son, and will read the wondrous story with grateful praise. Others, unfortunately, who know little, if anything at all, of the debt they owe to the Son of God, will celebrate, not in praise and humble prayer, but in blasphemous drunken revelry, without the least thought of the significance of the birth of the Man of Galilee. . . .

How can anyone read this touching story of the birth of Jesus Christ without wishing to forsake his sins? At this season of the year it is well for one and all—the king in his palace, if there are kings in palaces now, the peasant in his humble cottage, the rich and the poor alike—to bow the knee and pay honor to him who was without sin, whose life was spent in sacrifice and sorrow for the benefits of his fellow man; whose blood was shed as a sacrifice for sin. . . .

. . . What of this wonderful story? Have we permitted it to permeate and influence our lives? Have we accepted it in its full meaning without reservations? Do we believe that this babe was in very deed the only begotten Son of God in the flesh? Do we have abiding faith in his mission and are we willing to obediently follow him? If the world had so believed and had sincerely heeded his teachings, then it would not have been torn asunder by strife and wickedness all down through the ages. . . . There has been too much lip-service among the professed followers of the Son of God and too little real worship based upon the integrity of his teachings.

The angel declared to the shepherds on that glorious night, that he brought tidings of great joy which were for all people [see Luke 2:8–10], but quite generally the people everywhere on the face of the earth, have refused to receive the blessings of those tidings. They have not been willing to forsake their sins, to humble themselves and place their lives in harmony with the Master's teachings. . . .

Once again I plead to all men everywhere: Turn from your evil ways to the true worship of the Son of God, that your souls may be saved in his kingdom.[10]

Suggestions for Study and Teaching

Questions

- What do you do in your home to remember the Savior at Christmastime? What can we learn from President Smith's Christmas traditions? (See "From the Life of Joseph Fielding Smith.")

- Why do you think the story of Jesus Christ's birth "never grows old"? (See section 1.)

- Review President Smith's words about Jesus Christ coming to the world as a baby and enduring the difficulties of mortality (see section 2). What are your thoughts and feelings as you ponder the Savior's willingness to do this?

- Ponder the connection between the Savior's birth and the Savior's Atonement (see section 3). How can parents help their children gain this understanding? How can this understanding influence our Christmas traditions?

• What can we do to permit the story of the Savior's birth to "permeate and influence our lives"? (See section 4.)

Related Scriptures

Isaiah 53; Luke 1:26–35; 2; 1 Nephi 11:8–23

Teaching Help

Discussions in small groups "give a large number of people the opportunity to participate in a lesson. Individuals who are usually hesitant to participate might share ideas in small groups that they would not express in front of the entire group" (*Teaching, No Greater Call* [1999], 161).

Notes

1. "A Big Christmas Hug from Pres. Smith," *Church News,* Dec. 25, 1971, 3.

2. "A Big Christmas Hug from Pres. Smith," 3.

3. "Christmas Greetings from President Joseph Fielding Smith to the Members of the Church throughout the World," *Church News,* Dec. 19, 1970, 3.

4. *The Restoration of All Things* (1945), 279–80.

5. Personal correspondence, quoted in *Doctrines of Salvation,* ed. Bruce R. McConkie, 3 vols. (1954–56), 1:11.

6. Personal correspondence, quoted in *Doctrines of Salvation,* 1:32–33.

7. *Answers to Gospel Questions,* comp. Joseph Fielding Smith Jr., 5 vols. (1957–66), 2:134, 136.

8. "The Resurrection," *Improvement Era,* Dec. 1942, 780–81; see also *Doctrines of Salvation,* 2:259.

9. "Christmas Greetings," 3.

10. *The Restoration of All Things,* 278–79, 281–82, 286; punctuation standardized.

Preparing for the Coming of Our Lord

"Prepare ye the way of the Lord, and
make his paths straight, for the hour of
his coming is nigh" (D&C 133:17).

From the Life of Joseph Fielding Smith

President Joseph Fielding Smith once told a group of Latter-day Saints that he was "praying for the end of the world." He said, "If it came tomorrow I would be glad." In response to that declaration, a woman spoke out, loudly enough for others to hear. "Oh, I hope not," she said.

Sharing this experience some time later, President Smith taught:

"Do you not want the end of the world to come?

"Most people have the wrong idea of what is meant by the end of the world. . . .

". . . When Christ comes there will be an end to the world. . . . There will not be any war, any turmoil, envying, lying; there will be no wickedness. Men will learn then to love the Lord and keep His commandments, and if they don't they will not stay here. That's the end of the world, and that is what the Savior prayed for when His disciples came to Him and said, 'Teach us to pray.' What did He do? He taught them, 'Our Father who art in Heaven, hallowed be Thy name, Thy kingdom come, Thy will be done in earth as it is in heaven.' [See Luke 11:1–2.]

"That's what I'm praying for. The Lord was praying for the end of the world, and so am I."[1]

In sermons and writings, President Smith often quoted scriptural prophecies about the last days, the role of Joseph Smith in

"We long for the day when the Prince of Peace shall come."

preparing the way of the Lord, and the Savior's coming to the earth in glory. He expressed his deep feelings about these prophecies in the dedicatory prayer of the Ogden Utah Temple:

"As thou knowest, O our God, we are living in the last days when the signs of the times are being shown forth; when thou art hastening thy work in its time; and when we have already heard the voice of one crying in the wilderness: Prepare ye the way of the Lord and make his paths straight [see Matthew 3:3]. . . .

"O, our Father, we long for the day when the Prince of Peace shall come, when the earth shall rest and righteousness be found again upon her face; and it is our prayer, spoken out of humble and contrite hearts, that we shall abide the day and be found worthy to live with him whom thou hast appointed to stand as King of kings and Lord of lords, to whom be glory and honor and power and might both now and forever."[2]

Teachings of Joseph Fielding Smith

1

The coming of the Lord is near.

We are rapidly approaching the great day of the Lord, that time of "refreshing," when he will come in the clouds of heaven to take vengeance upon the ungodly and prepare the earth for the reign of peace for all those who are willing to abide in his law [see Acts 3:19–20].[3]

Many things have taken place . . . to impress faithful members of the Church with the fact that the coming of the Lord is near. The gospel has been restored. The Church has been fully organized. The priesthood has been conferred upon man. The various dispensations from the beginning have been revealed and their keys and authorities given to the Church. Israel has been and is being gathered to the land of Zion. The Jews are returning to Jerusalem. The gospel is being preached in all the world as a witness to every nation. Temples are being built, and ordinance work for the dead, as well as for the living, is performed in them. The hearts of the children have turned to their fathers, and the children are seeking after their dead. The covenants which the Lord promised to make with Israel in the latter days have been revealed, and thousands of gathered Israel have entered into them. Thus the work of the Lord is advancing, and all these things are signs of the near approach of our Lord. . . .

The words of the prophets are rapidly being fulfilled, but it is done on such natural principles that most of us fail to see it.

Joel promised that the Lord would pour out his spirit upon all flesh: the sons and daughters should prophesy, old men should dream dreams, and young men should see visions [see Joel 2:28–29]. . . .

Among the signs of the last days was an increase of learning. Daniel was commanded to ". . . shut up the words, and seal the book [of his prophecy], even to the time of the end: [and in that day] many shall run to and fro," said he "and knowledge shall be increased." (Dan. 12:4.) Are not the people "running to and fro" today as they never did before in the history of the world? . . .

. . . Is not knowledge increased? Was there ever a time in the history of the world when so much knowledge was poured out upon the people? But sad to say, the words of Paul are true—the people are "ever learning and never able to come to the knowledge of the truth." (2 Tim. 3:7.) . . .

Have we not had numerous rumors of wars? [See D&C 45:26.] Have we not had wars, such wars as the world never saw before? Is there not today commotion among the nations, and are not their rulers troubled? Have not kingdoms been overturned and great changes been made among nations? The whole earth is in commotion. Earthquakes in divers places are reported every day [see D&C 45:33]. . . .

Yet the old world goes on about its business paying very little heed to all the Lord has said and to all the signs and indications that have been given. Men harden their hearts and say ". . . that Christ delayeth his coming until the end of the earth." (D&C 45:26.)[4]

I was asked, not long ago, if I could tell when the Lord would come. I answered, "Yes," and I answer "Yes" now. I know when he will come. He will come tomorrow. We have his word for it. Let me read it:

"Behold, now it is called today until the coming of the Son of Man, and verily it is a day of sacrifice, and a day for the tithing of my people; for he that is tithed shall not be burned at his coming."

Now there is a discourse sufficient on tithing.

"For after today cometh the burning—this is speaking after the manner of the Lord—for verily I say, tomorrow all the proud and they that do wickedly shall be as stubble; and I will burn them up, for I am the Lord of Hosts; and I will not spare any that remain in Babylon." [D&C 64:23–24.]

So the Lord is coming, I say, tomorrow. Then let us be prepared.[5]

2

There will be a judgment when Christ comes.

The parable the Lord taught of the Wheat and the Tares had reference to the last days. According to the story a sower planted good seed in his field, but while he slept the enemy came and sowed tares in the field. When the blades began to show, the servants desired to go and pluck up the tares but the Lord commanded them to let both the wheat and the tares grow up together until the harvest was ripe, lest they root up the tender wheat while destroying the tares. Then at the end of the harvest, they were to go forth and gather the wheat and bind the tares to be burned. In the explanation of this parable, the Lord said to his disciples that "the harvest is the end of the world; and the reapers are the angels." [See Matthew 13:24–30, 36–43; D&C 86.][6]

The tares and the wheat are growing together and have been growing in the same field for all these years, but the day is near at hand when the wheat will be garnered, and the tares likewise will be gathered to be burned, and there will come a separation, the righteous from the wicked, and it behooves each one of us to keep the commandments of the Lord, to repent of our sins, to turn unto righteousness, if there is need of repentance in our hearts.[7]

Build up and strengthen the members of the Church in faith in God; goodness knows we need it. There are so many influences at work to divide us asunder, right among the members of the Church, and there is going to come, one of these days in the near future a

"We are rapidly approaching the great day of the Lord, that time of 'refreshing,' when he will come in the clouds of heaven."

separation of the wheat from the tares, and we are either wheat or tares. We are going to be on one side or the other.[8]

The day will come when we will not have *this* world. It will be changed. We will get a better world. We will get one that is righteous, because when Christ comes, he will cleanse the earth.

Read what is written in our scriptures. Read what he himself has said. When he comes, he will cleanse this earth from all its wickedness, and, speaking of the Church, he has said that he would send his angels and they would gather out of his kingdom, which is the Church, all things that offend [see Matthew 13:41].[9]

[The] great and dreadful day can be no other time but the coming of Jesus Christ to establish his kingdom in power among the righteous on the earth and to cleanse the earth from all iniquity. It will not be a day of fear and to cause dread in the hearts of the righteous, but it will be a great day of fear and terror to the ungodly. This we have learned from the words of our Savior himself, as he taught his disciples [see Matthew 24; Joseph Smith—Matthew 1].[10]

There shall be a judgment when Christ comes. We are informed that the books shall be opened, the dead shall be judged out of the things which are written in the books and among the books will be the book of life [see Revelation 20:12]. We shall see its pages. We shall see ourselves just as we are, and we are to understand with a righteous understanding that the judgments which are meted out to us are just and true, whether we come into the Kingdom of God, . . . to receive these glorious blessings or whether we are banished.[11]

I plead with the Latter-day Saints to stand firm and faithful in the discharge of every duty, keeping the commandments of the Lord, honoring the priesthood, that we may stand when the Lord comes—whether we be living or dead, it matters not,—to be partakers of this glory.[12]

3

To prepare for the coming of the Lord, we need to watch and pray and get our houses in order.

There are many events in the world today which indicate that the great day of the Lord is drawing near when the Redeemer will again appear to set up his kingdom in righteousness preparatory to the millennial reign. In the meantime it is the duty of members of the Church to seek for knowledge and to prepare themselves by study and by faith for the ushering in of that great and glorious day.[13]

We do not need to be worrying about the times and the seasons when Christ shall come, but we do need to watch and pray and be ready.[14]

I get annoyed sometimes at some of our elders who when speaking, say the Lord will come when we all become righteous enough to receive him. The Lord is not going to wait for us to get righteous. When he gets ready to come he is going to come—when the cup of iniquity is full—and if we are not righteous then, it will be just too bad for us for we will be classed among the ungodly, and we will be as stubble to be swept off the face of the earth, for the Lord says wickedness shall not stand.[15]

Shall we slumber on in utter oblivion or indifference to all that the Lord has given us as warning? I say unto you, "Watch therefore: for ye know not what hour your Lord doth come.

"But know this, that if the good man of the house had known in what watch the thief would come, he would have watched, and would not have suffered his house to be broken up.

"Therefore be ye also ready: for in such an hour as ye think not the Son of Man cometh." (Matt. 24:42–44.)

May we heed this warning given by the Lord and get our houses in order and be prepared for the coming of the Lord.[16]

―――――――――――――――――― 4 ――――――――――――――――――

Latter-day Saints can be instruments in God's hands to prepare a people for the Lord's coming.

Would it not be an extraordinarily strange thing if the Lord should come and begin his reign of peace, take vengeance on the wicked, cleansing the earth from sin, and not send messengers to prepare the way before him? Should we expect the Lord to come to judge the world without first giving it warning and preparing the means of escape for all who will repent?

When the angel Moroni visited young Joseph Smith, he prophesied of the Savior's Second Coming (see Joseph Smith—History 1:36–41).

Noah was sent to the world to warn it of the flood. If the people had hearkened they would have escaped. Moses was sent to lead Israel into the promised land, to fulfil the promises made to Abraham. John the Baptist was sent to prepare the way for the coming of Christ. In each instance the call came through the opening of the heavens. Isaiah, Jeremiah and other prophets, were sent to warn Israel and Judah before the scattering and captivity came upon them.

Had they given heed a different page of history would have been written. They had their chance to hear; they were warned and had the means of escape which they rejected.

The Lord promised to have the same interest in humanity preceding his second coming.[17]

Joseph Smith was sent to prepare the way for this second coming, by the proclamation of the fullness of the Gospel and the granting to all men the means of escape from iniquity and transgression.[18]

John on Patmos saw in vision in the last days an "angel fly in the midst of heaven, having the everlasting gospel to preach unto them that dwell on the earth, and to every nation, and kindred, and tongue and people." [Revelation 14:6.]

In fulfillment of this promise, Joseph Smith declared that Moroni, an ancient prophet on this continent, and now resurrected, taught him the gospel, giving him instruction in relation to the restoration of all things preceding the coming of Christ. And the Lord said: "For behold, the Lord God hath sent forth the angel crying through the midst of heaven, saying: Prepare ye the way of the Lord, and make his paths straight, for the hour of his coming is nigh." [D&C 133:17.]

Accepting this as true, Latter-day Saints believe that communication has been established with the heavens in modern times, and now the "Gospel of the Kingdom" is sent out as a witness to the world before Christ shall come [see Matthew 24:14].[19]

The Latter-day Saints may be considered strange and peculiar in believing that they have been called upon to fulfil this scripture [Matthew 24:14], but it is with full confidence that the Lord has spoken that they are diligently sending missionaries in to all parts of the earth. Moreover when all nations have heard this message as it has been revealed in these last days, then may we look forth for the coming of our Lord and Savior Jesus Christ, for at that day all nations will have been warned by the messengers who were sent unto them according to the Lord's promise.[20]

The gospel is for all men, and the Church shall be established everywhere, in all nations, even to the ends of the earth, before the second coming of the Son of Man. . . .

. . . He has set his hand the second time to gather Israel into the Church, and this time he will raise up congregations of his saints in all nations.[21]

From the dedicatory prayer for the Ogden Utah Temple:

O Father, hasten the day when righteousness shall prevail; when the rulers of nations shall open their borders to the preaching of the gospel; when the door of salvation shall swing wide open for the honest and upright and good among every people.

We pray for the spread of truth; we pray for the missionary cause; we seek strength and numbers and means to proclaim thy everlasting truths to more of thy other children in every nation, among every kindred, and speaking every tongue. . . .

. . . It is our desire to be instruments in thy hands to prepare a people for the coming of thy Son.[22]

------------------- ∎ 5 ∎ -------------------

The Millennium will be a time of peace and a time to labor in the work of the Lord.

The righteous will rejoice when he comes, because then peace will come to the earth, righteousness to the people, and that same spirit of peace and joy and happiness which prevailed upon this continent for two hundred years [see 4 Nephi 1:1–22] shall again be established among the people and eventually shall become universal, and Christ shall reign as Lord of lords and King of kings for a thousand years. We are looking forward to that time.[23]

For one thousand years shall this happy time of peace prevail and in due time all the inhabitants of the earth shall be brought into the fold of the Church.[24]

The gospel will be taught far more intensely and with greater power during [the] millennium, until all the inhabitants of the earth shall embrace it.[25]

Instead of being a time of rest, the Millennium is to be a time for all to labor. Idleness will not be found, better methods will be employed, not so much time will be consumed in the daily pursuits and more time will be given to the things of the Kingdom. The saints will be kept busy in the temples which shall be built in all parts of the land. In fact, so busy will they be that the temples will be occupied most of the time.[26]

There shall be mortality upon the face of the earth during the thousand years because of the great work that is to be accomplished, of salvation for the dead. During that thousand years of peace the great work of the Lord shall be in the temples, and into those temples the people shall go to labor for those who have passed beyond and who are waiting to have these ordinances which pertain to their salvation performed for them by those who still dwell in mortality upon the earth.[27]

It is our duty to save the dead and that work will continue during the Millennium until all are endowed and sealed who are entitled to this blessing.[28]

All those who have died in Christ shall come forth from the dead, at His coming, and shall dwell upon the earth as Christ shall be upon the earth during the millennium. They shall not remain here all the time during the thousand years, but they will mingle with those who are still here in mortal life. These resurrected Saints, and the Savior Himself, shall come to give instruction and guidance; to reveal unto us the things we ought to know; to give us information concerning the work in the temples of the Lord so we may do the work which is essential to the salvation of worthy men.[29]

The Lord has said through his servants that during the Millennium those who have passed beyond and have attained the resurrection will reveal in person to those who are still in mortality all the information which is required to complete the work of these who have passed from this life. Then the dead will have the privilege of making known the things they desire and are entitled to receive. In this way no soul will be neglected and the work of the Lord will be perfected.[30]

I pray every day of my life that the Lord will hasten His work. . . . I am praying for the end of the world because I want a better world. I want the coming of Christ. I want the reign of peace. I want the time to come when every man can live in peace and in the spirit of faith, humility and prayer.[31]

Suggestions for Study and Teaching

Questions

- How does the account in "From the Life of Joseph Fielding Smith" influence your feelings about the end of the world?

- How can the prophecies mentioned in section 1 help us prepare for the coming of the Lord?

- In section 2, review President Smith's teachings about the parable of the wheat and the tares. What can we do to be part of the "wheat"? What can we do to help our families and others?

- As we prepare for the coming of the Lord, what do you think it means to "watch and pray"? What do you think it means to "get our houses in order"? (See section 3.)

- President Smith prayed, "It is our desire to be instruments in thy hands to prepare a people for the coming of thy Son" (section 4). In what ways can we help others prepare for the Lord's coming?

- Review section 5. In what ways can we benefit now from knowing about what will happen in the Millennium?

Related Scriptures

Psalm 102:16; Isaiah 40:3–5; James 5:7–8; D&C 1:12; 39:20–21; 45:39, 56–59

Teaching Help

"The crowning, convincing, converting power of gospel teaching is manifest when an inspired teacher says, 'I know by the power of the Holy Ghost, by the revelations of the Holy Spirit to my soul, that the doctrines I have taught are true'" (Bruce R. McConkie, in *Teaching, No Greater Call* [1999], 43).

Notes

1. *The Signs of the Times* (1943), 103–5.
2. "Ogden Temple Dedicatory Prayer," *Ensign,* Mar. 1972, 10–11.
3. *The Restoration of All Things* (1945), 302.
4. In Conference Report, Apr. 1966, 12–14.
5. In Conference Report, Apr. 1935, 98; see also *Doctrines of Salvation,* ed. Bruce R. McConkie, 3 vols. (1954–56), 3:1.
6. "Watch Therefore," *Deseret News,* Aug. 2, 1941, Church section, 2; see also *Doctrines of Salvation,* 3:15.
7. In Conference Report, Apr. 1918, 156–57; see also *Doctrines of Salvation,* 3:15–16.
8. "How to Teach the Gospel at Home," *Relief Society Magazine,* Dec. 1931, 688; see also *Doctrines of Salvation,* 3:16.

9. In Conference Report, Apr. 1952, 28; italics in original.

10. "The Coming of Elijah," *Ensign,* Jan. 1972, 5.

11. "The Reign of Righteousness," *Deseret News,* Jan. 7, 1933, 7; see also *Doctrines of Salvation,* 3:60.

12. In Conference Report, Apr. 1935, 99; see also *Doctrines of Salvation,* 3:38.

13. *Answers to Gospel Questions,* comp. Joseph Fielding Smith Jr., 5 vols. (1957–66), 5:xii.

14. "A Warning Cry for Repentance," *Deseret News,* May 4, 1935, Church section, 6.

15. "A Warning Cry for Repentance," 8.

16. In Conference Report, Apr. 1966, 15.

17. "A Peculiar People: Modern Revelation—The Coming of Moroni," *Deseret News,* June 6, 1931, Church section, 8; see also *Doctrines of Salvation,* 3:3–4.

18. "A Peculiar People: Prophecy Being Fulfilled," *Deseret News,* Sept. 19, 1931, Church section, 6.

19. "A Peculiar People: Modern Revelation—The Coming of Moroni," 8; see also *Doctrines of Salvation,* 3:4–5.

20. "A Peculiar People: Prophecy Being Fulfilled," *Deseret News,* Nov. 7, 1931,

Church section, 6; see also *Doctrines of Salvation,* 3:6.

21. In Conference Report, British Area General Conference 1971, 176.

22. "Ogden Temple Dedicatory Prayer," 9, 11.

23. "The Right to Rule," *Deseret News,* Feb. 6, 1932, Church section, 8.

24. "Priesthood—Dispensation of the Fulness of Times," *Deseret News,* Aug. 19, 1933, 4; see also *Doctrines of Salvation,* 3:66.

25. "Churches on Earth During the Millennium," *Improvement Era,* Mar. 1955, 176; see also *Doctrines of Salvation,* 3:64.

26. *The Way to Perfection* (1931), 323–24.

27. "The Reign of Righteousness," 7; see also *Doctrines of Salvation,* 3:58.

28. In "Question Answered," *Deseret News,* Jan. 13, 1934, Church section, 8; see also *Doctrines of Salvation,* 2:166.

29. "The Reign of Righteousness," 7; see also *Doctrines of Salvation,* 3:59.

30. "Faith Leads to a Fulness of Truth and Righteousness," *Utah Genealogical and Historical Magazine,* Oct. 1930, 154; italics removed; see also *Doctrines of Salvation,* 3:65.

31. *The Signs of the Times,* 149.

List of Visuals

Cover: Background © Artbeats.

Page 5: *Young Joseph Fielding Smith Studying the Book of Mormon,* by Michael T. Malm. © Michael T. Malm.

Page 36: Detail from *I Saw a Light,* by Jon McNaughton. © Jon McNaughton.

Page 41: Detail from *The Lord Shewed Him All the Land,* by Walter Rane. © Intellectual Reserve, Inc.

Page 48: *(Christ) Rescue of the Lost Lamb,* by Minerva Teichert.

Page 53: *The Last Supper,* by Simon Dewey. © Simon Dewey.

Page 58: Detail from photograph © Corbis. Do not copy, download, or distribute.

Page 61: Detail from *Leaving the Garden of Eden,* by Joseph Brickey. © 1998 Joseph Brickey.

Page 66: Detail from *Christ in Gethsemane,* by Heinrich Hofmann. Courtesy C. Harrison Conroy Co., Inc.

Page 94: Detail from *Jesus Institutes the Sacrament,* by Gary E. Smith. © 1982 Gary E. Smith.

Page 104: *Joseph and Hyrum Smith Standing by River,* by Theodore S. Gorka. © 1996 Intellectual Reserve, Inc.

Page 109: Detail from *The First Vision,* by Del Parson. © 1987 Intellectual Reserve, Inc.

Page 112: *Martyrdom of Joseph and Hyrum,* by Gary E. Smith. © 1984 Intellectual Reserve, Inc.

Page 128: *An Angel Showing the Gold Plates to Joseph Smith, Oliver Cowdery, and David Whitmer,* by William L. Maughan. © 1988 William L. Maughan.

Page 132: *Eight Witnesses View the Book of Mormon Plates,* by Harold T. (Dale) Kilbourn. © Dale Kilbourn.

Page 143: Detail from *Jesus Teaching the People by the Seashore,* by James Tissot.

Page 152: *Melchizedek Priesthood Restoration,* by Minerva Teichert. Courtesy Church History Museum.

Page 156: *Elijah Appearing in the Kirtland Temple,* by Daniel A. Lewis. © 2007 Daniel A. Lewis.

Page 172: Detail from *My Baptism in Kyiv,* by Mykola Krisachenko. Courtesty Church History Museum.

Page 182: Detail from *Paul Bestowing the Holy Ghost,* by Michael T. Malm. © 2006 Michael T. Malm.

Page 228: Detail from *The Lord's Prayer,* by James Tissot.

Page 245: Detail from *A Word of Wisdom Revealed,* by Kenneth A. Corbett. © Kenneth A. Corbett.

Page 252: *Such as I Have I Give Thee,* by Walter Rane. © Intellectual Reserve, Inc.

Page 262: Photograph courtesy Church History Library and Archives.

Page 280: Detail from *Alma and Amulek in Prison,* by Gary L. Kapp. © Gary L. Kapp.

Page 310: Detail from *Behold the Lamb of God,* by Walter Rane. © Intellectual Reserve, Inc.

Page 314: *Christ in the Temple,* by Heinrich Hofmann. Courtesy C. Harrison Conroy Co., Inc.

Page 320: Detail from *Christ's Image,* by Heinrich Hofmann. Courtesy C. Harrison Conroy Co., Inc.

Page 324: *The Second Coming,* by Harry Anderson. © Intellectual Reserve, Inc.

Page 327: *The Angel Moroni Appears to Joseph Smith,* by Tom Lovell. © 2003 Intellectual Reserve, Inc.

Index

is family centered, 76
is for all people, 125, 265
is the sole hope of the world, 59,
271–73
restored through Joseph Smith,
110–11, 265
should be preached in simplicity,
271

Grant, Heber J., 141, 151

H

Heavenly Father
characteristics of, 38–44
exercising faith in, 38–39, 84–85
family of, all people's membership in, 40, 60, 254–55
invites all people to come unto
His Beloved Son, 45
is the Father of the spirits of all
people, 40, 254–55
knowledge of, lacking in the
world, 35, 39
love of, for us, 40–44
plan of, 44–45, 52, 59–69
sent His Only Begotten Son, 44,
315
wants us to return to Him, 44–45
weeps over His disobedient children, 42–44
work of, to bring to pass immortality and eternal life, 42

Hinckley, Gordon B., 1

Holy Ghost
Joseph Fielding Smith receives
guidance from, in his family,
181, 183
manifests the truth to all people,
145–46, 184
mission of, 183–84
power of, in speaking to individuals' spirits, 183–84
will not dwell in unholy tabernacles, 188

Holy Ghost, gift of
allows us to have the Holy Ghost
as a constant companion,
185–88
and the plan of salvation, 65
by the laying on of hands, 185
leads to revelations that guide
personal lives, 188–89
preparing to receive the blessings
of, 186–88

Home. *See* Family; Family home
evening; Marriage; Parents

I

Individual responsibility, 287–94

Industry. *See* Work

J

Jesus Christ
all things concentrated in and
around Him, 51
and Joseph Smith, 107–8
Atonement of, 44, 52, 62–68,
97–100, 107, 315–16
becoming sons and daughters of,
52–53
birth of, 52, 312–17
brings salvation from sin, 62–65
brings salvation from the Fall,
62–65
childhood and youth of, 313–15
directs the Church, 119–20
exercising faith in, 84–85
following the example of, 55–56,
168, 237
gaining a testimony of, 54
in this dispensation, 53–54
introduces the sacrament, 95–96
is the great prototype of priesthood service, 168
is the Only Begotten Son of God,
50–51
Joseph Fielding Smith's love for,
49–50

Latter-day Saints' belief in, 50–52

progressed from grace to grace until receiving a fulness, 313–15

remembering, at Christmastime, 311–12, 316–17

remembering, through the sacrament, 97–102

role of, in the plan of salvation, 44–45, 52, 62–68, 107

Second Coming of, 319, 321–23, 325–29

suffering of, in Gethsemane and on the cross, 62–64, 97–100

staying true to a testimony of, 53–55

See also Atonement of Jesus Christ; Second Coming of Jesus Christ

Joseph Smith. *See* Smith, Joseph

Joseph Fielding Smith. *See* Smith, Joseph Fielding

K

Keys of the priesthood. *See* Priesthood keys

Knowledge. *See* Learning

L

Language, reverence in, 246

Law

governs the universe and the kingdom of God, 230–31

obedience to, required for salvation, 65

Law of witnesses, 130–32

Learning

and discerning truth from falsehood, 142–43

from Church leaders, 144–45

from the scriptures, 134–36, 143–44, 148

is increased through righteous living, 146–49

most important, is gospel learning, 141–43

seeking, in many fields, 141–42

through guidance from the Holy Ghost, 145–46

through study, faith, and obedience, 145–46

Lee, Harold B., 31

Life, purpose of, 66–67

Living in the world but not of the world, 248

See also Worldliness

Love

among Latter-day Saints, 255–57

and appreciating people for themselves, 258–59

enhanced by knowledge that all people are God's children, 254–56

expressed through service, 257–58

for the Lord and others, leads to harmony with all sacred law, 259–60

includes being forgiving and seeing good in others, 256

Joseph Fielding Smith learns, from his horse Junie, 258–59

M

Marriage

celestial, is the crowning ordinance of the gospel, 194

celestial, will be available to all the faithful, 197–98

endures forever in the gospel plan, 194–96

faithfulness to, brings happiness and eternal blessings, 196–97